CHEF RONALDO'S
SABORES DE CUBA

DIABETES-FRIENDLY TRADITIONAL AND NUEVO CUBANO CUISINE

Director, Book Publishing, Abe Ogden; *Managing Editor,* Rebekah Renshaw; *Acquisitions Editor,* Victor Van Beuren; *Project Manager,* Lauren Wilson; *Production Manager and Composition,* Melissa Sprott; *Cover and Page Design,* Pixiedesign, LLC; *Photography,* Kelly Campbell Photography; *Printer,* Marquis Imprimeur.

Printed in Canada
1 3 5 7 9 10 8 6 4 2

The suggestions and information contained in this publication are generally consistent with the *Standards of Medical Care in Diabetes* and other policies of the American Diabetes Association, but they do not represent the policy or position of the Association or any of its boards or committees. Reasonable steps have been taken to ensure the accuracy of the information presented. However, the American Diabetes Association cannot ensure the safety or efficacy of any product or service described in this publication. Individuals are advised to consult a physician or other appropriate health care professional before undertaking any diet or exercise program or taking any medication referred to in this publication. Professionals must use and apply their own professional judgment, experience, and training and should not rely solely on the information contained in this publication before prescribing any diet, exercise, or medication. The American Diabetes Association—its officers, directors, employees, volunteers, and members—assumes no responsibility or liability for personal or other injury, loss, or damage that may result from the suggestions or information in this publication.

∞ The paper in this publication meets the requirements of the ANSI Standard Z39.48-1992 (permanence of paper).

American Diabetes Association titles may be purchased for business or promotional use or for special sales. To purchase more than 50 copies of this book at a discount, or for custom editions of this book with your logo, contact the American Diabetes Association at the address below or at booksales@diabetes.org.

American Diabetes Association
1701 North Beauregard Street
Alexandria, Virginia 22311

DOI: 10.2337/9781580406130

Library of Congress Cataloging-in-Publication Data
Names: Linares, Ronaldo, author. | Linares, Ronaldo. Chef Ronaldo's sabores de Cuba. Spanish. | American Diabetes Association.
Title: Chef Ronaldo's sabores de Cuba : diabetes-friendly traditional and nuevo cubano cuisine / Ronaldo Linares.
Other titles: Sabores de Cuba
Description: Alexandria [Virginia] : American Diabetes Association, 2016. | English and Spanish. | Includes bibliographical references and index.
Identifiers: LCCN 2015039804 | ISBN 9781580406130 (paperback)
Subjects: LCSH: Diabetes--Diet therapy--Recipes. | Cooking, Cuban. | BISAC: COOKING / Health & Healing / Diabetic & Sugar-Free. | COOKING / Regional & Ethnic / Caribbean & West Indian. | COOKING / Regional & Ethnic / Central American & South American. | HEALTH & FITNESS / Diseases / Diabetes. |
LCGFT: Cookbooks.
Classification: LCC RC662 .L56 2016 | DDC 641.597291--dc23 LC record available at http://lccn.loc.gov/2015039804

Director, publicación de libros, Abe Ogden; *editor general,* Rebekah Renshaw; *editor de adquisiciones,* Victor Van Beuren; *gerente de producción,* Lauren Wilson; *administradora de producción y composición,* Melissa Sprott; *diseño de páginas y portada,* Pixiedesign; *fotografía,* Kelly Campbell Photography; *imprenta,* Marquis Imprimeur.

Impreso en Canada
1 3 5 7 9 10 8 6 4 2

Las sugerencias e información contenidas en esta publicación en general son compatibles con los *Estándares de Atención Médica de la Diabetes* (*Standards of Medical Care in Diabetes*) y otras medidas de política de la Asociación Americana de la Diabetes, pero no representan la política ni posición de la Asociación ni de sus juntas o comités. Se han tomado medidas razonables para asegurar la exactitud de la información presentada. Sin embargo, la Asociación Americana de la Diabetes no puede asegurar la seguridad ni eficacia de ningún producto o servicio descrito en esta publicación. Se aconseja consultar con un médico o profesional de servicios de salud antes de iniciar un régimen alimentario o de ejercicio, o tomar algún medicamento mencionado en esta publicación. Los profesionales deben usar y aplicar su propio criterio, experiencia y capacitación profesional, y no deben basarse exclusivamente en la información que contiene esta publicación antes de recetar un régimen alimentario, de ejercicio y medicamentos. La Asociación Americana de la Diabetes —representada por sus funcionarios, directores, empleados, voluntarios y miembros— no asume ninguna responsabilidad ni obligación por lesión, pérdida o daño personal o de otro tipo que pueda ser resultado de las sugerencias o información en esta publicación.

∞ El papel de esta publicación cumple con los requisitos del Standard Z39.48-1992 de ANSI (permanencia del papel).

Es posible comprar las publicaciones de la Asociación Americana de la Diabetes para fines comerciales o promocionales, o para ventas especiales. Para comprar más de 50 copias de este libro con descuento o para ediciones especiales de este libro con su logotipo, comuníquese con la Asociación Americana de la Diabetes usando la dirección de abajo o booksales@diabetes.org.

American Diabetes Association
1701 North Beauregard Street
Alexandria, Virginia 22311

DOI: 10.2337/9781580406130

Datos de catalogación de publicaciones en la Biblioteca del Congreso
Names: Linares, Ronaldo, author. | Linares, Ronaldo. Sabores de Cuba del Chef Ronaldo. Español. | American Diabetes Association.
Title: Sabores de Cuba del Chef Ronaldo: Recetas para diabéticos de la cocina cubana tradicional y al estilo "Nuevo cubano"./ Ronaldo Linares.
Other titles: Sabores de Cuba
Description: Alexandria [Virginia]: American Diabetes Association, 2016. | English and Spanish. | Includes bibliographical references and index.
Identifiers: LCCN 2015039804 | ISBN 9781580406130 (paperback)
Subjects: LCSH: Diabetes--Diet therapy--Recipes. | Cooking, Cuban. | BISAC: COOKING / Health & Healing / Diabetic & Sugar-Free. | COOKING / Regional & Ethnic / Caribbean & West Indian. | COOKING / Regional & Ethnic / Central American & South American. | HEALTH & FITNESS / Diseases / Diabetes. |
LCGFT: Cookbooks.
Classification: LCC RC662 .L56 2016 | DDC 641.597291--dc23 LC record available at http://lccn.loc.gov/2015039804

DEDICATION

Dedicated to the moments in my life that made this dream possible
and the people who believed in me and helped me make my book a reality.

———————————————

DEDICATORIA

Dedicado a los momentos de mi vida que hicieron posible este sueño
y las personas que creyeron en mí y me ayudaron a hacer realidad este libro.

FOREWORD

FOOD, FAMILY, AND FITNESS: These are the driving forces behind young, accomplished chef Ronaldo Linares. Ronaldo grew up in Colombia and worked in the kitchen of his father's Cuban restaurant. This is where his life's journey began. The moment you start reading this cookbook, you will feel the fire of Ronaldo's Latin roots in every word.

Healthy eating and great flavor come together in this informative book; it's like an encyclopedia of Cuban cuisine. This collection of personal recipes is a diabetes-friendly tour-de-force of traditional and *nuevo* Cuban cooking. Ronaldo will teach you how to select the best ingredients when shopping at the farmers' market. And the glossary of ingredients and lists of pantry staples, kitchen essentials, and gluten-free flours in this book will prepare you for culinary success.

Diabetes is a personal subject for me. My grandfather suffered from this disease. So, as a chef, I realize the great responsibility of cooking for the public. I serve only healthful, fresh foods. As a culinary ambassador for the U.S. Department of Agriculture, I taught healthy cooking in the Philippines and Indonesia, and I've cooked with many of the best chefs in the world. So I know tasty, nutritious food.

When I met Ronaldo, the first thing he said was, "Chef, I love food—my passion is Cuban food." I have known Ronaldo for years as his mentor and his friend, but now he is *my* mentor. He is a talented chef who has appeared on several culinary television productions, and he's the Executive Chef at Martino's Cuban Restaurant. He also gives back to the community by teaching about nutrition and fitness. He hopes this book will inspire many more people to practice healthy eating habits.

Chef Ronaldo's Sabores de Cuba will teach you to cook from the heart, using healthy ingredients and traditional Cuban cooking methods. This book is your key to planning mouthwatering and wholesome meals. Use this book often and experience the flavors of Cuba Chef Ronaldo's way!

Andrew Gold
Culinary Educator / Executive Chef / Consultant
New York, NY

PRÓLOGO

LA COMIDA, LA FAMILIA Y LA SALUD: esto es lo que motiva al joven y exitoso chef Ronaldo Linares. Ronaldo creció en Colombia y trabajó en la cocina del restaurante cubano de su padre, donde dio los primeros pasos de lo que sería su carrera. Apenas abra este libro de cocina sentirá, en cada palabra, la pasión de las raíces latinas de Ronaldo.

Los platillos de este libro son sabrosos y saludables a la vez, y hay tanta información que es como una enciclopedia de la cocina cubana. Esta colección personal de recetas especiales para diabéticos es un recorrido por la cocina cubana tradicional y el estilo "Nuevo cubano". Ronaldo le enseñará cómo elegir los mejores ingredientes en el mercado de agricultores. Además, este libro contiene un glosario de ingredientes, listas de lo básico para la despensa y la cocina, y varios tipos de harina sin gluten que lo prepararán para el éxito culinario.

La diabetes es un tema personal para mí. Mi abuelo tenía la enfermedad. Así que, como chef, me doy cuenta de que cocinar para el público es una gran responsabilidad. Solo sirvo alimentos saludables y frescos. Como embajador culinario para el Departamento de Agricultura de Estados Unidos, enseñé cómo cocinar saludablemente en Filipinas e Indonesia, y he cocinado con muchos de los mejores chefs del mundo. De modo que sé cuándo un platillo es sabroso y nutritivo.

Cuando conocí a Ronaldo, lo primero que dijo fue: "Chef, me encanta la comida, y mi pasión es la cocina cubana". Conozco a Ronaldo desde hace años como su mentor y amigo. Ahora él es mi mentor. Es un talentoso chef que ha participado en varios programas culinarios en televisión y es el Chef ejecutivo del restaurante cubano Martino's. También aporta a la comunidad con sus clases de nutrición y aptitud física. Espera que este libro inspire a mucha gente a poner en práctica hábitos saludables de alimentación.

Los Sabores de Cuba del Chef Ronaldo le enseñarán a cocinar con el corazón, usando ingredientes saludables y métodos de la cocina cubana tradicional. Este libro es la clave para planear comida sana que le hará agua la boca. Use este libro con frecuencia y experimente los sabores de Cuba ¡al estilo de Ronaldo!

Andrew Gold
Educador de arte culinario / Chef ejecutivo / Consultor
New York, NY

TABLE OF CONTENTS

ÍNDICE

INTRODUCTION
FROM REFLECTION TO REALITY

SO HERE I AM, a Cuban, Colombian, Marine, and a salsa-dancing chef, making his dreams come true.

What is Latin food? Latin cuisine has a rich history. It's about family, tradition, layers of flavor, and the expression of one's country through food. I don't think there is anyone more passionate about Latin cuisine than me. That's probably what every Latino out there would say—that is the passion in all of us. For me Latin cuisine is a way to share the unique flavors that the warm climate in Latin America has to offer: the fruits, vegetables, tubers, and the delicious meats. Latin cuisine can take you on an emotional journey; it can leave you excited and speechless or make you grab the person next to you at the table and smile. That's the beauty of Latin cuisine—it allows you to express and convey emotions without words.

Let's get personal, *mi gente* (my people). This book is a manifestation of my love of food, family, and culture. I would like to share some of my life stories with you. I will try my hardest not to leave out anything about the journey that has led me to this moment, writing my first cookbook.

My journey started in Medellín, a city located almost in the center of Colombia with a population of 2.4 million people. Colombia is full of culture, food, beauty, and a feeling of joy only those who are native to the country can express. My memories of Medellín are mostly food-related and begin with my memory of *arepas* (corn patties) with scrambled eggs, tomatoes, and onions that had been sweated down to be almost candy-like. I remember the tantalizing flavors of fresh blood sausage stew with seasonal tubers. And the smells of rotisserie chicken that will beckon you from miles away and make you feel as if you're chasing the girl that got away. Finding the source of that smell always filled me with excitement, and my mouth would water as I got ready to dive in to that moist, perfectly seasoned chicken. If I could only tell you how much I miss the flavors and smells of Colombia in my everyday life. Yes, I can make these dishes anywhere, but the Colombian air, the beeping taxis, and especially the wonderful conversations that filled my time in Colombia are greatly missed. I think that great conversations and the laughter and tense moments that they bring add extra flavor to any meal. My childhood experiences with food in Colombia set me on the path to becoming a chef.

Now, years later, I find myself remembering those wonderful childhood years. It wasn't until recently that I truly realized how my early education in food, culture, and life impacted me. For example, I remember taking trips to the market with my mother every other day and being bored while I waited for her to pick out the best produce and meat. My mother would negotiate prices with the vendors and pick through all the produce, touching, smelling, and finally buying what seemed to be the perfect pieces. But I understand how lucky I was to be able to experience such events at an early age. Now I'm the weirdo picking up the fruits and vegetables at

INTRODUCCIÓN
DE LA REFLEXIÓN A LA REALIDAD

AQUÍ ME TIENEN: un cubano y colombiano, infante de Marina y chef que baila salsa y hace sus sueños realidad.

¿Qué es comida latina? La comida latina tiene una rica historia. Habla de familia, tradición, niveles de sabor, y es la expresión de patria por medio de los alimentos. Creo que no hay nadie a quien le apasione más que a mí la cocina latina. Todo latino por allí probablemente diga lo mismo; porque llevamos tanta pasión dentro. Para mí, la comida latina es una manera de compartir los sabores únicos que ofrece el clima cálido de Latinoamérica: las frutas, los vegetales, los tubérculos y las deliciosas carnes. La cocina latina puede llevarte por un recorrido emocional; te puede impresionar o dejar mudo, o hacer que le sonrías a la persona sentada a tu lado en la mesa. Eso es lo lindo de la comida latina: te permite expresar y trasmitir emociones sin palabras.

Hablemos claro, mi gente. Este libro es una manifestación de mi amor por la comida, familia y cultura. Quiero contarles algunas anécdotas de mi vida. Haré todo lo posible por no omitir nada sobre la trayectoria que me ha traído hasta aquí, a escribir mi primer libro de cocina.

Mi recorrido se inició en Medellín, ciudad ubicada prácticamente en el centro de Colombia, con una población de 2.4 millones de personas. Colombia está llena de cultura, comida, belleza y una alegría que solo los oriundos del país pueden expresar. Mis recuerdos de Medellín están mayormente relacionados a la comida y comienzan con mi recuerdo de las arepas (tortas de maíz) con huevos revueltos, tomate y cebolla sudada hasta casi saber a caramelo. Recuerdo los intensos sabores de un estofado de morcilla recién hecho y acompañado de tubérculos en temporada. Y los olores del pollo rostizado que te llaman de millas a la distancia y hacen que te sientas como si estuvieses tras una muchacha fuera de tu alcance. Encontrar el origen del olor siempre me llenaba de emoción, y se me hacía agua la boca mientras me disponía a meterle diente al pollo jugoso y perfectamente sazonado. Cómo quisiera poder decirles cuánto extraño todos los días los olores y sabores de Colombia. Sí, puedo preparar esos platillos en cualquier parte, pero extraño mucho el aire colombiano, el pitar de los taxis y especialmente las maravillosas conversaciones que ocuparon mi tiempo en Colombia. Pienso que las buenas conversaciones y las risas y momentos tensos que causan le dan un toque adicional de sabor a toda comida. Las experiencias de mi infancia, con la comida de Colombia, me llevaron a ser chef.

Ahora, años más tarde, noto que me pongo a recordar esos maravillosos años de mi niñez. Recién hace poco me di cuenta del impacto que tuvo en mí lo que aprendí de niño sobre la comida, la cultura y la vida. Por ejemplo, recuerdo cuando iba al mercado con mi mamá un día sí y un día no, y cómo me aburría mientras esperaba que seleccionara la mejor fruta, verduras y carne. Mi

the market, bringing them close to my nose and smelling them to see if they are just right, and lightly squeezing them to check for ripeness. My son, Liam, will probably look at me just as I looked at my mom. I'm looking forward to that!

So you've read through a few paragraphs of my story at this point. Are you still with me? Go ahead take a sip of *cafecito cubano* for energy. After that first sip, your arm hairs should stand up, your eyes should widen, and a smile should come to your face. Now we're ready to continue with the introduction to my cookbook. You must be asking yourself, "What about Cuba? Isn't this a Cuban cookbook?" Cuba is the salt that flavors my culinary journey. My mother was obviously a big influence on my relationship with food, but in order to fully understand my culinary connection to Cuba, we also need to talk about "the master"—my father.

To tell you the truth, my dad and I have a complex relationship, but it's a great one. Mr. Martin Reyes Reinaldo Linares (aka Papi) is every bit of 5' 4" tall with blond hair and blue eyes, and the presence of Clint Eastwood mixed with the culinary knowledge of French chef Jacques Pépin. Papi has a rich life story that only he can tell, but I will share a snippet of it with you. He was born on November 12, 1928, in Havana, Cuba. During his early years Cuba was rich, and he often tells me that everyone wanted to live in Cuba at that time. He loves to tell stories about Cuba, and he paints it as a paradise. These stories are told in great detail—my father gets up and draws each scene with the motions of his arms, sometimes breaking into a *pasodoble*—and they always bring great joy to his face. Some of the best times my father and I share involve his tales about the Cuba of the past.

When my father discussed Cuban culture with me, he would say, "Son, in Cuba the music, dancing, and food are similar to those of Colombia but are somehow mystical. Some of that magic was lost after Castro took over." I did not entirely understand what he meant, but somehow I imagined it. I imagined a country with people dancing in the streets, street vendors selling empanadas, fritters, and many more things. I was a kid and did not know any better. My first introduction to Cuban foods was the dishes my father would make at his restaurant and at home: the traditional *Ropa Vieja*, roast pork, *Boliche,* and (one of my favorites) blood sausage. Of course he made many other dishes, but those are the ones that stuck out to me as a 5-year-old kid. Those dishes left a flavor profile in my mind that would later fully reveal itself and lead me to become the man, husband, father, and chef I am today.

Now on to the book! I hope you have enjoyed my story, but it is time to cook. I have gathered the following recipes over the course of my life. In the coming chapters, I'll share the lessons I learned from my mother and father in the kitchen and from the time I spent with my grandma grinding corn for *arepas*. My culinary curiosity has led to many great opportunities and has sparked many wonderful relationships. My passion for food, especially Latin cuisine, has given me the strength to fight through adversity and reach for my goals. This book is my personal journey told through food. I hope these recipes will become favorites in your home.

So how does Cuban food fit into a diabetes meal plan? Cuban cuisine and other Latin cuisines are traditionally farm-to-table or butcher shop–to-table. Why not keep that tradition going? My experience cooking Cuban food over the last decade and my culinary memories of

madre negociaba precios con los vendedores e inspeccionaba los productos agrícolas tocándolos y oliéndolos, y finalmente compraba los que le parecían perfectos. Pero entiendo lo afortunado que fui de poder ser parte de experiencias así a temprana edad. Ahora soy yo el loco que agarra la fruta y las verduras en el mercado, se las lleva a la nariz y las huele para ver si están en el punto perfecto, y las aprieta un poco para ver si están maduras. Mi hijo, Liam, probablemente me va a mirar como yo miraba a mi mamá. ¡No veo las horas!

Ya han leído unos cuantos párrafos sobre mi historia. ¿Siguen allí? Adelante, tómense un sorbo de cafecito cubano para que les dé energía. Después del primer sorbo, hasta los vellos se ponen en posición de atención, los ojos se abren y una sonrisa se dibuja en el rostro. Ahora estamos listos para seguir con la introducción de mi libro de cocina. Probablemente se pregunten, ¿y Cuba? ¿No es un libro de cocina cubana?" Cuba es el toque de sabor que sazona mi experiencia culinaria. Es obvio que mi madre fue una gran influencia en mi relación con la comida, pero para comprender plenamente mi conexión culinaria con Cuba, también debemos hablar del "maestro": mi padre.

La verdad es que mi papá y yo tenemos una relación compleja pero muy buena. El Sr. Martín Reyes Reinaldo Linares (alias papi) mide 5' 4" (1.62 metros) y tiene pelo rubio y ojos azules, y el porte de Clint Eastwood combinado con los conocimientos culinarios del chef francés Jacques Pépin. Papi ha tenido una vida muy rica y solo él puede relatar su historia, pero les contaré un poquito. Nació el 12 de noviembre de 1928 en La Habana, Cuba. Durante su juventud, Cuba era muy próspera y a menudo me cuenta que todos querían vivir en Cuba en aquella época. Le encanta contar sobre Cuba y la pinta como el paraíso. Estas historias están llenas de detalles —mi padre se pone de pie y traza cada escena con ademanes que adorna a veces con un pasodoble— y siempre se le llena el rostro de alegría. Algunos de los mejores momentos que pasé con mi papá incluyen sus relatos sobre la Cuba del pasado.

Cuando mi padre hablaba conmigo sobre la cultura cubana, me decía, "Hijo, en Cuba la música, el baile y la comida son similares a los de Colombia pero de cierta manera, son místicos. Un poco de esa magia se perdió cuando Castro subió al mando". Yo no lograba comprender lo que quería decir, pero de cierta manera, me lo imaginaba. Me imaginaba un país donde la gente bailaba en las calles, donde los ambulantes vendían empanadas, frituras y muchas otras cosas. Era un niño, y ese era el límite de mi imaginación. Mi introducción a la comida cubana fueron los platillos que mi padre preparaba en su restaurante y en casa: la tradicional ropa vieja, el lechón asado, el boliche y (uno de mis preferidos) la morcilla. Por supuesto que preparaba muchos otros platillos, pero esos son los que más me gustaban cuando tenía yo 5 años. Estos platos dejaron en mi mente una serie de sabores que solo después se revelarían totalmente y me llevarían a ser la persona, el esposo, el padre y el chef que soy hoy.

Ahora, ¡al libro! Espero que hayan disfrutado mi historia, pero es hora de cocinar. Llevo toda una vida recopilando las siguientes recetas. En los próximos capítulos, compartiré las lecciones que aprendí en la cocina de mi madre y mi padre, y contaré del tiempo que pasé con mi abuela moliendo maíz para las arepas. Mi curiosidad culinaria me ha abierto muchas oportunidades y ha producido amistades maravillosas. Mi pasión por la comida, especialmente la latina, me ha dado la

my childhood in Colombia have inspired me to advocate for using fresh, healthful ingredients and robust flavors. The focus of this book is to make Cuban classics delicious and diabetes-friendly, and share my personal cooking style with some healthy "nuevo Cubano" treats. But whether you're cooking my recipes or yours, you should try to prepare your meals on the stovetop using fresh produce and meat and quality spices and herbs rather than hitting the "quick minute" button on your microwave. This book was created to help people control diabetes through food and get them back in the kitchen.

¡Buen provecho! Enjoy!

fuerza para luchar y sobreponerme a las adversidades, y alcanzar mis objetivos. Este libro relata mi experiencia particular por medio de la comida. Espero que estas recetas lleguen a estar entre las favoritas en su casa.

Entonces, ¿cómo se adecúa la comida cubana al plan de alimentación para la diabetes? En la cocina cubana y otras cocinas latinoamericanas, la comida tradicionalmente va del huerto o del carnicero a la mesa. ¿Por qué no continuar la tradición? Mi experiencia de la última década de preparar comida cubana y los recuerdos culinarios de mi infancia en Colombia me han inspirado a promover el uso de ingredientes frescos y saludables, y sabores intensos. Este libro pone énfasis en hacer que los clásicos platos cubanos sean deliciosos y buenos para las personas con diabetes, además de infundir mi estilo personal de cocina a unos cuantos manjares saludables de la "nueva cocina cubana". Pero ya sea preparen mis recetas o las suyas, deben tratar de hacerlo en la estufa, usando fruta y verduras frescas, y especias y hierbas de calidad, en vez de apretar el botón de cocción rápida en el microondas. Este libro se creó para ayudar a las personas a controlarse la diabetes por medio de la comida y para hacer que vuelvan a la cocina.

¡Buen provecho! ¡Disfruten!

WHY THE FARMERS' MARKET?

FARMERS' MARKETS have become more and more popular over the last 5 years. Many people are starting to take control of their lives (and health) by cooking whole foods at home. This makes me happy. Every time farmers' market season rolls around I get excited. Farmers' markets mean delicious in-season produce that can keep your family healthy and happy, and save you money.

Think about it, guys: the people who sell produce at farmers' markets are hard-working Americans. When you shop at a farmers' market, you're helping to support their families. And at most farmers' markets, negotiating prices is acceptable, which means more money in your pocket.

My whole point of view about farmers' markets comes from my excellent experiences in New Jersey, and I know there are 49 other states that have wonderful farmers' markets, so I hope you can all relate. Here are the reasons I dance my way to the farmers' market once a week:

- Going to the farmers' market is a great way to get the family together once a week for a fun morning in the sun.
- These markets allow you to connect with your community and the farmers who work so hard to bring you high-quality, healthy foods.
- I enjoy the fresh smells of the variety of produce available.
- Nothing says "fresh" like seeing the dirt on vegetables that were just picked hours before.
- Farmers' markets are a great place for kids to learn about hard work and the foods they eat; they allow kids to see where the life of a vegetable begins before it becomes a delicious dish.
- I love the inspiration you get from seeing the abundance of produce available. You don't always know what you plan to cook before going to the market, but somehow the market inspires you.

I start going to the farmers' market at the end of April to see what goodies have arrived. The excitement of the market at the beginning of every year is great; families walk around checking out the goods, and chefs come on a mission to pick the best produce available and make one hell of a dish that night. It is fascinating how many personalities you come across at the farmers' market.

So let's talk produce. *What should I buy? What do I look for? Is it fresh? How much should I get? Should I ask the farmer for advice?* These are questions that I ask myself at the farmers' market. So I come prepared and make sure I get what is in season during the time that I go. The seasons may be a little different where you are, so the availability of the produce in the following lists may vary depending on the climate in your area.

FARMERS' MARKET AT SPRINGTIME

Spring always reminds me of the trips my mother and I made to the markets in Colombia. If you could only see

¿POR QUÉ EL MERCADO DE AGRICULTORES?

EN LOS ÚLTIMOS CINCO AÑOS, los mercados de agricultores se han vuelto cada vez más populares. Muchas personas están empezando a tomar el control de su vida (y salud) al cocinar alimentos naturales en casa. Esto me hace feliz. Me emociono cada vez que llega la temporada del mercado de agricultores. Ofrecen deliciosos vegetales y frutas de temporada que pueden mantener a su familia sana y feliz, además de ahorrarles dinero.

Piénsenlo, amigos: las personas que venden sus productos en los mercados de agricultores son estadounidenses que trabajan muy duro. Cuando ustedes compran en un mercado de agricultores, los están ayudando a mantener a su familia. Y en la mayoría de los mercados de agricultores, se acepta regatear, lo que quiere decir que su dinero rendirá más.

Mi opinión sobre los mercados de agricultores proviene de mis excelentes experiencias en Nueva Jersey, y sé que hay otros 49 estados que tienen maravillosos mercados de agricultores, así que espero que todos puedan identificarse. Estas son las razones por las que una vez por semana voy bailando al mercado:

- Ir al mercado es una gran manera de congregar a la familia una vez por semana para pasar una divertida mañana bajo el sol.
- Estos mercados les permiten estar en contacto con su comunidad y los agricultores que trabajan tan duro para ofrecerles alimentos sanos de alta calidad.
- Disfruto los olores frescos de la variedad de productos agrícolas disponibles.
- Las verduras con "tierrita" porque fueron cosechadas hace apenas unas horas son la viva imagen de la frescura.
- Los mercados de agricultores son un lugar ideal para que los niños aprendan sobre el trabajo duro y los alimentos que consumen; permiten que los niños vean el inicio del ciclo de vida de un vegetal antes de ser parte de un platillo delicioso.
- Me encanta la inspiración que nace de ver la abundancia de productos agrícolas. Uno no siempre sabe qué va a cocinar antes de salir al mercado, pero de alguna manera, este inspira.

Comienzo a ir al mercado de agricultores a fines de abril para ver qué ha llegado. Cada año, al principio de la temporada, se siente la emoción en el mercado; las familias pasean examinando la mercadería, y los chefs acuden con la misión de escoger los mejores productos disponibles y preparar un plato sensacional esa noche. Es fascinante ver a todos los personajes que uno encuentra en el mercado de agricultores.

Entonces, hablemos de frutas y verduras. ¿Qué debo comprar? ¿Qué debo buscar? ¿Está fresco? ¿Cuánto debo comprar? ¿Debo pedirle consejos al agricultor? Estas son las preguntas que me hago en el mercado de agricultores. Así que voy preparado y me aseguro de comprar lo que está en temporada cuando voy. Quizá

the massive buildings filled with farmers trying to sell their bounty! There was so much beauty under one roof: bright colors, people trying to haggle a lower price, and endless rows of produce. Spring always takes me back to my time spent in Medellín, Colombia. Here's a list of great spring-time ingredients to look for at the market, along with descriptions to help you choose the freshest products:

- Arugula—dark green leaves, bright aroma.

- Asparagus—smooth skin, bright green color, freshly cut ends.

- Chard (also found in the summer and early fall)—crisp stems, bright colors, freshly cut ends.

- Fava beans—firm pods (larger pods are great for soups or stews).

- Fiddleheads—tight coils, bright green color (best if eaten right away).

- Green garlic (similar to a scallion but with a garlicky flavor)—crisp, bright green stalks (make sure they are not wilted).

- Herbs—bright colors, nice aroma, firm.

- Lettuce (also found in the summer and fall)—whole heads, unwashed (there is less chance of bacteria being introduced to unwashed lettuce).

- Mint—strong leaves, strong mint smell.

- Radishes—deep colors, stems attached, firm.

- Scallions—firm stalks, strong scent, untouched ends.

- Spinach—bright green, fresh aroma, crisp.

- Thyme—strong stems, bright leaves, strong aroma.

- Wild mushrooms (also found in the summer and fall)—earthy smells, firm look, avoid if they smell moldy.

FARMERS' MARKET IN THE SUMMER AND FALL

Get there early, *mi gente*! The crowds wake up a little earlier during summertime. It also seems like the mood changes; the warmer weather tends to bring festive music, more kids, and more produce to the market. As the summer dies down and the fall rolls in, the season of squash, brussels sprouts, and pumpkin begins. Here's the produce to look for in the summer and fall:

- Broccoli—tight green florets, firm stalks.

- Brussels sprouts (try to get them on their stalk; there's nothing fresher than that)—green sprouts, no browning on the leaves.

- Cabbage—heavy heads, crisp leaves, fresh stems.

- Carrots—deep orange color, tops attached, firm.

- Cauliflower—bright white florets, tight, firm stalks.

- Celery—firm stalks, fresh leaves, firm texture.

- Cherries—shiny, plum colored, green stems.

- Corn (look for it early in the harvest because that's when it is sweetest).

- Garlic (best flavor is in late summer and early fall).

- Kale—firm stalks, crisp leaves, bright green color.

- Nectarines (my wife's favorite)—bright color, beautiful citrus smell.

- Onions (sweetest early in the summer; as onions age, the flavor gets stronger).

- Oregano—firm stems, crisp leaves, bright smell.

- Peaches—deep golden color, smooth skin, wonderful peachy smell.

las estaciones sean un poco diferentes donde viven, por lo que la disponibilidad de productos en las siguientes listas puede variar, según el clima en su zona.

EL MERCADO DE AGRICULTORES EN LA PRIMAVERA

La primavera siempre me recuerda las veces que mi madre y yo íbamos al mercado en Colombia. ¡Si pudieran ver los enormes locales llenos de agricultores que trataban de vender su cosecha! Había tanta belleza bajo un solo techo: colores vivos, gente tratando de regatear y obtener un precio más bajo, y filas interminables de productos agrícolas. La primavera siempre hace que me remonte a los años que viví en Medellín, Colombia. Esta es una lista de fabulosos ingredientes de primavera que pueden buscar en el mercado, además de descripciones, para ayudarlos a elegir los productos más frescos:

- Acelga (también se encuentra en el verano y a principios de otoño)—tallos crujientes, colores vivos, extremos recién cortados.
- Ajo verde (similar al cebollín pero con sabor a ajo)—tallos frescos, de color muy verde. Asegúrense de que no estén marchitos.
- Brotes de helecho—volutas apretadas, de color muy verde (son mejores si se comen enseguida).
- Cebollines—tallos firmes, olor fuerte, extremos no cortados.
- Champiñones silvestres (también se encuentran en el verano y otoño)—olor terroso, aspecto firme, se deben evitar si huelen a moho.
- Espárragos—piel lisa, color verde brillante, con los extremos recién cortados.

- Espinaca — color verde vivo, aroma fresco, crujiente.
- Habas—vainas firmes (las vainas más grandes son ideales para sopas o guisos).
- Hierbas—colores vivos, aroma agradable, firmes.
- Lechuga (también se encuentra en el verano y otoño)—cogollos enteros, sin lavar (cuando está sin lavar hay menor posibilidad de que estén contaminadas de bacterias).
- Menta—Hojas fuertes, olor fuerte a menta.
- Rábanos—color intenso, firmes, con tallo.
- Rúcula o arúgula—hojas de color verde oscuro, aroma fuerte.
- Tomillo—tallos fuertes, hojas brillantes, aroma fuerte.

EL MERCADO DE AGRICULTORES EN EL VERANO Y OTOÑO

¡Lleguen temprano, mi gente! Las multitudes se despiertan un poco antes durante el verano. El estado de ánimo también parece cambiar; el clima más caluroso tiende a hacer que haya música festiva, más niños y más productos agrícolas en el mercado. Al aproximarse el fin del verano e iniciarse el otoño, comienza la temporada del zapallo, los calabacines y las coles de Bruselas. Busquen estos productos en el verano y otoño:

- Ajo (sabe mejor al final del verano y principios de otoño).
- Apio—tallos y textura firmes, hojas frescas.
- Brócoli—con flores verdes apretadas y tallos firmes.
- Calabacín—cáscara lisa, textura firme, extremos con el corte fresco.

- Potatoes (also found in the winter)—firm, smooth skin, earthy smell.

- Pumpkins—hard shells, heavy (if they are light, they are dry).

- Strawberries—bright colors, sweet aroma, smooth skin, not dry.

- Sweet peppers—bright deep color, smooth skin, green stem.

- Tomatoes—smooth skin, fresh smell.

- Winter squash (the varieties seem endless)—firm, thick, heavy (if they are light, they are dry).

- Zucchini—smooth skin, firm texture, freshly cut ends.

LET'S TALK PREPARATION

Now what do we do with all of this amazing produce once we get home? That's easy, start cooking and creating! Use this book for inspiration and get creative with the produce. The recipes in this chapter are guides—feel free to add or subtract as you wish (and as your meal plan allows). All I ask is that you use the recipes to make your dishes taste amazing.

Thanks to the cooking "gods" and modern technology, we have many ways to cook vegetables. From roasting to sautéing to steaming, and even poaching, there is more than one way to eat your vegetables. Each style of cooking brings out certain characteristics of the vegetables you prepare; go ahead and find your favorite cooking method.

What is my favorite way to cook vegetables? I would have to say roasting them. This method allows deep flavors to develop while the vegetables cook in the oven. The only drawback is that roasting takes time. But the wait has its rewards.

I wish you luck and hope to run into you at the farmers' market!

- Calabaza—cáscara dura, pesada (si no pesa mucho es que está seca).

- Calabaza de invierno—(las variedades parecen infinitas), textura firme, gruesa y pesada (si no pesa mucho es que está seca).

- Cebollas (son más dulces a comienzos de verano; con el tiempo, el sabor de la cebolla se vuelve más fuerte).

- Cerezas—lustrosas, de color ciruela, con tallos verdes.

- Col—cabeza pesada, hojas y tallos frescos.

- Col rizada—tallo firme, hojas frescas y crujientes, de color verde intenso.

- Coles de Bruselas—(trate de conseguirlas en racimo, que es su estado más fresco), brotes verdes sin hojas pardas.

- Coliflor—con florecillas de vivo color blanco, apretadas, con tallo firme.

- Duraznos—de color dorado intenso, textura suave, maravilloso olor característico.

- Fresas—de color vivo y aroma dulce, superficie lisa, no seca.

- Maíz (búsquelo cuando recién salga la cosecha pues es más dulce).

- Nectarinas—(las preferidas de mi esposa), de color vivo, con un rico olor cítrico.

- Orégano—tallos firmes, hojas frescas, aromático.

- Papas—(también se encuentran en invierno), firmes, cáscara suave, aroma a tierra.

- Pimientos—tallos verdes, textura lisa y colores brillantes e intensos.

- Tomates—cáscara lisa, aroma fresco.

- Zanahorias—de color naranja intenso, con hojas, firmes.

HABLEMOS DE LA PREPARACIÓN

Ahora, ¿qué hacemos una vez que llegamos a casa con todos estos maravillosos vegetales y frutas? Es fácil, ¡comenzar a cocinar y crear! Usen este libro para inspirarse y ser creativos con los productos agrícolas. Las recetas de este capítulo son guías; no duden en añadir o quitar como deseen (y conforme lo permita su plan de alimentación). Lo único que pido es que usen las recetas para hacer que sus platos sepan de maravillas.

Gracias a todos los "dioses" de la cocina y la tecnología moderna, hay muchas formas de preparar vegetales. Hay más de una manera de comer los vegetales, desde asados, salteados, cocidos al vapor e incluso escalfados. Cada estilo de cocina resalta ciertas características de las hortalizas que se preparan; adelante y encuentren su método preferido.

¿Cuál es mi manera favorita de preparar vegetales? Diría que asarlos. Este método de cocción en el horno permite que los vegetales revelen sus sabores más intensos. La única desventaja es que asarlos toma tiempo. Pero la espera tiene sus recompensas.

Les deseo suerte y ¡espero encontrarme con ustedes en el mercado!

CHEF RONALDO'S GLOSSARY

THERE ARE MANY cooking terms and ingredients that are particular to Latin cuisine, and it seems each country in Latin America—Cuba, Colombia, Peru, Puerto Rico, Brazil, Chile, Ecuador, Argentina, Venezuela, Uruguay, Paraguay, and so on—has slightly different meanings for the same terms and ingredients. The beautiful thing is that we can all understand each other; cooking is an amazing art that gathers us all at the dinner table with amazing smells, textures, flavors, and conversation. Here are some of the terms and ingredients that matter to me. Hopefully they will become part of your culinary vocabulary as you cook your way through this book.

AVOCADO *(AGUACATE)*: We are used to seeing small Hass avocados and California avocados in the U.S., but the avocados I grew up with were large and green. Their texture was like butter when ripe, and they were mildly sweet. Avocados are a truly unique ingredient. They have tons of vitamins, minerals, fiber, and healthy monounsaturated fats to help keep your body going. The recipes in the book call for the Hass avocado.

AVOCADO OIL *(ACEITE DE AGUACATE)*: Avocado oil has tons of monounsaturated fat that is good for your heart. Most of the recipes in this book call for avocado oil.

BANANAS: One of my favorite fruits out there is the banana. I especially love to eat bananas before a workout. They give me the right amount of energy for an hour of exercise. An excellent source of potassium and fiber, bananas really are a great fruit. But be careful because size does matter here; the bigger the banana, the more carbohydrate it contains. So please be mindful of serving size and carbohydrate content when you eat bananas.

BLACK BEANS *(FRIJOLES NEGROS)*: Black beans are a staple in many Latin cuisines, especially in the Cuban kitchen. They are a great source of protein, dietary fiber, and deliciousness. I know they take time to cook, but it is worth the wait.

CILANTRO (OR FRESH CORIANDER): Cilantro is a fresh herb that looks very similar to parsley until you put your nose close to it and its wonderful, vibrant smell wakes your nose up! Cilantro is very strong and is often used in stews, salads, and as a finisher or garnish for many dishes.

COCONUT *(COCO)*: We're all familiar with the amazing fruit that palm trees give us. Not only do we get the meat from coconuts but also the wonderful coconut water. One of my favorite health benefits of coconuts is the high level of potassium in both the meat and the water, which makes coconuts a great substitute if you don't like bananas. (But keep in mind that coconut is high in saturated fat.) Coconut water is also a great way to replenish electrolytes such as potassium, after a hard workout. Be sure to avoid coconut water with added sugars.

CUMIN *(COMINO)*: I love cumin! If you don't have it in your pantry, stop reading and go buy it. This seed packs

GLOSARIO DEL CHEF RONALDO

HAY MUCHOS TÉRMINOS e ingredientes que son inherentes a la comida latina y, según parece, cada país latinoamericano —Cuba, Colombia, Perú, Puerto Rico, Brasil, Chile, Ecuador, Argentina, Venezuela, Uruguay, Paraguay, etc.— atribuye significados ligeramente diferentes a los mismos términos e ingredientes. Lo lindo es que podemos entendernos; cocinar es un arte maravilloso que nos congrega a todos ante la mesa con fabulosos olores, texturas, sabores y conversación. Estos son algunos de los términos e ingredientes que son importantes para mí. Espero que se hagan parte de su vocabulario culinario a medida que preparen las recetas de este libro.

ACEITE DE AGUACATE: El aceite de aguacate tiene muchísima grasa monoinsaturada, que es buena para el corazón. La mayoría de las recetas de este libro usan aceite de aguacate.

AGUACATE (PALTA): Estamos acostumbrados a ver los pequeños aguacates Hass y los de California en Estados Unidos, pero los aguacates de mi infancia eran grandes y verdes. Su textura cuando estaban maduros era como la de la mantequilla, y eran ligeramente dulces. Los aguacates realmente son un ingrediente extraordinario. Tienen muchas vitaminas, minerales, fibra y saludables grasas monoinsaturadas, que le dan energía al cuerpo. En las recetas de este libro se usan aguacates Hass.

BONIATO: Los boniatos blancos usualmente se encuentran en Florida, pero me gusta usarlos como sustitutos de los boniatos rojos cuando puedo. La batata o el boniato blanco es más dulce que el boniato más común y ofrece beneficios muy positivos para la salud. Este es un excelente dato para las personas con diabetes: Debido a su bajo índice glucémico, las batatas o boniatos, si se comen en cantidades moderadas, pueden tener menos impacto en el nivel de glucosa que otros tipos de tubérculos. Pero de todos modos tienen carbohidratos, o sea que coman porciones pequeñas. Además, son una excelente fuente de fibra alimentaria, vitamina A y vitamina C.

CALABAZA: Existen varios tipos de calabaza, y todos tienen sabor y textura diferente, pero de todos modos, son bastante parecidos. Se puede asar la calabaza por sí sola, agregarse a guisos o preparar sopas con ella. Contiene mucha vitamina A y potasio.

CILANTRO (CULANTRO): El cilantro es una hierba fresca de apariencia muy similar a la del perejil, pero cuando se pone cerca de la nariz, ¡su maravilloso y fuerte sabor te despierta el olfato! El cilantro es muy fuerte y se usa con frecuencia en guisos, ensaladas o para adornar o darles el toque final a muchos platillos.

COCO: Todos conocemos el estupendo fruto que nos brindan las palmas. No solo aprovechamos la pulpa del coco, sino también su maravillosa agua. Uno de los beneficios de salud que más me gusta del coco es el alto contenido de potasio que contienen tanto la pulpa como el agua, así que, si no les gusta el plátano, el coco puede ser un

some serious flavor, and it plays well with other ingredients. You can buy ground cumin or the whole seed at the supermarket. Let's talk health benefits: this little seed contains some iron, calcium, and potassium among other nutrients. Yes, my mind is blown!

DRY BAY LEAF *(HOJAS DE LAUREL)*: This amazing leaf does wonders in the kitchen. It adds an earthy note to any stew, braise, roast, or soup. This is a must-have ingredient and, frankly, it's one of my favorites to use.

FLANK STEAK *(FALDA)*: This meat is used in the famous Cuban dish *Ropa Vieja* and in stews. The longer you cook this meat, the more it begins to fall apart (just like old clothes that become loose and shredded over time). Flank steak is a great source of protein, and it's lean so the fat content is low.

GREEN PLANTAIN *(PLÁTANO VERDE)*: Green plantains are a staple in my kitchen. They are often fried, but why not cook them in the oven and call them "Twice-Baked *Tostones*"? It sounds absolutely crazy, but it tastes so good. *Plátanos* are a great source of vitamin C, potassium, and fiber. And by baking these bad boys instead of frying them, we get to enjoy the health benefits of plantains without extra fat.

KOSHER SALT *(SAL KOSHER)*: Kosher salt is a variety of salt with a large grain size. Why use this salt? A little goes a long way in your cooking. Remember that salt is the vessel to bring out all the amazing flavors of your ingredients, but you should use it only in small amounts to keep your recipes healthy.

LIMES *(LIMAS)*: I love some good limes, especially when you finish your dishes with them. Whether you're spritzing the juice on a piece of fish, in a stew or soup, or even on

a mango, lime adds the acidity that some dishes need. Lime juice will become a favorite weapon in your culinary arsenal.

MAMEY SAPOTE: This ingredient is a lot of fun to say, and it is the king of fruits as far as Cubans are concerned. The fruit is the size of a sweet potato, and it has rough skin. The salmon color of the fruit is beautiful, and the flesh gives easily when ripe. *Mamey sapote* is very hard to find, but if you do find it, make a nice smoothie and enjoy the amazing flavor.

MANGO: Like many other fruits, mango has different stages of ripeness. It matures from green to yellow and finally to red. It starts out tart, but when it has fully ripened it is nice and sweet. In order to get the most nutritional benefit out of a mango you should eat it whole instead of drinking the juice—that way you maximize the fiber content. Always eat fruit in small portions because it does contain natural sugars and carbohydrate.

ORANGES *(NARANJAS)*: Any variety of orange can be used in the recipes in this book (though many call for navel oranges). We all know oranges contain a kick-butt amount of vitamin C, which makes them great ingredients for salads, drinks, roasts, and marinades.

OREGANO *(ORÉGANO)*: A staple ingredient in many Cuban kitchens, oregano can be used fresh, dried, or ground. It adds an excellent flavor to roasts, braises, stews, salads, and marinades. This little herb also contains vitamin K, fiber, and antioxidants (when consumed fresh). It's a pretty cool herb if you ask me.

PUMPKIN *(CALABAZA)*: There are several types of pumpkin out there and all of them have different flavor profiles and textures, but they're all still relatively similar.

excelente sustituto. (Eso sí, tengan en cuenta que el coco tiene mucha grasa saturada.) El agua de coco también es una gran manera de remplazar electrolitos como el potasio después de hacer mucho ejercicio. Pero debemos evitar el agua de coco con azúcar agregada.

COMINO: ¡Me encanta el comino! Si no lo tienen en la despensa, dejen de leer y vayan a comprarlo. Esta semilla tiene mucho sabor y va bien con otros ingredientes. Pueden comprar el comino en polvo o la semilla entera en el supermercado. Hablemos de sus beneficios para la salud: esta semillita contiene hierro, calcio y potasio, entre otros nutrientes. Sí, ¡impresionante!

CÚRCUMA (AZAFRÁN DE LA INDIA, AMARILLITO, PALILLO): Los cubanos típicamente usan el bijol, un colorante amarillo, en la cocina, pero a mí me gusta la cúrcuma porque da un lindo color amarillo, acompañado de ciertos beneficios para la salud. La cúrcuma contiene agentes antiinflamatorios en cantidades pequeñas, que pueden beneficiar a las personas con artritis e hinchazón de las articulaciones, además de ayudarlas a recuperarse después de hacer ejercicio.

FALDA: Este corte de carne se usa en el famoso platillo cubano llamado ropa vieja así como en guisos. Cuando esta carne se cuece por mucho tiempo, comienza a deshilacharse (igual que las prendas viejas, que se deshilan y hacen trizas con el tiempo). La falda es una excelente fuente de proteína y tiene poca grasa, por ser magra.

FRIJOLES NEGROS: Los frijoles negros son un ingrediente básico en la cocina de muchos países latinoamericanos, particularmente la cubana. Son una excelente fuente de proteína, fibra alimentaria y sabor. Sé que su preparación toma tiempo, pero la espera vale la pena.

HOJAS DE LAUREL: Esta fabulosa hoja hace maravillas en la cocina. Le da un toque natural a cualquier guiso, estofado, asado o sopa. Es un ingrediente esencial y, francamente, uno de mis preferidos.

LIMAS (LIMONES VERDES): Me encantan las limas o limones verdes, particularmente como toque final de los platillos. Cuando se le echa un chorrito de limón verde a ya sea, el pescado, un guiso, una sopa o incluso a un mango, el limón verde aporta la acidez que ciertos platillos necesitan. El limón verde pasará a ser una de sus armas favoritas en el arsenal culinario.

MAMEY ZAPOTE: El nombre de este ingrediente es divertido. Se trata de la reina de las frutas, según los cubanos. Es del tamaño de una batata y tiene la corteza áspera. El color salmón de la fruta es bello, y la pulpa se deshace fácilmente cuando madura. Es muy difícil encontrar el mamey zapote, pero si lo llegan a hallar, preparen un rico batido y disfruten el maravilloso sabor.

MANGO: Como muchas otras frutas, el mango tiene diferentes etapas de madurez. A medida que madura pasa de ser verde a amarillo y, finalmente, rojo. Al comienzo es ácido, pero cuando madura del todo es dulce. Para obtener el máximo beneficio nutricional del mango, deben comerlo entero en vez de beber su jugo, para maximizar el contenido de fibra. Siempre coman porciones pequeñas de la fruta porque contiene azúcar natural y carbohidratos.

NARANJAS: Se puede usar cualquier variedad de naranja en las recetas de este libro. Todos sabemos que las naranjas contienen abundante vitamina C, lo que las hace un excelente ingrediente de ensaladas, bebidas, asados y adobos.

Pumpkin can be roasted on its own, added to stews, or made into a soup. It contains good amounts of vitamin A and potassium.

SOFRITO: There is no good English translation for this word. So what is *sofrito*? It's a combination of herbs, citrus, spices, and veggies, and it is the base for many of my Cuban dishes. You can make different types of *sofrito* depending on what you're cooking—this is a great time to use your creativity and let your cooking knowledge take over. It just has to taste good.

TURMERIC (CÚRCUMA): Cubans typically use *bijol,* a yellow coloring, in their cooking, but I like turmeric because it gives you a beautiful yellow color *and* some health benefits to go with it. Turmeric contains small amounts of anti-inflammatory agents, which can help people with arthritis and joint swelling and can aid in recovery after workouts.

WHITE SWEET POTATO (BONIATO): White sweet potatoes are typically found in Florida, but I like to use them as a substitute for sweet potatoes when I can. White sweet potatoes have a sweeter flavor than regular sweet potatoes and provide some really great health benefits. Here is a great fact for people with diabetes: Due to their low glycemic index, sweet potatoes may have a little less impact on blood glucose levels than other potatoes if eaten in small amounts. But they still have carbohydrate, so keep your portions small. They are also a great source of dietary fiber, vitamin A, and vitamin C.

YUCCA: The variety of yucca we find in supermarkets is sweet yucca. It tastes a bit like a potato, only better. There are two layers of skin you must peel before preparing yucca: the thick outer brown layer, and the inner pink layer. The vegetable is generally boiled or thinly sliced and baked to make chips before eating. It is also great in stews because it holds up very well to long cooking times. Yucca packs a lot of carbohydrate, so be mindful of your portions when eating this vegetable.

ORÉGANO: El orégano es un ingrediente básico de muchas recetas cubanas y se puede usar fresco, seco o molido. Le da un excelente toque de sabor a los asados, guisos, estofados, ensaladas y adobos. Esta hierbita también contiene vitamina K, fibra y antioxidantes (cuando se consume fresco). Es una hierba fabulosa, en mi opinión.

PLÁTANO (BANANA, GUINEO): Una de mis frutas favoritas es el plátano. Me gusta en particular comer plátanos antes de hacer ejercicio. Me dan la cantidad necesaria de energía para una hora de ejercicio. Son una excelente fuente de potasio y fibra, una fruta realmente fabulosa. Pero cuidado con el tamaño, pues es importante en este contexto; cuanto más grande el plátano, más carbohidratos tiene. O sea que tengan en cuenta el tamaño de la porción y cantidad de carbohidratos cuando coman plátanos.

PLÁTANO VERDE: Los plátanos verdes son básicos en mi cocina. A menudo se fríen, pero ¿por qué no meterlos al horno y llamarlos "Tostones horneados dos veces"? Suena de locos, pero saben muy bien. Los plátanos son una gran fuente de vitamina C, potasio y fibra. Y cuando se preparan en el horno en vez de freírlos, podemos gozar de los beneficios del plátano sin la grasa adicional.

SAL *KOSHER*: La sal *kosher* es una variedad de sal de grano grande. ¿Por qué se usa este tipo de sal? Un poquito produce grandes resultados. Recuerden que la sal es la manera de resaltar todos los sabores maravillosos de los ingredientes, pero solo deben usarla en cantidades pequeñas para que sus recetas sigan siendo saludables.

SOFRITO: ¿Qué es el sofrito? Es una combinación de hierbas, fruta cítrica, especias y vegetales, y es la base de muchos de mis platos cubanos. Se puede preparar una variedad de sofritos, según lo que se va a cocinar. Es una gran oportunidad de ser creativos y dar rienda suelta a nuestros conocimientos de cocina. Simplemente tiene que saber bien.

YUCA (MANDIOCA): La variedad de yuca que se encuentra en los supermercados es la dulce. Tiene un sabor parecido al de la papa, pero mejor. Se pelan dos capas de piel antes de preparar la yuca: la exterior, que es gruesa y marrón, y la interior que es rosada. Antes de comer estos tubérculos, por lo general se hierven o se cortan en rodajas finas que se hornean para hacer hojuelas. También es muy buena en guisos, pues no se deshace por más que se cueza. La yuca tiene muchos carbohidratos, o sea que tengan en cuenta el tamaño de la porción cuando coman estos vegetales.

YOUR PANTRY THE RONALDO WAY

A WELL-STOCKED PANTRY is essential to a healthy home. It also saves time and money. Who doesn't love that? Below you'll find tips and a list of staple ingredients to help you create the perfect pantry.

Many of us use our pantry space to store plastic bags and other household items. But we can do better, people! Here are some tips for utilizing pantry space to create a hub of health for the greater good of our families:

- Collect clear glass or plastic storage containers in various sizes (gallon, quart, pint, half-pint). Use these to store dry ingredients. If you can see inside the container, you'll know exactly what you have and how much you have.

- Store the healthiest foods at eye level. If you keep treats such as cookies or chips in the house, store them on a high shelf or towards the back so you don't see them and aren't tempted to eat them.

- Keep your pantry neat and organized. When it looks good, you'll feel good!

- Take a bi-weekly inventory of what you have in the pantry so you don't buy duplicate items. This will also keep the pantry items you have fresh in your mind, which may be helpful when meal planning.

- Invest in labels or a label maker and properly label your containers so you don't have to play the "what is in the jar" game.

PANTRY STAPLES

Avocado oil	Kosher salt
Beef stock (quart size, unsalted)*	Lentils (dried)
Black beans (dried and canned)	Limes
Canned tomatoes (crushed)	Nuts (almonds, walnuts, pine nuts)
Canned tuna (in water)	Olive oil
Chicken stock (quart size, unsalted)*	Pepper
Coconut oil	Red beans (dried and canned)
Garbanzo beans (dried and canned)	Tomato paste
Garlic	Vegetable stock (quart size, unsalted)*

* Stocks are flavorful and affordable. I keep at least 3 of each flavor on hand at all times.

UNA DESPENSA "A LA RONALDO"

UNA DESPENSA BIEN SURTIDA es esencial para un hogar saludable. También ahorra tiempo y dinero. ¿Y a quién no le gusta eso? A continuación encontrarán consejos y una lista de ingredientes básicos que los ayudarán a crear la despensa perfecta.

Muchos usamos la despensa para guardar bolsas de plástico y otros artículos domésticos. Pero, ¡amigos, podemos hacer algo mejor! Estos consejos sobre el uso del espacio en la despensa ayudan a crear un centro de salud, para beneficio de nuestras familias:

- Coleccionen recipientes de vidrio o plástico de diversos tamaños para guardar las cosas (de galón, cuarto de galón, pinta, media pinta). Úsenlos para guardar ingredientes secos. Si pueden ver el interior del recipiente, sabrán exactamente qué y cuánto tienen.
- Guarden los alimentos más saludables a la altura de los ojos. Si tienen golosinas como galletas o papitas en casa, pónganlas en una repisa alta o hacia atrás, escondidas, para que no se vean tentados de comerlas.
- Mantengan la despensa ordenada y organizada. Cuando luce bien, ¡nos hace sentir bien!
- Cada dos semanas, hagan un inventario de lo que tienen en la despensa para que no compren lo mismo. Esto también les recordará lo que tienen en ella, lo que puede ayudarlos con la planificación de las comidas.
- Inviertan en etiquetas o una maquinita para hacer etiquetas, y marquen debidamente los recipientes para que no tengan que adivinar qué hay en cada frasco.

ARTÍCULOS BÁSICOS PARA SU DESPENSA

Aceite de aguacate	Frijoles colorados (secos y enlatados)
Aceite de coco	Garbanzos (secos y enlatados)
Aceite de oliva	Lentejas (secas)
Ajo	Limas o limones verdes
Atún enlatado (en agua)	Nueces (almendras, piñones, de nogal)
Caldo de pollo (cuarto de galón, sin sal)*	Pasta de tomate
Caldo de res (cuarto de galón, sin sal)*	Pimienta
Caldo vegetal (cuarto de galón, sin sal)*	Sal *kosher*
Frijoles negros (secos y enlatados)	Tomates enlatados (aplastados)

* Los caldos tienen mucho sabor y son económicos. En todo momento tengo a la mano por lo menos tres de cada sabor.

ALL ABOUT OILS

Avocado oil has a 500°F smoke point. It is a healthy fat and a good way to add monounsaturated fats to your cooking. It's great for dressings, shakes, and high-heat cooking.

Coconut oil can add a unique flavor to baked goods, and research is ongoing into possible health benefits.

SPICES

Allspice

Bay leaf (dried)

Cayenne pepper

Cinnamon (ground)

Coriander (ground)

Cumin (ground)

Curry powder

Garlic powder

Onion powder

Nutmeg (ground)

Smoked paprika

Saffron

Oregano (dried)

Thyme

SAZÓN (RONALDO'S SPECIAL BLEND)

SERVES: 16
SERVING SIZE: Approximately 1/4 teaspoon

2 teaspoons coarse kosher salt
1 teaspoon cracked black pepper
1/4 teaspoon ground cumin
1/2 teaspoon garlic powder
1 teaspoon dried oregano
1/8 teaspoon ground nutmeg

Talk about awesome flavor! I always have this special, multipurpose blend on hand for when I need to add a quick dash of seasoning to a dish. This also works well as a rub for chicken, beef, and pork. Remember, a little goes a very long way with this sazón—it adds great flavor and a beautiful aroma, and it will make your palate very happy. Go ahead, make some and store it in a glass jar. Just remember to label it.

EXCHANGES/CHOICES
free food

CALORIES 0 | **CALORIES FROM FAT** 0 | **TOTAL FAT** 0g | **SATURATED FAT** 0g | **TRANS FAT** 0g
CHOLESTEROL 0mg | **SODIUM** 240mg | **POTASSIUM** 0mg | **TOTAL CARBOHYDRATE** 0g
DIETARY FIBER 0g | **SUGARS** 0g | **PROTEIN** 0g | **PHOSPHORUS** 0mg

TODO ACERCA DE LOS ACEITES

El aceite de aguacate tiene un punto de ahumado de 500°F. Es una grasa saludable y una buena manera de agregar grasas monoinsaturadas a sus comidas. Es fabuloso en aliños, batidos y los alimentos preparados a temperatura alta.

El aceite de coco puede darle un original toque de sabor a los productos de repostería, y actualmente se investigan sus beneficios para la salud.

ESPECIAS

Ajo en polvo	Hoja de laurel
Azafrán	Nuez moscada molida
Canela	Orégano seco
Cebolla en polvo	Pimentón español ahumado *(paprika)*
Cilantro (molido)	Pimienta de cayena
Comino	Pimienta inglesa o de Jamaica *(allspice)*
Curry en polvo	Tomillo

SAZÓN (MEZCLA ESPECIAL DE RONALDO)

RINDE: 16 porciones
TAMAÑO DE LA PORCIÓN: Aproximadamente 1/4 cdta.

2 cdtas. de sal kosher gruesa
1 cdta. de pimienta negra gruesa
1/4 cdta. de comino
1/2 cdta. de ajo en polvo
1 cdta. de orégano seco
1/8 cdta. de nuez moscada molida

¡Esto es lo mejor para realzar el sabor! Siempre tengo a la mano esta mezcla especial para cuando necesito condimentar algo rápidamente. Es muy buena con el pollo, la carne de res y el cerdo. Recuerden que solo necesitan un poquito de esta sazón, pues tiene mucho sabor, además de un gran aroma, y el paladar se lo agradecerá. Adelante, prepárenla y pónganla en un frasco de vidrio. No se olviden de ponerle una etiqueta.

SELECCIONES/INTERCAMBIOS
No cuenta

CALORÍAS 0 | **CALORÍAS DE GRASA** 0 | **TOTAL DE GRASA** 0g | **GRASA SATURADA** 0g **GRASA TRANS** 0g | **COLESTEROL** 0mg | **SODIO** 240mg | **POTASIO** 0mg | **TOTAL DE CARBOHIDRATOS** 0g | **FIBRA ALIMENTARIA** 0g | **AZÚCARES** 0g | **PROTEÍNA** 0g | **FÓSFORO** 0mg

Whole Grains

Barley

Brown Rice

Farro

Oatmeal

Quinoa

Baking

Agave nectar

All-purpose flour

Baking powder

Baking soda

Cocoa powder (unsweetened)

Coconut (unsweetened)

Self-rising flour

Sugar (in moderation)

Whole-wheat flour

Gluten-Free Flours

Almond flour

Brown rice flour

Cornstarch

Millet or Montina flour

Potato starch

Tapioca starch

Teff flour

White rice flour

White sorghum flour

Xanthan or guar gum

Yucca flour

GRANOS ENTEROS

Arroz integral

Avena

Cebada

Farro

Quinua

REPOSTERÍA

Azúcar (en moderación)

Bicarbonato de sodio

Cacao en polvo (sin endulzar)

Coco (sin endulzar)

Harina de trigo integral

Harina preparada

Harina sin preparar

Néctar de agave

Polvo de hornear

HARINAS SIN GLUTEN

Fécula de papa

Fécula de tapioca

Goma xantana o guar

Harina de almendras

Harina de arroz blanco

Harina de arroz integral

Harina de mijo o Montina

Harina de sorgo blanco

Harina de tef

Harina de yuca

Maicena (de maíz)

KITCHEN ESSENTIALS

NOW THAT WE GOT the pantry out of the way, it is time to see what we have in the kitchen cupboards and the oven drawer (where we Latinos used to store pots) so we're prepared to tackle the recipes in this book. This list is just a guide, *mi gente*, but I believe that some of these must-have tools really optimize your cooking at home. So let's get this going!

RONALDO'S TOP FOUR:

1. A smile.
2. Love.
3. Music (I like salsa and some Latin hip hop).
4. A good outfit (When your family or guests see you looking good, they feel good too!).

Now let's have a look at our culinary arsenal!

COOKING TOOLS

4 LARGE CUTTING BOARDS: They're perfect for cutting red meat, poultry, pork, and greens, and other tasks. I prefer wooden cutting boards.

PRESSURE COOKER: An easy tool to make rice, soups, stews, and other goodies.

SMALL, MEDIUM, AND LARGE POTS: For cooking stocks, soups, and stews.

DUTCH OVEN: Great for making stews both inside the house and on the grill.

LARGE CAST IRON SKILLET: Use it to sauté, braise, grill, and prepare Spanish tortillas.

SMALL CAST IRON SKILLET: To sauté and grill smaller items.

SMALL, MEDIUM, AND LARGE NONSTICK PANS

BOTTLE OPENER: For opening wine and beer.

LIME SQUEEZER: How many times have you squirted citrus juice in your eyes because you decided to squeeze the fruit by hand? Probably a handful of times. A lime squeezer does 3 things—it extracts all the juice while saving you time and protecting your eyes.

CAN OPENER: Spend the money on a solid one. Dollar store can openers rust and break too easily.

MEDIUM AND LARGE STRAINERS

MEDIUM-SIZE FLOUR SIFTER

LARGE WOK: I mainly use a wok to fry things or prepare nice sautés. It gives the food a unique flavor.

PARING KNIFE: I like using German or Japanese knives.

CHEF'S KNIFE: I like using German or Japanese knives.

BONING KNIFE: Try to use one with a 5-inch blade. This is your dirty work knife. You can use it to debone a chicken or a pig if you are up to it.

LO ESENCIAL PARA LA COCINA

AHORA QUE TENEMOS la despensa llena, es hora de ver qué tenemos en los muebles de la cocina y la gaveta del horno (donde los latinos guardamos las ollas) a fin de tener lo necesario para preparar las recetas de este libro. La lista es apenas una guía, mi gente, pero creo que algunos de estos utensilios esenciales realmente optimizan la preparación de alimentos en casa. ¡Manos a la obra!

LOS CUATRO ELEMENTOS BÁSICOS DE RONALDO:

1. Una sonrisa

2. Amor

3. Música (me gusta la salsa y un poco de hip hop latino)

4. Un buen atuendo (cuando los familiares o invitados te ven bien, ¡se sienten bien también!)

Ahora, ¡echémosle un vistazo a nuestro arsenal culinario!

UTENSILIOS DE COCINA

4 TABLAS GRANDES DE CORTAR: Son perfectas para cortar carne roja, aves, cerdo, verduras y otras tareas esenciales. Prefiero las tablas de madera.

OLLA A PRESIÓN: Un utensilio que facilita la preparación de arroz, sopas, guisos y otras maravillas.

OLLAS PEQUEÑAS, MEDIANAS Y GRANDES: Para preparar caldos, sopas y guisos.

OLLA CON TAPA, PESADA *(DUTCH OVEN)***:** Excelente para hacer guisos en casa y a la parrilla.

SARTÉN GRANDE DE HIERRO FUNDIDO: Se usa para saltear, guisar, asar y preparar tortilla española.

SARTÉN PEQUEÑA DE HIERRO FUNDIDO: Para saltear y asar cosas pequeñas.

OLLAS PEQUEÑAS, MEDIANAS Y GRANDES EN LAS QUE NO SE PEGUEN LOS ALIMENTOS

SACACORCHOS Y ABRIDOR DE BOTELLAS: Para abrir el vino y la cerveza.

EXPRIMIDOR: ¿Cuántas veces les ha caído jugo cítrico en los ojos porque decidieron exprimir la fruta a mano? Probablemente varias. Un exprimidor hace tres cosas: extrae todo el jugo mientras les ahorra tiempo y les protege los ojos.

ABRELATAS: Inviertan en uno bueno. Los abridores de la tienda de a dólar se oxidan y rompen fácilmente.

COLADOR MEDIANO Y GRANDE

CERNIDOR MEDIANO

WOK GRANDE: Uso el wok principalmente para freír o preparar salteados deliciosos. Le da un sabor especial a la comida.

PEELER: Williams-Sonoma has a clear plastic one that works like magic.

FOOD PROCESSOR: Everyone loves a food processor, and it cuts down on preparation time.

KITCHENAID MIXER: This gadget is expensive, but it has so many uses and it will last forever. I've had mine for 10 years now, and it's still going strong.

SMALL AND MEDIUM WHISKS

TONGS

HAND (IMMERSION) BLENDER: Great for finishing sauces, whipping, or quick blending.

SLOTTED SERVING SPOON

REGULAR SERVING SPOON

PLASTIC AND METAL SPATULAS

2 ROASTING PANS: They should be big enough to fit your oven.

POULTRY SHEARS OR A CLEAVER: I prefer the cleaver.

LARGE ROLLING PIN: Handy for rolling out dough and keeping people out of the kitchen while you chef it up. Ha-ha!

RAMEKINS: For preparing flan, custards, and bread puddings.

MORTAR AND PESTLE: These tools are great for crushing herbs and spices and making the ever-famous guacamole.

ESPRESSO MAKER: If you are making Cuban-inspired food, you should drink Cuban coffee!

SQUEEZE BOTTLES: Use these to serve sauces and oils. They also make measuring a lot easier.

FOOD SCALE

12 KITCHEN TOWELS: Why 12? Because messes can pop up at any time, *mi gente!*

PARCHMENT PAPER

Meal Preparation

Let's talk meal preparation! When I say "meal preparation," I mean a form of batch cooking to prepare you for the week ahead. With our busy lifestyles, nothing could set you up better for the coming week than having meals ready for you in the refrigerator. All you have to do is place a precooked dish in the microwave for 2–3 minutes and you'll have a great homemade meal that will fuel you for the next couple of hours.

So when is a good time to do said meal preparation? I think Sunday is a perfect day to do so (though a different day may be better for you). My friend Helen preps while watching *novelas* on Sunday afternoons; I prep watching the Giants play. Get up early on your prep day and make a menu that includes three different proteins, a blend of your favorite vegetables, and two or three different starches. This way you can change up the flavor at each meal and give yourself some variety, which is always the key to not getting bored with your meals. I like to stick to one vegetable blend per week, but I change it week to week to keep us from having the same thing all the time.

Throughout this book you will find recipes that are perfect for meal preparation, and I will indicate the recipes that I think are better options for early prepara-

CUCHILLO PARA PELAR: Me gusta usar cuchillos alemanes o japoneses.

CUCHILLO DE CHEF: Me gusta usar cuchillos alemanes o japoneses.

CUCHILLO PARA DESHUESAR: Prueben uno con una cuchilla de 5 pulgadas. Se trata del cuchillo para tareas pesadas. Lo pueden usar para deshuesar un pollo o cerdo si están dispuestos a hacerlo.

PELADOR: Williams-Sonoma tiene uno de plástico trasparente que es mágico.

PROCESADOR DE ALIMENTOS: A todos les gusta el procesador de alimentos, porque acorta el tiempo de preparación.

BATIDORA KITCHENAID: Este implemento es caro pero tiene muchos usos y dura para siempre. Tengo la mía desde hace 10 años y todavía está en perfecto estado.

BATIDOR DE MANO PEQUEÑO Y MEDIANO

PINZAS

BATIDORA A MANO (DE INMERSIÓN): Fabulosa para darle el toque final a las salsas y batir rápidamente.

ESPUMADERA

CUCHARÓN REGULAR PARA SERVIR

ESPÁTULAS DE PLÁSTICO Y METAL

2 ASADERAS: Deben ser suficientemente grandes para el horno.

TIJERAS O CUCHILLO DE CARNICERO PARA AVE DE CORRAL: Prefiero el cuchillo de carnicero.

RODILLO GRANDE: Es práctico para estirar masas y mantener a la gente fuera de la cocina mientras estás ocupado. ¡Jajá!

TARTERAS INDIVIDUALES: Para preparar flan, natilla y pudín de pan.

MAJA Y MORTERO: Estos utensilios son excelentes para aplastar hierbas y especias, y hacer el famoso guacamole.

CAFETERA DE *ESPRESSO*: Si están preparando comida a la cubana, ¡tienen que beber café cubano!

BOTELLAS PARA APRETAR: Úsenlas para servir salsas y aceites. También facilitan mucho la medición.

BALANZA DE ALIMENTOS

12 SECADORES DE COCINA: ¿Por qué 12? Porque ensuciamos a cada rato, ¡mi gente!

PAPEL MANTEQUILLA

PREPARACIÓN DE ALIMENTOS

¡Hablemos de la preparación de alimentos! Cuando digo "preparación de alimentos", me refiero a cuando preparamos una gran cantidad de comida y nos alistamos para la semana siguiente. Con nuestro atareado estilo de vida, nada mejor que empezar la semana con comidas listas en el refrigerador. Todo lo que tienen que hacer es colocar un platillo precocido en el microondas por 2-3 minutos y tendrán una fabulosa comida hecha en casa y que los llenará de energía por un par de horas.

Entonces, ¿cuál es el mejor momento para la preparación de alimentos? Pienso que el domingo es el día

tion than others. You can use the Side Dishes chapter (page 94) to select a vegetable dish for the week, and you can make a protein from the Surf and Turf chapter (page 224), or if you are a stew fan, grab a protein from Stews: Feeding the Whole Family (page 80). You see how easy it is? That's why you will love this book; most of the thinking has been taken out of the equation. The only question you have to ask yourself is, "How adventurous do I want to become?"

Now you have everything you need to get cooking, *mi gente*! I hope the recipes in this book will speak to your heart and help you become an even healthier version of yourself for the rest of your life. *Toma! (The word "toma" literally means to take or to capture. I use it throughout the book to convey a sense of victory or accomplishment. It's a great way to say, "That dish came out great!")*

perfecto para hacerlo (aunque quizá otro día sea mejor para ustedes). Mi amiga Helen cocina mientras ve novelas los domingos por la tarde; yo preparo los alimentos mientras veo los partidos de los Giants. Levántense temprano el día de preparación y hagan un menú que incluya tres proteínas diferentes, una combinación de sus vegetales preferidos y dos o tres almidones distintos. Esta es una manera de cambiar el sabor de cada comida y tener un poco de variedad, que es la clave para no aburrirse de lo que se come. Me gusta limitarme a una combinación de vegetales por semana, pero voy variando de una semana a otra para evitar hacer lo mismo todo el tiempo.

En todo este libro encontrarán recetas perfectas para la preparación de alimentos, e indicaré las recetas que pienso que son mejores opciones que otras para preparar con anticipación. Pueden usar el capítulo de Acompañantes (pág. 94) para seleccionar un plato de vegetales para la semana, y pueden hacer una proteína del capítulo de Mar y tierra (pág. 224) o, si son aficionados a los guisos, usar una proteína de Sancochos para alimentar a toda la familia (pág. 80). ¿Ven qué fácil es? Por eso les encantará este libro; no es necesario pensar mucho. Lo único que se deben preguntar es "¿Cuán intrépido quiero ser?" Ahora, ¡ya tienen todo lo que necesitan para cocinar, mi gente! Espero que estas recetas les lleguen al fondo del alma y los ayuden a ser una versión más saludable de ustedes mismos el resto de su vida. ¡Toma! (*Uso esta palabra en todo el libro para trasmitir la sensación de victoria o logro. Es una excelente manera de decir, "¡Ese platillo salió fabuloso!"*)

GLUTEN-FREE FLOUR SUBSTITUTES

TODAY MANY PEOPLE suffer from some kind of gluten intolerance or allergy, and some people, like me, choose to live a gluten-free lifestyle for their health. We all know traditional desserts are not the best for people because they are high in carbohydrate, unhealthy fats, and calories. And desserts made with wheat flour cannot be eaten by people on a gluten-free diet. But if you live a gluten-free lifestyle, you can eat gluten-free, flour–based desserts in small portions. That sounds pretty cool to me! So I asked myself, "How can this be done?" And I did what anyone would do—I jumped on the Internet. I researched, and researched, and researched, and I finally compiled great lists of gluten-free flours and flour blends. The ingredients below are available at health-food stores, by mail order, and increasingly at supermarkets. Bob's Red Mill is a good brand for gluten-free products.

Gluten-Free Flours

I am always looking online for great-tasting, healthy, and gluten-free flours. I'm not sure about you, but I know when I go to my local health-food store and look at the plethora of gluten-free flours, I am overwhelmed by the selection. I used to go home with nothing and just use whatever I had in the pantry. But with some research and experimenting I've come up with some of the best available gluten-free flours for your everyday needs

BROWN RICE FLOUR: A great alternative to wheat flour, brown rice flour also adds protein, iron, fiber, and B vita-

mins to your diet. Its use is not limited to baking; it could be used to coat fish, meat, or chicken for baking—or if you feel brave, you can make some pasta with it.

FAVA BEAN FLOUR: This flour is a great source of protein (a perk for vegetarians), iron, and fiber. Use this flour in combination with other gluten-free flours. It does not do well alone.

GARBANZO BEAN FLOUR: Loaded with protein, fiber, and iron, garbanzo bean flour is excellent for making pizza crusts or breads. You can also use it to thicken stews, soups, or sauces.

MILLET FLOUR: This flour is a great source of protein, essential amino acids, and fibers. Millet flour is so versatile due to its mild flavor that you can use it in savory or sweet baking.

QUINOA FLOUR: Quinoa is one of the oldest cultivated grains in the world, and it makes one of the most nutritious grain flours on the market. Quinoa flour is a great source of protein and amino acids. It is also a great replacement for wheat flour in cookies, pancakes, oven-baked breaded chicken, and many other things.

TAPIOCA STARCH/FLOUR: This flour is made from the starch of the yucca root. It has many uses, including thickening sauces, pie fillings, and soups. It can also add some chewiness to your favorite cookies. For best results, combine it with other gluten-free flours.

SUSTITUTOS DE HARINA SIN GLUTEN

HOY EN DÍA MUCHA GENTE tiene algún tipo de intolerancia o alergia al gluten y algunas personas, como yo, optan por comer sin gluten por el bien de su salud. Todos sabemos que los postres tradicionales no son los mejores para la gente pues tienen muchos carbohidratos, grasas poco saludables y calorías. Y las personas que omiten el gluten en su alimentación no pueden comer los postres hechos con harina de trigo. Pero si no comen gluten, pueden probar porciones pequeñas de postres hechos con harina sin gluten. ¡Suena perfecto! O sea que me pregunté, "¿Cómo se puede lograr?" Hice lo que haría cualquiera: recurrí al Internet. Investigué e investigué sin parar, y finalmente hice listas de harinas y mezclas de harina sin gluten. Los ingredientes de abajo se venden en las tiendas de alimentos saludables, por correo y, cada vez más, en los supermercados. La marca Bob's Red Mill tiene muchos productos sin gluten.

Harinas sin gluten

Siempre busco en Internet harinas saludables, sin gluten y sabrosas. No sé si les pasa, pero cuando voy a la tienda de alimentos saludables y veo la gran variedad de harinas sin gluten, me abruma la selección. Solía irme a casa con las manos vacías y simplemente usaba lo que tenía en la despensa. Pero con un poco de investigación y experimentación, he encontrado algunas de las mejores harinas sin gluten a la venta, para sus necesidades cotidianas.

FÉCULA/HARINA DE TAPIOCA: Esta harina se hace con el almidón de la yuca. Tiene muchos usos, entre ellos espesar salsas, rellenos de tartas y sopas. También hace que sus galletas preferidas sean un poco chiclosas. Para obtener los mejores resultados, combínenla con otras harinas sin gluten.

HARINA DE ARROZ INTEGRAL: Una excelente alternativa a la harina de trigo, la harina de arroz integral aporta también proteína, hierro, fibra y vitaminas B a su alimentación. Su uso no se limita a la repostería; se puede usar para cubrir el pescado, la carne de res o el pollo antes de hornear, o si se atreven, para hacer fideos con ella.

HARINA DE GARBANZOS: Está repleta de proteína, fibra y hierro, y es excelente para hacer la masa de pizza o pan. También la pueden usar para espesar guisos, sopas o salsas.

HARINA DE GOMA XANTANA: Este es un agente vegetal para espesar y estabilizar. ¿Por qué se debe usar en la repostería? Imita lo que el gluten hace al hornear, o sea que la masa hecha con goma xantana tiene elasticidad, espesor y la conocida textura de masa.

HARINA DE HABAS: Este tipo de harina es una excelente fuente de proteína (un beneficio para los vegetarianos), hierro y fibra. Usen esta harina en combinación con otras sin gluten, no sola.

HARINA DE MIJO: Esta harina es una excelente fuente de proteína, aminoácidos esenciales y fibra. La harina de mijo es muy versátil debido a su sabor neutral, y la pueden usar en alimentos dulces o salados.

WHITE SORGHUM FLOUR: This flour has many benefits—it's nutritious and it adds incredible flavor to your baking. One of my favorite things about white sorghum flour is the fact that the starch and protein in the flour take longer to digest than in other flours.

WHOLE-GRAIN TEFF FLOUR: Teff is an ancient east African cereal grass. It is commonly used in Ethiopian households and as a substitute for all-purpose flour. This flour is a good source of fiber, protein, iron, amino acids, vitamin C, and calcium. You could call it a nutritional powerhouse.

XANTHAN GUM: This is a plant-based thickening and stabilizing agent. Why use this in baking? It imitates what gluten does in baking, so dough made with xanthan gum has elasticity, thickness, and that familiar doughy texture.

Gluten-Free Flour Blends

Here are the gluten-free flour blends that I've found to be useful. You can make these blends ahead of time, place them in the proper container, and store them in the pantry.

ALL-PURPOSE FLOUR BLEND (SERVING SIZE—1 CUP):
Use this blend for all your gluten-free baking needs.

1/2 cup rice flour
1/4 cup tapioca starch/flour
1/4 cup cornstarch or potato starch

HIGH-FIBER FLOUR BLEND (SERVING SIZE—1 CUP):
This high-fiber blend works for breads, pancakes, snack bars, and cookies that contain chocolate, warm spices, raisins, or other fruits. It is not suited to delicately flavored recipes, such as sugar cookies, crepes, cream puffs, birthday cakes, or cupcakes.

1 cup brown rice flour or sorghum flour
1/2 cup teff flour (preferably light)
1/2 cup millet flour or Montina flour
2/3 cup tapioca starch/flour
1/3 cup cornstarch or potato starch

HIGH-PROTEIN FLOUR BLEND (SERVING SIZE—1 CUP):
This nutritious blend works best in baked goods that require elasticity, such as wraps and pie crusts.

1 1/4 cups bean flour (bean of your choice), garbanzo bean flour, or soy flour
1 cup arrowroot starch, cornstarch, or potato starch
1 cup white rice or brown rice flour

SELF-RISING FLOUR BLEND (SERVING SIZE—1 CUP):
Use this blend for muffins, scones, cakes, cupcakes, or any recipe that uses baking powder for leavening.

1 1/4 cups white sorghum flour
1 1/4 cups white rice flour
1/2 cup tapioca starch/flour
2 teaspoons xanthan or guar gum
4 teaspoons baking powder
1/2 teaspoon salt

HARINA DE QUINUA: La quinua es uno de los granos de cultivo más antiguos del mundo y produce uno de los tipos de harina de grano más nutritivos a la venta. La harina de quinua es una excelente fuente de proteína y aminoácidos. También es un sustituto fabuloso para la harina de trigo en galletas, panqueques, pollo empanizado al horno y muchos otros.

HARINA DE SORGO BLANCO: Esta harina tiene muchos beneficios: es nutritiva y le da un toque adicional de fabuloso sabor a los productos horneados. Una de las cosas que me gustan más de la harina de sorgo blanco es el hecho que toma más tiempo digerir el almidón y la proteína de este tipo de harina que otros.

HARINA DE *TEF* DE GRANO INTEGRAL: El *tef* es una antigua hierba del este de África que se come como cereal. Se usa mucho en los hogares etíopes y es un buen sustituto para la harina sin preparar. Esta harina es una buena fuente de fibra, proteína, hierro, aminoácidos, vitamina C y calcio. Se puede decir que está repleta de nutrientes.

Mezclas de harina sin gluten

Estas son algunas mezclas de harina sin gluten que me parecen útiles. Se preparan estas mezclas con anticipación, se colocan en el debido recipiente y se guardan en la despensa.

MEZCLA DE HARINA SIN PREPARAR
(TAMAÑO DE LA PORCIÓN—1 TAZA):

Use esta mezcla para evitar el gluten en toda su repostería.

1/2 taza de harina de arroz
1/4 taza de fécula/harina de tapioca
1/4 taza de maicena o fécula de papa

MEZCLA DE HARINA CON MUCHA FIBRA
(TAMAÑO DE LA PORCIÓN—1 TAZA):

Esta mezcla con mucha fibra es buena para panes, panqueques, barras que se comen de bocadillo y galletas que contienen chocolate, especias fuertes, pasas y otras frutas. No es apropiada para recetas de sabor delicado, como las galletas de azúcar, los *crepes*, las bolitas rellenas de crema, los pasteles de cumpleaños o los bizcochitos.

1 taza de harina de arroz integral o de sorgo
1/2 taza de harina de *tef* (de preferencia, *light*)
1/2 taza de harina de mijo o Montina
2/3 taza de fécula/harina de tapioca
1/3 taza de maicena o fécula de papa

MEZCLA DE HARINA CON MUCHA PROTEÍNA
(TAMAÑO DE LA PORCIÓN—1 TAZA):

Esta nutritiva mezcla es muy buena para productos horneados que requieren elasticidad, como los *wraps* y la masa de tarta.

1 1/4 tazas de harina de menestra (la que prefieran), harina de garbanzos o harina de soya
1 taza de fécula de arrurruz, maicena o fécula de papa
1 taza de harina de arroz blanco o integral

MEZCLA DE HARINA PREPARADA
(TAMAÑO DE LA PORCIÓN—1 TAZA):

Usen esta mezcla para panecillos, bollos, pasteles, bizcochitos o cualquier receta que use polvo de hornear como levadura.

1 1/4 tazas de harina de sorgo blanco
1 1/4 tazas de harina de arroz blanco
1/2 taza de fécula/harina de tapioca
2 cdtas. de goma xantana o *guar*
4 cdtas. de polvo de hornear
1/2 cdta. de sal

THE CUBAN CLASSICS
LOS CLÁSICOS CUBANOS

This chapter covers the Cuban dishes that I learned from my father and those I learned along my culinary journey. I apologize if I've left out any of your favorites; if I were to put every single classic Cuban dish into one book, it would be too big.

Este capítulo incluye los platillos clásicos cubanos que aprendí de mi padre y los que he aprendido a lo largo de mi experiencia culinaria. Les pido disculpas si he omitido uno de sus preferidos; si incluyese todos los platos clásicos cubanos en un libro, sería demasiado voluminoso.

—Chef Ronaldo

PLANTAIN MASH (MOFONGO)

PREP TIME: 10 minutes
COOKING TIME: 30 minutes
SERVES: 4
SERVING SIZE: 1/2 cup

1 cup unsalted vegetable stock
2 small ripe plantains, peel removed and cut into 4 pieces each
Parchment paper
1 teaspoon ground nutmeg
1 teaspoon ground cinnamon
1/2 teaspoon kosher salt
1 teaspoon cracked black pepper

1. Preheat oven to 400°F.

2. In a saucepan, bring vegetable stock to a rolling simmer and set aside.

3. Place plantains on a baking sheet lined with parchment paper and bake until plantains are fork tender, about 15–20 minutes.

4. Once plantains are tender, remove them from the oven and place them in a food processor along with 3/4 cup vegetable stock, nutmeg, cinnamon, salt, and pepper. Pulsate 10 times (1 second per pulse). When mash reaches a dough-like consistency, remove it from the food processor.

5. To form the plantain mash, place it in a bowl lined with plastic wrap. Press mixture down to remove any air bubbles, then flip it onto a plate. Remove the bowl and serve.

RONALDO'S TIP

Only add 3/4 cup stock to the food processor at first, then add the rest in small batches if needed. If you add all the stock at once, you might end up with mash that has a batter-like consistency.

EXCHANGES/CHOICES
2 starch

CALORIES 130 | **CALORIES FROM FAT** 0 | **TOTAL FAT** 0g | **SATURATED FAT** 0.2g | **TRANS FAT** 0g
CHOLESTEROL 0mg | **SODIUM** 285mg | **POTASSIUM** 515mg | **TOTAL CARBOHYDRATE** 34g
DIETARY FIBER 3g | **SUGARS** 15g | **PROTEIN** 1g | **PHOSPHORUS** 35mg

MOFONGO O PURÉ DE PLÁTANO

TIEMPO DE PREPARACIÓN: 10 minutos
TIEMPO DE COCCIÓN: 30 minutos
RINDE: 4 porciones
TAMAÑO DE LA PORCIÓN: 1/2 taza

1 taza de caldo vegetal sin sal
2 plátanos maduros pequeños, sin
    cáscara, cada uno cortado en 4 trozos
Papel mantequilla
1 cdta. de nuez moscada molida
1 cdta. de canela molida
1/2 cdta. de sal *kosher*
1 cdta. de pimienta negra gruesa

1. Calentar el horno a 400°F.

2. En una olla, calentar el caldo vegetal hasta que dé un hervor y poner de lado.

3. Colocar los plátanos en una lata para hornear, forrada con papel mantequilla y hornear hasta que los plátanos estén blandos cuando se pinchan con un tenedor, aproximadamente 15-20 minutos.

4. Colocar los plátanos en un procesador de alimentos con 3/4 taza de caldo vegetal, nuez moscada, canela, sal y pimienta. Prender y apagar 10 veces (1 segundo cada vez). Cuando el puré tenga consistencia de masa, retirarlo del procesador de alimentos.

5. Para darle forma al puré, colocarlo en una vasija cubierta con plástico. Presionar la mezcla para eliminar las burbujas y luego voltearla sobre un plato. Retirar la vasija y servir.

CONSEJO DE RONALDO

Solo se debe agregar 3/4 taza de caldo al procesador de alimentos inicialmente y luego agregar poco a poco según sea necesario. Si se agrega todo el caldo a la vez, la consistencia puede ser de mezcla en vez de masa.

SELECCIONES/INTERCAMBIOS
2 almidones

CALORÍAS 130 | **CALORÍAS DE GRASA** 0 | **TOTAL DE GRASA** 0g | **GRASA SATURADA** 0.2g | **GRASA TRANS** 0g
COLESTEROL 0mg | **SODIO** 285mg | **POTASIO** 515mg | **TOTAL DE CARBOHIDRATOS** 34g
FIBRA ALIMENTARIA 3g | **AZÚCARES** 15g | **PROTEÍNA** 1g | **FÓSFORO** 35mg

Cuban-Style Stuffed Potato

PREP TIME: 10 minutes
COOKING TIME: 1 hour 5 minutes
SERVES: 12
SERVING SIZE: 1 stuffed potato (3 ounces)

2 quarts cold water
(for cooking potatoes)
2 pounds sweet potatoes, peeled, cut
into cubes, and placed in cold water
1 teaspoon kosher salt
Parchment paper
2 cups Cuban-Inspired Turkey *Picadillo*
(page 54)
3 eggs, beaten (place in refrigerator until
ready to use)
2 cups brown rice bread crumbs
1 teaspoon dried oregano
1 teaspoon garlic powder

1. Preheat oven to 350°F.

2. In a large pot, bring water, potatoes, salt to a boil. Once potatoes start boiling, reduce heat and simmer about 20 minutes, or until potatoes are falling apart.

3. Strain out water, return potatoes to the pot, and mash with a potato masher (have yourself a little fun and turn on the salsa music).

4. Using a food processor, purée the potatoes in batches (at least 4 batches to get a better purée). Once all the potatoes have been puréed, place the mixture on a parchment paper–lined baking sheet, spread it out evenly, and let it rest at room temperature about 15 minutes.

5. Form the rested puréed potato into 12 medium-size (3-ounce) balls and with a tablespoon make a small well in the center of each ball. Fill the wells with *picadillo* and reshape the balls.

6. Grab 2 large bowls and fill one with eggs and the other with brown rice bread crumbs. Mix oregano and garlic powder into bread crumbs. Cover each potato ball with egg, dredge with brown rice bread crumbs, and place in refrigerator for 10 minutes so breading can set.

7. Remove stuffed potatoes *(papas rellenas)* from refrigerator and place on a parchment paper–lined tray. Leave about 1 inch between potato balls. Bake for 30 minutes, remove from oven, and enjoy!

RONALDO'S TIP

You can find brown rice bread crumbs in the gluten-free section of most supermarkets.

EXCHANGES/CHOICES
1 1/2 starch, 1/2 fat

CALORIES 140 | **CALORIES FROM FAT** 25 | **TOTAL FAT** 3g | **SATURATED FAT** 1g | **TRANS FAT** 0g
CHOLESTEROL 55mg | **SODIUM** 160mg | **POTASSIUM** 360mg | **TOTAL CARBOHYDRATE** 21g
DIETARY FIBER 3g | **SUGARS** 5g | **PROTEIN** 6g | **PHOSPHORUS** 95mg

PAPA RELLENA AL ESTILO CUBANO

TIEMPO DE PREPARACIÓN: 10 minutos
TIEMPO DE COCCIÓN: 1 hora, 5 minutos
RINDE: 12 porciones
TAMAÑO DE LA PORCIÓN: 1 papa rellena
   (3 onzas)

---

2 cuartos de galón de agua fría
   (para cocer las papas)
2 libras de batatas o boniatos, pelados,
   cortados en cubos y en agua fría
1 cdta. de sal *kosher*
Papel mantequilla
2 tazas de picadillo de pavo a la cubana
   (pág. 55)
3 huevos batidos (refrigerar hasta que
   sea el momento de usarlos).
2 tazas de arroz integral molido
1 cdta. de orégano seco
1 cdta. de ajo en polvo

1. Calentar el horno a 350°F.

2. En una olla grande, llevar el agua, las papas y la sal a un hervor. Una vez que las papas comiencen a hervir, bajar la temperatura y cocer a fuego lento unos 20 minutos, hasta que las papas se deshagan.

3. Escurrir el agua, volver a poner las papas en la olla y aplastar con un prensapapas (diviértanse un poco y pongan un poco de música salsa).

4. Con un procesador de alimentos, aplastar las papas en tandas (por lo menos 4 tandas para que el puré salga mejor). Una vez terminado el puré, colocar la mezcla en una lata cubierta de papel mantequilla, repartiéndola uniformemente, y poner de lado a temperatura ambiente unos 15 minutos.

5. Con el puré asentado, hacer 12 bolas (de 3 onzas) de tamaño mediano y con una cuchara de servir hacer un pocito en el centro de cada bola. Llenar los pozos con picadillo y darles forma a las bolas.

6. Tomar 2 tazones grandes y llenar uno con los huevos y el otro con el arroz integral molido. Mezclar orégano y ajo en polvo con el arroz molido. Cubrir cada bola de papa con huevo, echar encima el arroz molido y colocar en el refrigerador 10 minutos para que el arroz se adhiera bien.

7. Retirar las papas rellenas del refrigerador y colocar en una lata con papel mantequilla. Dejar aproximadamente 1 pulgada entre cada bola de puré. Hornear 30 minutos, sacar del horno ¡y disfrutar!

CONSEJO DE RONALDO

Puede encontrar arroz molido integral en la sección de productos sin gluten de la mayoría de los supermercados.

SELECCIONES/INTERCAMBIOS
1 1/2 almidones, 1/2 grasa

CALORÍAS 140 | **CALORÍAS DE GRASA** 25 | **TOTAL DE GRASA** 3g | **GRASA SATURADA** 1g | **GRASA TRANS** 0g
COLESTEROL 55mg | **SODIO** 160mg | **POTASIO** 360mg | **TOTAL DE CARBOHIDRATOS** 21g
FIBRA ALIMENTARIA 3g | **AZÚCARES** 5g | **PROTEÍNA** 6g | **FÓSFORO** 95mg

GREEN PLANTAIN *MOFONGO*

PREP TIME: 10 minutes
COOKING TIME: 45 minutes
SERVES: 4
SERVING SIZE: 1/2 cup

2 green plantains, peels removed

1/4 cup washed and cubed red pepper
(1/8-inch cubes)

1/8 cup washed and cubed green
pepper (1/8-inch cubes)

1/8 cup cubed Spanish onion
(1/8-inch cubes)

2 cloves garlic, peeled and finely
chopped

1 cup unsalted chicken stock

1 teaspoon dried oregano

1 dried bay leaf

1. Preheat oven 400°F.

2. Cut plantains into 1-inch rounds and place into a baking dish.

3. Add all the remaining ingredients to a mixing bowl and toss together.
   Place mixture into the baking dish with plantains and cover with foil.
   Bake for 45 minutes.

4. Remove from oven and place all ingredients into a metal bowl. Remove the
   bay leaf. Using a fork or potato masher, gently mash the mixture. (If you have a
   mortar and pestle, you may use this to gently mash the mixture instead.)

5. Line a separate bowl with plastic wrap and add the mashed mixture. Press
   down firmly to pack the *mofongo* into the bowl. Flip the bowl upside down onto
   a plate to transfer mixture. Remove bowl and serve.

EXCHANGES/CHOICES
2 starch

CALORIES 130 | **CALORIES FROM FAT** 10 | **TOTAL FAT** 1g | **SATURATED FAT** 0g | **TRANS FAT** 0g
CHOLESTEROL 0mg | **SODIUM** 20mg | **POTASSIUM** 530mg | **TOTAL CARBOHYDRATE** 30g
DIETARY FIBER 2g | **SUGARS** 14g | **PROTEIN** 3g | **PHOSPHORUS** 55mg

MOFONGO DE PLÁTANO VERDE

TIEMPO DE PREPARACIÓN: 10 minutos
TIEMPO DE COCCIÓN: 45 minutos
RINDE: 4 porciones
TAMAÑO DE LA PORCIÓN: 1/2 taza

2 plátanos verdes, sin cáscara

1/4 taza de pimiento rojo, lavado y cortado en cubos de 1/8 pulgada

1/8 taza de pimiento verde lavado y cortado en cubos de 1/8 pulgada

1/8 taza de cebolla española, pelada y cortada en cubos de 1/8 pulgada

2 dientes de ajo, pelados y finamente picados

1 taza de caldo de pollo sin sal

1 cdta. de orégano seco

1 hoja de laurel

1. Calentar el horno a 400°F.

2. Cortar los plátanos en tajadas de 1 pulgada y colocar en una asadera.

3. Añadir todos los ingredientes restantes en un tazón y mezclar. Colocar la mezcla en la asadera con los plátanos y cubrir con papel aluminio. Hornear 45 minutos.

4. Retirar del horno y colocar todos los ingredientes en una vasija de metal. Sacar la hoja de laurel. Usar un prensapapas o tenedor para aplastar la mezcla suavemente. (Si tiene mortero y maja se puede utilizar en vez para aplastar suavemente la mezcla).

5. Cubrir otra vasija con plástico y añadir el puré. Presionar firmemente el mofongo en la vasija. Voltear la vasija boca abajo sobre una fuente para transferir la mezcla. Retirar la vasija y servir.

SELECCIONES/INTERCAMBIOS
2 almidones

CALORÍAS 130 | CALORÍAS DE GRASA 10 | TOTAL DE GRASA 1g | GRASA SATURADA 0g | GRASA TRANS 0g
COLESTEROL 0mg | SODIO 20mg | POTASIO 530mg | TOTAL DE CARBOHIDRATOS 30g
FIBRA ALIMENTARIA 2g | AZÚCARES 14g | PROTEÍNA 3g | FÓSFORO 55mg

CONGRÍ LIGHT (CUBAN BLACK BEANS AND RICE)

The name may seem funny, but I wanted to bring a little humor to the dish. I know congrí (black beans and rice) is congrí, but why not make it healthier with some brown rice and add a little nutty flavor to the dish? I love congrí and the flavors the dish brings to the party. The smells of bay leaves, oregano, and tender beans are truly magical. This is the type of dish that takes a while to master, but I know this recipe will guide you in the right direction. Be patient when cooking beans; if you've cooked fresh beans before, you know they take a while. Gracias!

PREP TIME: 20 minutes
COOKING TIME: 1 hour
SERVES: 10
SERVING SIZE: 3/4 cup

10 ounces dried black beans, sorted and rinsed (1 1/2 cups)
4 cups water, divided (use more if needed)
1/2 cup uncooked brown rice
1 teaspoon sea salt
1 1/2 teaspoons avocado oil, divided
1 teaspoon garlic powder
1 cup finely chopped green pepper
1/2 cup finely chopped red pepper
1 cup finely chopped Spanish onion
2 tablespoons finely chopped garlic
1 1/2 tablespoons dried oregano
1 1/2 teaspoons ground cumin
3 dried bay leaves

1. Into a stovetop pressure cooker, add rinsed beans and 3 cups water, and cover. Place pressure cooker on stove and set on high heat. Once the beans start boiling, lower heat to medium and cook beans until they are tender, about 45 minutes. Make sure beans are submerged in water while they cook; add more water if needed.

2. Once beans are tender, add rice, 1 cup water, salt, and 1/2 teaspoon avocado oil. Stir well and add the remaining ingredients. Stir once more with spoon, and make sure to put a little hip into it.

3. Make sure there is about 3/4 inch of water above the beans. Cover the mixture, and put heat on medium-low. Cook for 15 minutes, or until rice is tender. Once the *congrí* is done, fluff with a fork and serve. Enjoy!

EXCHANGES/CHOICES
1 1/2 starch, 1 lean protein

CALORIES 160 | **CALORIES FROM FAT** 20 | **TOTAL FAT** 2g | **SATURATED FAT** 0g | **TRANS FAT** 0g | **CHOLESTEROL** 0mg | **SODIUM** 190mg | **POTASSIUM** 540mg | **TOTAL CARBOHYDRATE** 29g | **DIETARY FIBER** 6g | **SUGARS** 2g | **PROTEIN** 7g | **PHOSPHORUS** 165mg

Congrí *LIGHT* (Frijoles Negros y Arroz a la Cubana)

El nombre quizá suene gracioso pero quería darle un toque de humor al plato. Sé que la combinación de arroz y frijoles negros es congrí, pero ¿por qué no hacerlo más saludable con arroz integral y darle un poco de sabor a nuez al platillo? Me encanta el congrí y los sabores que el plato aporta a la fiesta. El olor de las hojas de laurel, el orégano y los frijoles tiernos son realmente mágicos. Toma un tiempo llegar a dominar este tipo de plato, pero sé que esta receta los guiará en el sentido correcto. Sean pacientes al preparar los frijoles; si han hecho frijoles frescos antes, saben que toman tiempo. ¡Gracias!

TIEMPO DE PREPARACIÓN: 20 minutos
TIEMPO DE COCCIÓN: 1 hora
RINDE: 10 porciones
TAMAÑO DE LA PORCIÓN: 3/4 taza

---

10 onzas de frijoles negros secos, limpios y enjuagados (1 1/2 tazas)

4 tazas de agua, en partes (usar más de ser necesario)

1/2 taza de arroz integral sin cocer

1 cdta. de sal marina

1 1/2 cdtas. de aceite de aguacate, en partes

1 cdta. de ajo en polvo

1 taza de pimiento verde, finamente picado

1/2 taza de pimiento rojo, finamente picado

1 taza de cebolla española, finamente picada

2 cdas. de ajo, finamente picado

1 1/2 cdas. de orégano seco

1 1/2 cdtas. de comino

3 hojas de laurel

1. En una olla a presión, echar los frijoles enjuagados y 3 tazas de agua, y tapar. Colocar la olla a presión sobre la estufa y prender a fuego alto. Una vez que los frijoles comiencen a hervir, bajar el fuego a medio y cocer los frijoles hasta que estén tiernos, aproximadamente 45 minutos. Asegurarse de que los frijoles estén sumergidos en agua mientras se cuecen; agregar más agua si es necesario).

2. Una vez que los frijoles estén blandos, añadir el arroz, 1 taza de agua, sal y 1/2 cdta. de aceite de aguacate. Mezclar bien y añadir el resto de los ingredientes. Revolver una vez más con un cucharón y no olvidarse de meterle un poco de la cadera.

3. Asegurarse de que haya 3/4 pulgada de agua encima de los frijoles. Tapar y poner el fuego en medio bajo. Cocer 15 minutos o hasta que el arroz esté blando. Una vez hecho el congrí, granear con un tenedor y servir. ¡A disfrutar!

SELECCIONES/INTERCAMBIOS
1 1/2 almidones, 1 proteína magra

CALORÍAS 160 | **CALORÍAS DE GRASA** 20 | **TOTAL DE GRASA** 2g | **GRASA SATURADA** 0g | **GRASA TRANS** 0g
COLESTEROL 0mg | **SODIO** 190mg | **POTASIO** 540mg | **TOTAL DE CARBOHIDRATOS** 29g
FIBRA ALIMENTARIA 6g | **AZÚCARES** 2g | **PROTEÍNA** 7g | **FÓSFORO** 165mg

SLOW-COOKER CHICKEN AND RICE

This recipe is very simple, but that's the point. Chicken and rice should not be complicated; it should be easy, fun, and exciting! I use a slow cooker because that's what I like, but you can always use a pressure cooker or even a large saucepan for this dish. If you do decide to use a pressure cooker or saucepan, make it a point to control the heat. You don't want to burn the rice.

PREP TIME: 10 minutes
COOKING TIME: 1 hour
SERVES: 8
SERVING SIZE: 1 cup

2 cups uncooked brown rice

1 cup washed and cubed carrots (1/4-inch cubes)

1/2 cup cubed Spanish onion (1/4-inch cubes)

1/4 cup washed and cubed red pepper (1/4-inch cubes)

2 cloves garlic, peeled and finely chopped

2 tablespoons finely chopped cilantro

16 ounces chicken breasts, cut into 1/2-inch cubes

1 teaspoon kosher salt

1/4 teaspoon cracked black pepper

1/4 teaspoon ground cumin

2 dried bay leaves

2 1/2 teaspoons turmeric

1 teaspoon finely chopped fresh oregano leaves

1 tablespoon avocado oil

3 1/2 cups water

1. Gather all the ingredients before you begin making this recipe. Once you are set up, add all the ingredients except the water to slow cooker and stir with a spoon so the ingredients distribute evenly. Add water and stir once more.

2. Turn slow cooker to highest setting. Once mixture comes to a simmer in the slow cooker, stir and cover with a lid.

3. Reduce heat to low and set timer for 1 hour. Do not overcook. When the timer goes off, enjoy the dish!

RONALDO'S TIP

While the chicken and rice cook, prepare any other dishes for your dinner with some great salsa music in the background. The rice in this dish should be fluffy; grab a fork and fluff it a little before serving. *Toma*!

EXCHANGES/CHOICES
2 1/2 starch, 2 lean protein

CALORIES 280 | **CALORIES FROM FAT** 45 | **TOTAL FAT** 5g | **SATURATED FAT** 1g | **TRANS FAT** 0g
CHOLESTEROL 40mg | **SODIUM** 340mg | **POTASSIUM** 440mg | **TOTAL CARBOHYDRATE** 41g
DIETARY FIBER 3g | **SUGARS** 2g | **PROTEIN** 17g | **PHOSPHORUS** 265mg

ARROZ CON POLLO HECHO EN OLLA DE COCCIÓN LENTA

Esta receta es muy sencilla, pero ese es el punto. El arroz con pollo no tiene que ser complicado; debe ser ¡fácil, divertido y emocionante! Uso una olla de cocción lenta porque me gusta así, pero siempre se puede utilizar una olla a presión o incluso una olla regular grande para este plato. Si deciden utilizar una olla a presión o cacerola, vigilen la temperatura. No quemen el arroz.

TIEMPO DE PREPARACIÓN: 10 minutos
TIEMPO DE COCCIÓN: 1 hora
RINDE: 8 porciones
TAMAÑO DE LA PORCIÓN: 1 taza

2 tazas de arroz integral sin cocer

1 taza de zanahorias lavadas y cortadas en cubos de 1/4 de pulgada

1/2 taza de cebolla española, lavada y cortada en cubos de 1/4 de pulgada

1/4 taza de pimiento rojo, lavado y cortado en cubos de 1/4 de pulgada

2 dientes de ajo, pelados y finamente picados

2 cdas. de cilantro, finamente picado

16 onzas de pechuga de pollo, en cubos de 1/2 pulgada

1 cdta. de sal *kosher*

1/4 cdta. de pimienta negra gruesa

1/4 cdta. de comino

2 hojas de laurel

2 1/2 cdtas. de cúrcuma o palillo molido

1 cdta. de hojas de orégano fresco, finamente picadas

1 cda. de aceite de aguacate

3 1/2 tazas de agua

1. Reunir todos los ingredientes antes de empezar a preparar esta receta. Una vez que están listos, agregar todos los ingredientes excepto el agua a la olla y revolver con un cucharón para distribuir los ingredientes uniformemente. Agregar agua y revolver una vez más.

2. Prender la olla de cocción lenta a la graduación más alta. Una vez que la mezcla comience a hervir en la olla de cocción lenta, revolver y tapar.

3. Bajar la temperatura y prender la alarma para dentro de 1 hora. No cocer en exceso. Cuando suene la alarma, ¡disfrutar el plato!

> **CONSEJO DE RONALDO**
>
> Mientras el pollo y el arroz se cuecen, se pueden preparar otros platos para la cena con fabulosa música salsa de fondo. El arroz en este plato debe quedar graneado; granéenlo un poco con un tenedor antes de servir. ¡Toma!

SELECCIONES/INTERCAMBIOS
2 1/2 almidones, 2 proteínas magras

CALORÍAS 280 | **CALORÍAS DE GRASA** 45 | **TOTAL DE GRASA** 5g | **GRASA SATURADA** 1g | **GRASA TRANS** 0g | **COLESTEROL** 40mg | **SODIO** 340mg | **POTASIO** 440mg | **TOTAL DE CARBOHIDRATOS** 41g | **FIBRA ALIMENTARIA** 3g | **AZÚCARES** 2g | **PROTEÍNA** 17g | **FÓSFORO** 265mg

MOJO-MARINATED PORK TENDERLOIN *(PERNIL)*

This recipe takes the classic pork shoulder dish (pernil) and makes it healthier while still giving you the amazing Cubano flavor that we love. I have substituted pork tenderloin for pork shoulder in this version of the recipe. I can hear my father's voice screaming at me, "Oye, chico, what are you doing changing the dish?" I'm not changing the essence of the dish, I'm just modifying it so people can enjoy it in a healthier way.

PREP TIME: 25 minutes
COOKING TIME: 15–20 minutes
SERVES: 5
SERVING SIZE: 1 (4-ounce) piece pork

2 navel oranges, peeled and cut in half
2 lemons, peeled
1 teaspoon kosher salt
1/2 teaspoon cracked black pepper
1/4 teaspoon ground cumin
1/4 teaspoon garlic powder
2 tablespoons distilled vinegar
2 stems fresh thyme, leaves removed
   from stem
1 (20-ounce) pork tenderloin
Nonstick cooking spray

1. Preheat oven to 400°F.

2. Grab your blender to make the *mojo* marinade. Add oranges, lemons, salt, pepper, cumin, garlic powder, vinegar, and fresh thyme leaves into the blender. Pulsate the mixture 4 times, then purée for 1 minute. Set aside 4 ounces *mojo* and add the rest to a resealable plastic bag.

3. Remove the silver skin from the pork tenderloin. Add pork tenderloin to the resealable plastic bag with the *mojo*. Marinate pork for at least 20 minutes in the fridge.

4. Remove the pork tenderloin from the bag (discarding the marinade in the bag) and pat dry with a paper towel. Preheat an ovenproof sauté pan over medium heat, spray with nonstick cooking spray, and wait 10 seconds for oil to come up to temperature. Brown both sides of pork tenderloin in the pan, then place pan in the oven for 15–20 minutes. Internal temperature of cooked pork should read 145°F.

5. Remove pork from oven and let it rest for a few minutes so juices redistribute. Drizzle some of the reserved *mojo* marinade on the pork, and serve.

EXCHANGES/CHOICES
1/2 fruit, 3 lean protein

CALORIES 160 | **CALORIES FROM FAT** 25 | **TOTAL FAT** 3g | **SATURATED FAT** 1g | **TRANS FAT** 0g
CHOLESTEROL 75mg | **SODIUM** 450mg | **POTASSIUM** 590mg | **TOTAL CARBOHYDRATE** 10g
DIETARY FIBER 2g | **SUGARS** 5g | **PROTEIN** 25g | **PHOSPHORUS** 300mg

LOMO DE CERDO ADOBADO CON MOJO

La receta clásica usa hombro de cerdo, pero yo uso pernil en esta versión, porque lo hace más saludable, sin perder el fabuloso sabor cubano que nos encanta. Puedo oír la voz de mi padre gritándome, "Oye, chico, ¿qué estás haciendo? ¿Cambiando el plato?" No estoy cambiando la esencia del plato; simplemente estoy modificándola para que la gente pueda disfrutarlo de una manera más saludable.

TIEMPO DE PREPARACIÓN: 25 minutos
TIEMPO DE COCCIÓN: 15-20 minutos
RINDE: 5 porciones
TAMAÑO DE LA PORCIÓN: 1 trozo
(de 4 onzas) de carne de cerdo

---

2 naranjas, peladas y cortadas
   por la mitad
2 limones, pelados
1 cdta. de sal *kosher*
1/2 cdta. de pimienta negra gruesa
1/4 cdta. de comino
1/4 cdta. de ajo en polvo
2 cdas. de vinagre destilado
Hojas de 2 ramitos de tomillo fresco,
   descartar tallos
1 lomo de cerdo de 20 onzas
Aceite en aerosol

1. Calentar el horno a 400°F.

2. Usar la licuadora para preparar el mojo. Poner las naranjas, limones, sal, pimienta, comino, ajo en polvo, vinagre y hojas de tomillo fresco en la licuadora. Prender y apagar cuatro veces, luego licuar 1 minuto. Guardar 4 onzas del mojo y colocar el resto del mojo en una bolsa de plástico con cierre.

3. Retirar la piel plateada del lomo. Meter el lomo a la bolsa de plástico con mojo. Adobar el cerdo por lo menos 20 minutos en el refrigerador.

4. Retirar el lomo de la bolsa (y descartar el adobo en la bolsa). Secarlo con una toalla de papel. Calentar una sartén para saltear que se pueda meter al horno a fuego medio, echarle aceite en aerosol y esperar 10 segundos para que el aceite alcance la temperatura necesaria. Dorar ambos lados del lomo en la sartén y luego colocar la sartén en el horno de 15-20 minutos. La temperatura interna del cerdo cocido debe llegar a 145°F.

5. Retirar el cerdo del horno y ponerlo de lado unos minutos para que los jugos se redistribuyan. Echarle al cerdo un poco del mojo reservado y servir.

SELECCIONES/INTERCAMBIOS
1/2 fruta, 3 carnes magras

CALORÍAS 160 | **CALORÍAS DE GRASA** 25 | **TOTAL DE GRASA** 3g | **GRASA SATURADA** 1g | **GRASA TRANS** 0g
COLESTEROL 75mg | **SODIO** 450mg | **POTASIO** 590mg | **TOTAL DE CARBOHIDRATOS** 10g
FIBRA ALIMENTARIA 2g | **AZÚCARES** 5g | **PROTEÍNA** 25g | **FÓSFORO** 300mg

Old-Fashioned *Ropa Vieja*

There is nothing better than a good Ropa Vieja, which translates to "old clothes." The dish takes its name from a legend that says that after the Castro regime took over Cuba, the people were left with nothing, and a new way of life began. People were said to be so poor that they had to cook down old clothing, add a bunch of spices and broth, and wait until the clothes fell apart to eat them. In this recipe we are using top round steak.

PREP TIME: 20 minutes
COOKING TIME: 2 hours
SERVES: 5
SERVING SIZE: 1 cup

1 cup washed and sliced red pepper
(1/4-inch-thick slices), core reserved
1 cup washed and sliced green pepper
(1/4-inch-thick slices), core reserved
1 cup apple cider vinegar
1 tablespoon black peppercorns
1 bunch cilantro
2 teaspoons garlic powder
2 quarts water
20 ounces top round steak
1 tablespoon avocado oil
1 cup sliced onion
(1/4-inch-thick slices)
2 cloves garlic, finely chopped
1/2 teaspoon ground cumin
1 teaspoon Spanish smoked paprika
1/2 teaspoon dried oregano
3/4 teaspoon sea salt
1 teaspoon cracked black pepper
1 tablespoon tomato paste
6 ounces canned diced tomatoes
8 pitted green olives, finely chopped
2 dried bay leaves
3 tablespoons cilantro, finely chopped

1. In a large stockpot, add the cores of the red and green pepper, apple cider vinegar, peppercorns, cilantro bunch, garlic powder, and water. Bring to a boil and add top round steak. Reduce heat and simmer steak for 1 hour 30 minutes, until the meat is tender.

2. Remove top round steak from water and shred the meat with a set of tongs. Place meat on a plate and cover with a damp towel; set aside. Reserve 3 cups stock for sauce.

3. Preheat a large sauté pan over medium heat, add avocado oil, and wait 10 seconds for oil to heat. Add red pepper, green pepper, onion, and garlic; sauté 1 minute on high heat.

4. Reduce heat to medium-low. Add cumin, smoked paprika, oregano, salt, pepper, and tomato paste. Sauté for 3 minutes so flavors can marry.

5. Add diced tomatoes, olives, reserved stock, and bay leaves, and simmer for 10 minutes on medium-low heat.

6. Add shredded steak to sauce and simmer for 10 minutes. Fold in chopped cilantro, and serve.

EXCHANGES/CHOICES
4 lean protein

CALORIES 160 | **CALORIES FROM FAT** 35 | **TOTAL FAT** 4g | **SATURATED FAT** 1.5g | **TRANS FAT** 0g | **CHOLESTEROL** 70mg | **SODIUM** 360mg | **POTASSIUM** 530mg | **TOTAL CARBOHYDRATE** 3g | **DIETARY FIBER** 1g | **SUGARS** 1g | **PROTEIN** 28g | **PHOSPHORUS** 270mg

ROPA VIEJA A LA ANTIGUA

No hay nada mejor que un buen plato de ropa vieja. Toma su nombre de una leyenda que dice que después de que Castro asumió el mando de Cuba, la gente se quedó sin nada y comenzó una nueva forma de vida. Se decía que los pobladores de la isla eran tan pobres que tenían que cocinar ropa vieja, añadir muchas especias y caldo, y esperar hasta que la ropa se deshilachara para comer. En esta receta usamos asado redondo (top round steak).

TIEMPO DE PREPARACIÓN: 20 minutos
TIEMPO DE COCCIÓN: 2 horas
RINDE: 5 porciones
TAMAÑO DE LA PORCIÓN: 1 taza

1 taza de pimiento rojo, lavado y cortado en tajadas de 1/4 de pulgada, guardando el centro

1 taza de pimiento verde, lavado y cortado en tajadas de ¼ de pulgada, guardando el centro

1 taza de vinagre de sidra de manzana

1 cda. de granos de pimienta negra

1 manojo de cilantro

2 cdtas. de ajo en polvo

2 cuartos de galón de agua (2 litros)

20 onzas de asado redondo de res

1 cda. de aceite de aguacate

1 taza de cebolla, cortada en tajadas de 1/4 de pulgada

2 dientes de ajo, finamente picado

1/2 cdta. de comino

1 cdta. de pimentón español ahumado (*paprika*)

1/2 cdta. de orégano seco

3/4 cdta. de sal marina

1 cdta. de pimienta negra gruesa

1 cda. de pasta de tomate

6 onzas de tomates enlatados, en cubos

8 aceitunas verdes sin semilla, finamente picadas

2 hojas de laurel

3 cdas. de cilantro finamente picado

1. En una olla grande, echar los centros del pimiento rojo y verde, vinagre de manzana, granos de pimienta, manojo de cilantro, ajo en polvo y agua. Hacer hervir y agregar la carne. Bajar la temperatura y cocer a fuego lento 1 hora y media, hasta que la carne esté blanda.

2. Retirar la carne del agua y desmenuzarla con tenazas. Colocar la carne en una fuente, taparla con un paño húmedo y poner de lado. Guardar 3 tazas de caldo para la salsa.

3. Calentar una sartén grande sobre fuego medio, agregar el aceite de aguacate y esperar 10 segundos para que se caliente. Agregar el pimiento rojo, pimiento verde, cebolla y ajo, y saltear 1 minuto a fuego alto.

4. Bajar la temperatura a media baja. Agregar el comino, pimentón, orégano, sal, pimienta y pasta de tomate. Saltear 3 minutos para que los sabores se impregnen.

5. Agregar el tomate en cubos, aceitunas, las 3 tazas de caldo y hojas de laurel, y cocer 10 minutos a fuego medio bajo.

6. Agregar la carne deshilachada a la salsa y cocer a fuego lento 10 minutos. Incorporar el cilantro picado y servir.

SELECCIONES/INTERCAMBIOS
4 proteínas magras

CALORÍAS 160 | **CALORÍAS DE GRASA** 35 | **TOTAL DE GRASA** 4g | **GRASA SATURADA** 1.5g | **GRASA TRANS** 0g
COLESTEROL 70mg | **SODIO** 360mg | **POTASIO** 530mg | **TOTAL DE CARBOHIDRATOS** 3g
FIBRA ALIMENTARIA 1g | **AZÚCARES** 1g | **PROTEÍNA** 28g | **FÓSFORO** 270mg

CUBAN-STYLE BRAISED OXTAILS

I was pretty young when I first had this dish. I remember it was so delicious, tender, juicy, and full of flavor! The meat of the oxtail seems to extract the flavors from the sofrito (sauce) and create a perfect balance. Every bite is as good as the first one, but the best thing about the dish is the bone. It's traditional to suck out all the juices form the bone— it's like a second dish hidden in behind the meat.

PREP TIME: 30 minutes
COOKING TIME: 2 hours 50 minutes
SERVES: 10
SERVING SIZE: 6 ounces stew
(bone in the meat)

---

1 1/2 pounds bone-in oxtails (to yield
  16 ounces cooked), fat trimmed off
1 cup cubed yellow onion
  (1/4-inch cubes)
4 washed and cubed plum tomatoes
  (1/4-inch cubes)
1 1/2 cups washed and cubed carrots
  (1/4-inch cubes)
1 tablespoon tomato paste
3 cloves garlic, finely chopped
1 teaspoon kosher salt
1 tablespoon cracked black pepper
1 tablespoon dried oregano
4 sprigs thyme
1/2 cup red wine
4 cups vegetable stock

1. Preheat Dutch oven or stew pot, add oxtails, and brown on all sides. (No oil is needed here. The fat from the oxtail will help with the browning.)

2. Remove browned oxtails from Dutch oven, add onions, tomatoes, and carrots, and sauté until vegetables are translucent or shiny.

3. Add tomato paste, garlic, salt, pepper, oregano, and thyme, and stir for 1 minute. Reduce heat to medium and add red wine. Simmer for 1 minute.

4. Return oxtails to Dutch oven or pot and add the vegetable stock. Reduce heat to low and cover, leaving lid slightly ajar. Cook for 2 hours and 30 minutes. You will know oxtails are done when the meat pulls away from the bone.

5. Skim excess fat from the top, remove thyme sprigs, and serve with a small ladle.

EXCHANGES/CHOICES
1 vegetable, 2 medium-fat protein

CALORIES 170 | **CALORIES FROM FAT** 60 | **TOTAL FAT** 7g | **SATURATED FAT** 2.5g | **TRANS FAT** 0g
CHOLESTEROL 50mg | **SODIUM** 360mg | **POTASSIUM** 500mg | **TOTAL CARBOHYDRATE** 9g
DIETARY FIBER 2g | **SUGARS** 4g | **PROTEIN** 17g | **PHOSPHORUS** 170mg

RABO DE BUEY GUISADO A LA CUBANA

Era bastante chico cuando comí este plato por primera vez. Recuerdo que era ¡delicioso, suave, jugoso y sabroso! La carne del rabo parece extraer los sabores del sofrito y crear un equilibrio perfecto. Cada bocado es tan bueno como el primero, pero lo mejor del plato es el hueso. Lo tradicional es chupar todo el jugo del hueso; es como si la carne escondiera un segundo plato.

TIEMPO DE PREPARACIÓN: 30 minutos
TIEMPO DE COCCIÓN: 2 horas y 50 minutos
RINDE: 10 porciones
TAMAÑO DE LA PORCIÓN: 6 onzas de guiso
(carne con hueso)

---

1 1/2 libras de rabo de buey con hueso, desgrasado y que al cocer dé 16 onzas

1 taza de cebolla amarilla, pelada y cortada en cubos de 1/4 de pulgada

4 tomates cerezos, lavados y cortados en cubos de 1/4 de pulgada

1 1/2 tazas de zanahorias lavadas y cortadas en cubos de 1/4 de pulgada

1 cda. de pasta de tomate

3 dientes de ajo, finamente picados

1 cdta. de sal *kosher*

1 cda. de pimienta negra gruesa

1 cda. de orégano seco

4 ramitos de tomillo

1/2 taza de vino tinto

4 tazas de caldo vegetal

1. Calentar una olla para guisar o con tapa, añadir los rabos y dorar todo alrededor. (No es necesario usar aceite. La grasa del rabo ayudará a que se dore).

2. Retirar los rabos dorados de la olla y agregar la cebolla, los tomates y las zanahorias, y saltear hasta que los vegetales estén traslúcidos o relucientes.

3. Agregar la pasta de tomate, el ajo, la sal, la pimienta, el orégano y el tomillo, y revolver 1 minuto. Bajar el fuego a medio y agregar el vino tinto. Cocer a fuego lento 1 minuto.

4. Volver a poner los rabos en la olla y agregar el caldo vegetal. Bajar la temperatura y tapar a medias. Cocer 2 horas y media. Sabrán que los rabos están cocidos cuando la carne se desprenda de los huesos.

5. Eliminar la grasa de encima, retirar las ramitas de tomillo y servir con un cucharón pequeño.

SELECCIONES/INTERCAMBIOS
1 vegetal, 2 proteínas con grasa moderada

CALORÍAS 170 | **CALORÍAS DE GRASA** 60 | **TOTAL DE GRASA** 7g | **GRASA SATURADA** 2.5g | **GRASA TRANS** 0g | **COLESTEROL** 50mg | **SODIO** 360mg | **POTASIO** 500mg | **TOTAL DE CARBOHIDRATOS** 9g | **FIBRA ALIMENTARIA** 2g | **AZÚCARES** 4g | **PROTEÍNA** 17g | **FÓSFORO** 170mg

CUBAN-INSPIRED TURKEY *PICADILLO*

PREP TIME: 20 minutes
COOKING TIME: 50 minutes
SERVES: 6
SERVING SIZE: 3/4 cup

1 tablespoon avocado oil
1 pound ground turkey (93% lean)
1/4 teaspoon kosher salt
2 teaspoons cracked black pepper
1 tablespoon Spanish smoked paprika
1/2 teaspoon ground cumin
1 tablespoon dried oregano
1 cup cubed Spanish onion
1/2 cup washed and cubed roasted
   red pepper
1/2 cup washed and cubed green
   pepper
2 ounces Spanish olives, pitted and
   cubed
3 tablespoons raisins, finely chopped
1 tablespoon tomato paste
2 ounces red Burgundy wine
6 ounces crushed tomatoes
1 cup unsalted chicken stock

1. Preheat large skillet, and add avocado oil and turkey. Season with salt, pepper, smoked paprika, cumin, and oregano, and stir until turkey is cooked through. Remove from skillet and set aside.

2. In the same skillet, add onion, roasted red pepper, green pepper, olives, and raisins, and sauté on medium-low heat until veggies are translucent.

3. Add the tomato paste and cook mixture for an additional 2 minutes. Add red wine and reduce for 5 minutes. Reduce heat to low and cook for about 10 minutes.

4. Transfer ground turkey back to the skillet. Add crushed tomatoes and chicken stock, and simmer for an additional 20 minutes, until all the flavors have married. Serve.

RONALDO'S TIP

You must let this dish simmer so all the flavors can develop and stay true to the *sazón cubana*.

EXCHANGES/CHOICES
1/2 other carbohydrate, 1 vegetable,
2 lean protein, 1 fat, 1/2 alcohol

CALORIES 260 | **CALORIES FROM FAT** 90 | **TOTAL FAT** 10g | **SATURATED FAT** 2g | **TRANS FAT** 0g
CHOLESTEROL 60mg | **SODIUM** 350mg | **POTASSIUM** 520mg | **TOTAL CARBOHYDRATE** 15g
DIETARY FIBER 3g | **SUGARS** 8g | **PROTEIN** 17g | **PHOSPHORUS** 200mg

PICADILLO DE PAVO A LA CUBANA

TIEMPO DE PREPARACIÓN: 20 minutos
TIEMPO DE COCCIÓN: 50 minutos
RINDE: 6 porciones
TAMAÑO DE LA PORCIÓN: 3/4 taza

1 cda. de aceite de aguacate
1 libra de carne molida de pavo
(93% magra)
1/4 cdta. de sal *kosher*
2 cdtas. de pimienta negra gruesa
1 cda. de pimentón español ahumado
(paprika)
1/2 cdta. de comino
1 cda. de orégano seco
1 taza de cebolla española, en cubos
1/2 taza de pimiento rojo, lavado, cortado en cubos y asado
1/2 taza de pimiento verde, lavado y
cortado en cubos
2 onzas de aceitunas españolas, sin
semillas y en cubos
3 cdas. de pasas, finamente picadas
1 cda. de pasta de tomate
2 onzas de vino tinto Borgoña
6 onzas de tomate aplastado
1 taza de caldo de pollo sin sal

1. Calentar una sartén grande y agregar el aceite de aguacate y pavo. Sazonar con sal, pimienta, pimentón, comino y orégano, y revolver hasta que el pavo esté cocido. Retirar de la sartén y poner de lado.

2. En la misma sartén, agregar la cebolla, el pimiento rojo asado, el pimiento verde, las aceitunas y las pasas, y saltear a fuego medio bajo hasta que los vegetales estén traslúcidos.

3. Agregar la pasta de tomate y cocer la mezcla 2 minutos más. Agregar el vino tinto y reducir 5 minutos. Bajar la temperatura y cocer unos 10 minutos.

4. Pasar el pavo a la sartén, agregar el tomate aplastado y el caldo de pollo, y cocer a fuego lento 20 minutos, hasta que los sabores se impregnen. Servir.

CONSEJO DE RONALDO

Deben cocer este plato a fuego lento para que todos los sabores salgan a relucir y sean fieles a la sazón cubana.

SELECCIONES/INTERCAMBIOS
1/2 otro carbohidrato, 1 vegetal,
2 proteínas magras, 1 grasa, 1/2 alcohol

CALORÍAS 260 | **CALORÍAS DE GRASA** 90 | **TOTAL DE GRASA** 10g | **GRASA SATURADA** 2g | **GRASA TRANS** 0g
COLESTEROL 60mg | **SODIO** 350mg | **POTASIO** 520mg | **TOTAL DE CARBOHIDRATOS** 15g
FIBRA ALIMENTARIA 3g | **AZÚCARES** 8g | **PROTEÍNA** 17g | **FÓSFORO** 200mg

ABUELA'S MOJO SPATCHCOCK CHICKEN

Nothing brings me back to my childhood like chicken. I love chicken! It was something I ate almost every day as a young child in Colombia. The best chicken I ever had was my abuela's—it was always juicy and just right. This is my version of her recipe. Please enjoy these flavors from my life.

PREP TIME: 25 minutes
COOKING TIME: 1 hour
SERVES: 10
SERVING SIZE: 4 ounces chicken

1 (2 1/2-pound) whole chicken, skin and backbone removed

1 1/4 teaspoons kosher salt, divided

2 teaspoons cracked black pepper, divided

3 navel oranges, seeded and juiced into a bowl

3 cloves garlic, peeled and minced

1 teaspoon cracked black pepper

4 sprigs thyme, leaves removed from stem

1/4 teaspoon dried oregano

1. Preheat oven to 400°F.

2. Place the chicken (with backbone and skin already removed) on a baking sheet with chicken innards facing down. (Don't worry, the chicken will taste amazing even without the skin.) Season with 3/4 teaspoon salt and 1 teaspoon pepper, and gently massage them into the chicken skin.

3. Grab the bowl with the orange juice and add garlic, 1/2 teaspoon salt, 1 teaspoon pepper, thyme, and oregano. Whisk ingredients together to incorporate the flavors. Set this *mojo* aside.

4. Place chicken in the oven and cook for 1 hour, basting chicken with the *mojo* every 10 minutes.

5. After 1 hour has elapsed, insert a meat thermometer into the thickest part of the chicken breast. The thermometer should read 160°F. Let chicken rest before serving. (If we cook the chicken all the way to the indicated temperature of 165°F, the residual cooking might make it dry. So I recommend taking it out at around 160°F and letting the chicken rest for 15 minutes, until the residual cooking brings the temperature up to 165°F.) Remove the chicken from the bones before serving. Enjoy and *toma*!

EXCHANGES/CHOICES
1 vegetable, 3 1/2 lean protein

CALORIES 160 | **CALORIES FROM FAT** 25 | **TOTAL FAT** 3g | **SATURATED FAT** 1g | **TRANS FAT** 0g
CHOLESTEROL 80mg | **SODIUM** 290mg | **POTASSIUM** 460mg | **TOTAL CARBOHYDRATE** 6g
DIETARY FIBER 1g | **SUGARS** 4g | **PROTEIN** 26g | **PHOSPHORUS** 255mg

POLLO ASADO CON MOJO DE LA ABUELA

Nada hace que me remonte a mi infancia como el pollo. ¡Me encanta! Lo comía casi todos los días de niño en Colombia. El mejor pollo que he comido es el preparado por mi abuela, que siempre estaba jugoso y perfecto. Esta es mi versión de su receta. Por favor, disfruten los sabores de mi vida.

TIEMPO DE PREPARACIÓN: 25 minutos
TIEMPO DE COCCIÓN: 1 hora
RINDE: 10 porciones
TAMAÑO DE LA PORCIÓN: 4 onzas de pollo

---

1 pollo entero (2 1/2 libras), sin piel ni columna

1 1/4 cdtas. de sal *kosher*, en partes

2 cdtas. de pimienta negra gruesa, en partes

3 naranjas, sin semillas, exprimidas en un recipiente

3 dientes de ajo, pelados y picados

1 cdta. de pimienta negra gruesa

Hojas de 4 ramitas de tomillo, descartar tallos

1/4 cdta. de orégano seco

1. Calentar el horno a 400°F.

2. Colocar el pollo (sin la columna y piel) en una asadera con las menudencias hacia abajo. (No se preocupen, el pollo sabrá maravilloso por más que no tenga piel). Sazonar con 3/4 cdta. de sal y 1 cdta. de pimienta. Frotarlas delicadamente en el pollo.

3. En la vasija con jugo de naranja agregar el ajo, 1/2 cdta. de sal, 1 cdta. de pimienta, el tomillo y orégano. Mezclar los ingredientes para incorporar los sabores. Poner el mojo de lado.

4. Hornear el pollo 1 hora, bañándolo con el mojo cada 10 minutos.

5. Al cabo de 1 hora, insertar un termómetro de carne en la parte más gruesa de la pechuga de pollo. La temperatura debe ser 160°F. Poner el pollo de lado un rato antes de servir. (Si se cocina el pollo hasta la temperatura indicada de 165°F, cocerlo más tiempo podría hacer que se seque. Por eso recomiendo sacarlo cuando alcance 160°F y poner el pollo de lado 15 minutos, hasta que el calor residual eleve la temperatura a 165°F). Deshuesar el pollo antes de servir. A disfrutar. ¡Toma!

SELECCIONES/INTERCAMBIOS
1 vegetal, 3 1/2 proteínas magras

CALORÍAS 160 | **CALORÍAS DE GRASA** 25 | **TOTAL DE GRASA** 3g | **GRASA SATURADA** 1g | **GRASA TRANS** 0g | **COLESTEROL** 80mg | **SODIO** 290mg | **POTASIO** 460mg | **TOTAL DE CARBOHIDRATOS** 6g | **FIBRA ALIMENTARIA** 1g | **AZÚCARES** 4g | **PROTEÍNA** 26g | **FÓSFORO** 255mg

Fresh-Water Cod *a la Vizcaína*

The first time I ever experienced this dish was around 1996–1997 at Martino's Cuban Restaurant in New Jersey, the restaurant my family and I have been putting our blood, sweat, and tears into for the last 23 years. Wow! It's hard to wrap my head around that. My father added this dish to the menu as a special, and I watched like a hawk as he made it. This dish is put together like a beautiful dance, like a pasodoble. The recipe has a few steps, but it's all worth it. This one's for you, Papi!

PREP TIME: 20 minutes
COOKING TIME: 40 minutes
SERVES: 4
SERVING SIZE: 1 piece cod and 1/2 cup sauce

16 ounces fresh-water cod, cut into
    4-ounce pieces
4 tablespoons tapioca flour
1 cup low-sodium canned crushed
    tomatoes
1/2 cup finely chopped Spanish onion
    (about 1/2 medium onion)
1/4 cup finely chopped red pepper
    (about 1/2 small red pepper)
3 cloves garlic, peeled and finely
    chopped
1/2 cup pitted Manzanillo olives,
    drained and finely chopped
1/4 teaspoon kosher salt
1/4 teaspoon cracked black pepper
1 teaspoon Spanish smoked paprika
1 teaspoon avocado oil
1 dried bay leaf
1 cup unsalted chicken stock
1 tablespoon finely chopped cilantro
1 lime, cut into 4 pieces

1. Place cod pieces on a baking sheet lined with a paper towel and pat dry both sides of fish.

2. Add tapioca flour to a small bowl and dredge each piece of cod in flour. Shake off any excess flour and place fish in the fridge.

3. Add crushed tomatoes, onions, red pepper, garlic, olives, salt, pepper, and smoked paprika to a bowl, and mix well with a spoon.

4. Remove cod from the fridge. Preheat a large nonstick pan over medium heat, add avocado oil, and wait a few seconds for oil to heat up. Add cod to the pan skin side down. Once skin side is browned, flip fish, brown other side, and set fish aside.

5. Using the same pan, add all ingredients from the bowl and bring to a simmer. Reduce heat so that only small bubbles break the surface of the sauce. Add the bay leaf and chicken stock, and let the sauce develop for 25 minutes. Add cod pieces to sauce and cook for an additional 5 minutes.

6. Turn off the heat. Add cilantro and lightly fold it in around fish. To serve add 1 piece fish and about 1/2 cup sauce to each plate. Garnish with a little spritz of lime.

EXCHANGES/CHOICES
2 vegetable, 3 lean protein

CALORIES 170 | CALORIES FROM FAT 45 | TOTAL FAT 5g | SATURATED FAT 1g | TRANS FAT 0g
CHOLESTEROL 50mg | SODIUM 430mg | POTASSIUM 640mg | TOTAL CARBOHYDRATE 13g
DIETARY FIBER 3g | SUGARS 3g | PROTEIN 22g | PHOSPHORUS 250mg

BACALAO DE AGUA DULCE A LA VIZCAÍNA

La primera vez que probé este plato fue alrededor de 1996-1997 en Martino's en Nueva Jersey, el restaurante cubano al que mi familia y yo le hemos dedicado sangre, sudor y lágrimas en los últimos 23 años. ¡Vaya! ¡Cómo pasan los años! Mi padre agregó este platillo al menú especial, y lo observé atentamente mientras lo preparaba. Este plato se hace como un lindo baile, como un pasodoble. La receta tiene varios pasos, pero vale la pena. ¡Esta es para ti, papi!

TIEMPO DE PREPARACIÓN: 20 minutos
TIEMPO DE COCCIÓN: 40 minutos
RINDE: 4 porciones
TAMAÑO DE LA PORCIÓN: 1 trozo de bacalao y 1/2 taza de salsa

---

16 onzas de bacalao de agua dulce, cortado en trozos de 4 onzas

4 cdas. de harina de tapioca

1 taza de tomate enlatado con poca sal, aplastado

1/2 taza de cebolla española, finamente picada (aproximadamente 1/2 cebolla mediana)

1/4 taza de pimiento rojo, finamente picado (aproximadamente 1/2 pimiento rojo)

3 dientes de ajo, pelados y finamente picados

1/2 taza de aceitunas deshuesadas tipo manzanillo, escurridas y picadas

1/4 cdta. de sal *kosher*

1/4 cdta. de pimienta negra gruesa

1 cdta. de pimentón español ahumado (paprika)

1 cdta. de aceite de aguacate

1 hoja de laurel

1 taza de caldo de pollo sin sal

1 cda. de cilantro finamente picado

1 lima o limón verde, cortado en 4 trozos

1. Colocar los trozos de bacalao en una asadera cubierta con papel toalla y secar ambos lados del pescado.

2. Agregar la harina de tapioca a una vasija pequeña y espolvorear cada trozo de bacalao con harina. Sacudir para eliminar el exceso de harina y colocar el pescado en el refrigerador.

3. Añadir el tomate aplastado, la cebolla, el pimiento rojo, el ajo, las aceitunas, la sal, la pimienta y el pimentón a una vasija, y mezclar bien con una cuchara.

4. Sacar el bacalao del refrigerador. Calentar una sartén antiadherente grande a fuego medio, agregar el aceite de aguacate y esperar unos segundos para que el aceite se caliente. Poner el bacalao en la asadera con la piel hacia abajo. Una vez que se dore la piel, voltear el pescado, dorar el otro lado y ponerlo de lado.

5. Agregar a la misma sartén todos los ingredientes de la vasija y hacer hervir a fuego lento. Bajar la temperatura para que a la salsa solo le salgan burbujas pequeñas. Agregar el laurel y el caldo de pollo, y cocer la salsa 25 minutos. Agregar los trozos de bacalao a la salsa y cocer 5 minutos adicionales.

6. Apagar el fuego. Agregar el cilantro y mezclarlo un poco alrededor del pescado. Al servir poner un trozo de pescado en cada plato y agregar aproximadamente 1/2 taza de salsa. Echarle un poco de jugo de limón verde.

SELECCIONES/INTERCAMBIOS
2 vegetales, 3 proteínas magras

CALORÍAS 170 | **CALORÍAS DE GRASA** 45 | **TOTAL DE GRASA** 5g | **GRASA SATURADA** 1g | **GRASA TRANS** 0g
COLESTEROL 50mg | **SODIO** 430mg | **POTASIO** 640mg | **TOTAL DE CARBOHIDRATOS** 13g
FIBRA ALIMENTARIA 3g | **AZÚCARES** 3g | **PROTEÍNA** 22g | **FÓSFORO** 250mg

CILANTRO-MARINATED TILAPIA

PREP TIME: 10 minutes
COOKING TIME: 15 minutes
SERVES: 3
SERVING SIZE: 1 (4-ounce) piece

12 ounces fresh tilapia
2 tablespoons finely chopped cilantro
1 tablespoon lime juice
Dash ground cumin
Dash cracked black pepper
1/2 teaspoon kosher salt
Parchment paper

1. Preheat oven to 350°F.

2. Cut tilapia into 3 equal pieces (about 4 ounces each). Place tilapia pieces into a resealable plastic bag. Add cilantro, lime juice, cumin, black pepper, and salt. Seal bag and gently mix all ingredients in the bag. (This is the best way to get the *sazón* deep into the tilapia.)

3. Line a baking sheet with parchment paper, place tilapia fillets on the sheet, and cook in oven for 15 minutes.

4. Remove from oven and let fish rest for a few minutes before serving.

EXCHANGES/CHOICES
3 lean protein

CALORIES 110 | **CALORIES FROM FAT** 20 | **TOTAL FAT** 2g | **SATURATED FAT** 1g | **TRANS FAT** 0g
CHOLESTEROL 55mg | **SODIUM** 0mg | **POTASSIUM** 370mg | **TOTAL CARBOHYDRATE** 1g
DIETARY FIBER 0g | **SUGARS** 0g | **PROTEIN** 23g | **PHOSPHORUS** 200mg

TILAPIA ADOBADA CON CILANTRO

TIEMPO DE PREPARACIÓN: 10 minutos
TIEMPO DE COCCIÓN: 15 minutos
RINDE: 3 porciones
TAMAÑO DE LA PORCIÓN: 1 trozo (de 4 onzas)

12 onzas de tilapia fresca
2 cdas. de cilantro finamente picado
1 cda. de jugo de lima o limón verde
Un poco de comino
Un poco de pimienta negra gruesa
1/2 cdta. de sal *kosher*
Papel mantequilla

1. Calentar el horno a 350°F.

2. Cortar la tilapia en tres trozos iguales (de aproximadamente 4 onzas cada uno). Colocar los trozos de tilapia en una bolsa de plástico con cierre. Agregar el cilantro, jugo de limón, comino, pimienta negra y sal. Cerrar la bolsa y mezclar delicadamente todos los ingredientes en la bolsa. (Esta es la mejor manera de sazonar bien la tilapia).

3. Poner papel mantequilla en una asadera, colocar los filetes de tilapia en la asadera y hornear 15 minutos.

4. Retirar del horno y poner el pescado de lado unos minutos antes de servir.

SELECCIONES/INTERCAMBIOS
3 proteínas magras

CALORÍAS 110 | **CALORÍAS DE GRASA** 20 | **TOTAL DE GRASA** 2g | **GRASA SATURADA** 1g | **GRASA TRANS** 0g
COLESTEROL 55mg | **SODIO** 0mg | **POTASIO** 370mg | **TOTAL DE CARBOHIDRATOS** 1g
FIBRA ALIMENTARIA 0g | **AZÚCARES** 0g | **PROTEÍNA** 23g | **FÓSFORO** 200mg

Little-Neck Clams with Garlic and Cilantro

PREP TIME: 10 minutes
COOKING TIME: 5–10 minutes
SERVES: 4
SERVING SIZE: 10 clams

40 little neck clams

3 cloves garlic, peeled and finely chopped

2 cups unsalted chicken stock

1 teaspoon kosher salt

1/4 teaspoon black cracked pepper

3 tablespoons finely chopped cilantro

2 teaspoons fresh thyme leaves

1 tablespoon lime juice

1. In a large pan or pot, add clams, garlic, chicken stock, salt, and pepper, and bring to a simmer, stirring constantly. Stir until all clams open up, add the cilantro, fresh thyme leaves, and lime juice, and mix well.

2. Turn off the heat and discard any clams that haven't opened up. Enjoy!

EXCHANGES/CHOICES
1 lean protein

CALORIES 40 | **CALORIES FROM FAT** 10 | **TOTAL FAT** 1g | **SATURATED FAT** 0g | **TRANS FAT** 0g
CHOLESTEROL 10mg | **SODIUM** 420mg | **POTASSIUM** 70mg | **TOTAL CARBOHYDRATE** 3g
DIETARY FIBER 0g | **SUGARS** 0g | **PROTEIN** 6g | **PHOSPHORUS** 90mg

ALMEJITAS CON AJO Y CILANTRO

TIEMPO DE PREPARACIÓN: 10 minutos
TIEMPO DE COCCIÓN: 5-10 minutos
RINDE: 4 porciones
TAMAÑO DE LA PORCIÓN: 10 almejas

40 almejitas (tipo *little neck*)

3 dientes de ajo, pelados y finamente picados

2 tazas de caldo de pollo sin sal

1 cdta. de sal *kosher*

1/4 cdta. de pimienta negra gruesa

3 cdas. de cilantro finamente picado

2 cdtas. de hojas de tomillo fresco, sin tallos

1 cda. de jugo de lima o limón verde

1. En una sartén u olla grande, poner las almejas, el ajo, caldo de pollo, sal y pimienta y hervir a fuego lento, revolviendo constantemente. Revolver hasta que todas las almejas se abran, añadir el cilantro, el jugo de limón verde y las hojas de tomillo fresco, y mezclar bien.

2. Apagar el fuego y desechar cualquier almeja que no se haya abierto. ¡A disfrutar!

SELECCIONES/INTERCAMBIOS
1 proteína magra

CALORÍAS 40 | **CALORÍAS DE GRASA** 10 | **TOTAL DE GRASA** 1g | **GRASA SATURADA** 0g | **GRASA TRANS** 0g
COLESTEROL 10mg | **SODIO** 420mg | **POTASIO** 70mg | **TOTAL DE CARBOHIDRATOS** 3g
FIBRA ALIMENTARIA 0g | **AZÚCARES** 0g | **PROTEÍNA** 6g | **FÓSFORO** 90mg

Garbanzos with Cilantro Chutney

I didn't start eating garbanzo beans regularly until about 2 years ago. They happened to be on a menu in a soup, and they were so delicious. My wife and kid love them, so I wanted to include them as part of the "sazón" of this book. The key to cooking garbanzo beans is time; this recipe will make them perfectly tender and delicious—so be patient.

PREP TIME: 15 minutes
COOKING TIME: 5 hours
SERVES: 6
SERVING SIZE: 1/2 cup

6 cups water, divided
10 ounces dried garbanzo beans
4 tablespoons finely chopped cilantro
1/2 cup finely chopped Spanish onion
2 tablespoons lime juice
1 1/2 teaspoons kosher salt
1/8 teaspoon cracked black pepper
1/8 teaspoon ground cumin
1/4 teaspoon dried oregano
1/4 teaspoon garlic powder

1. Bring large pot of water to a boil, then remove from heat. Add garbanzo beans to the water and let them soak for 1 hour.

2. Drain garbanzo beans and add to a pot with 4 cups water. Cook over low heat for 4 hours, or until tender. One hour into cooking add remaining 2 cups water.

3. With 30 minutes cooking time remaining, add cilantro, onion, lime juice, salt, pepper, cumin, oregano, and garlic powder, and stir into the garbanzo beans.

4. When garbanzo beans are tender, remove from heat and serve.

RONALDO'S TIP

This is a great dish to make on a Monday and eat for the rest of the week. It reheats beautifully, and the flavors improve and develop over time.

EXCHANGES/CHOICES
1 1/2 starch, 1 1/2 lean protein

CALORIES 180 | **CALORIES FROM FAT** 25 | **TOTAL FAT** 3g | **SATURATED FAT** 0g | **TRANS FAT** 0g | **CHOLESTEROL** 0mg | **SODIUM** 420mg | **POTASSIUM** 450mg | **TOTAL CARBOHYDRATE** 30g | **DIETARY FIBER** 9g | **SUGARS** 6g | **PROTEIN** 9g | **PHOSPHORUS** 180mg

GARBANZOS CON *CHUTNEY* DE CILANTRO

Recién hace dos años comencé a comer garbanzos con regularidad. Fue de casualidad, porque eran parte de una sopa del menú y sabían a maravillas. A mi esposa y mi hijo les encantan, y por eso los quise incluir como parte de la "sazón" de este libro. La clave para preparar garbanzos es el tiempo; esta receta hará que se pongan perfectamente blandos y deliciosos, así que tengan paciencia.

TIEMPO DE PREPARACIÓN: 15 minutos
TIEMPO DE COCCIÓN: 5 horas
RINDE: 6 porciones
TAMAÑO DE LA PORCIÓN: 1/2 taza

6 tazas de agua, en partes
10 onzas de garbanzos secos
4 cdas. de cilantro finamente picado
1/2 taza de cebolla española, finamente picada
2 cdas. de jugo de lima o limón verde
1 1/2 cdtas. de sal *kosher*
1/8 cdta. de pimienta negra gruesa
1/8 cdta. de comino
1/4 cdta. de orégano seco
1/4 cdta. de ajo en polvo

1. En una olla grande hervir agua y luego retirar del fuego. Echar los garbanzos al agua y remojar una hora.

2. Escurrir los garbanzos y echarlos a la olla con 4 tazas de agua. Cocerlos a fuego lento 4 horas o hasta que estén blandos. Tras cocerlos una hora agregar las 2 tazas restantes de agua.

3. Cuando falten 30 minutos de cocción, agregar a los garbanzos el cilantro, cebolla, jugo de limón, sal, pimienta, comino, orégano y ajo en polvo y revolver.

4. Cuando los garbanzos estén blandos, retirar del fuego y servir.

CONSEJO DE RONALDO

Este es un plato perfecto para preparar un lunes y comer el resto de la semana. Queda muy bien recalentado, y los sabores se acentúan con el tiempo.

SELECCIONES/INTERCAMBIOS
1 1/2 almidones, 1 1/2 proteínas magras

CALORÍAS 180 | **CALORÍAS DE GRASA** 25 | **TOTAL DE GRASA** 3g | **GRASA SATURADA** 0g | **GRASA TRANS** 0g
COLESTEROL 0mg | **SODIO** 420mg | **POTASIO** 450mg | **TOTAL DE CARBOHIDRATOS** 30g
FIBRA ALIMENTARIA 9g | **AZÚCARES** 6g | **PROTEÍNA** 9g | **FÓSFORO** 180mg

HEMINGWAY SANGRIA

This was always a family favorite at the table growing up; I would always see the sangria floating around. This is the beefed up version; the version my family had was the sangria that already came premade. That always cracked me up because by adding fruit, they made it their own. I remember making this sangria the first time for them; they were like "there is no such thing as a white sangria." As soon as it touched their lips, they asked for more and more. Now every time they come over to the house, they always ask for that Hemingway Sangria. It is always interesting that even something simple like a drink brings back so many memories.

PREP TIME: 20 minutes
REFRIGERATION TIME: 2 hours
SERVES: 8
SERVING SIZE: 4 ounces

1 (750-mL) bottle white wine, preferably Chablis

3 ounces triple sec

3 ounces gold rum

1 cup peeled and cubed pineapple (1/4-inch cubes)

1 medium mango, cut into 1/4-inch cubes (1 cup)

2 tablespoons lime juice

1 teaspoon lime zest

2 oranges, juiced

1 lime, thinly sliced

1 (750-mL) bottle diet tonic water

1 cup mint leaves, washed, torn into pieces, and placed in fridge covered

1. To a large vessel, add wine, triple sec, rum, pineapple, mango, lime juice, lime zest, orange juice, and lime slices. Cover tightly with plastic wrap and put mixture in the fridge for 2 hours.

2. Remove sangria from fridge, add tonic water and mint leaves, and serve.

EXCHANGES/CHOICES
1 other carbohydrate, 1 alcohol

CALORIES 170 | **CALORIES FROM FAT** 0 | **TOTAL FAT** 0g | **SATURATED FAT** 0g | **TRANS FAT** 0g
CHOLESTEROL 0mg | **SODIUM** 15mg | **POTASSIUM** 210mg | **TOTAL CARBOHYDRATE** 15g
DIETARY FIBER 0g | **SUGARS** 10g | **PROTEIN** 1g | **PHOSPHORUS** 35mg

SANGRÍA A LA HEMINGWAY

Durante mi infancia, esta siempre fue una de las recetas preferidas de mi familia; siempre veía sangría en la mesa. Esta versión es mejorada; la versión de mi familia era la sangría que venía ya preparada. Eso siempre me hacía reír pues le daban un toque personal al agregar un poco de fruta. Recuerdo que cuando les preparé esta sangría por primera vez, me dijeron: "No existe la sangría blanca". Apenas se la llevaron a la boca, me pidieron más y más. Ahora cada vez que vienen a casa me piden sangría a la Hemingway. Es interesante que incluso algo simple como una bebida traiga tantos recuerdos.

TIEMPO DE PREPARACIÓN: 20 minutos
TIEMPO DE REFRIGERACIÓN: 2 horas
RINDE: 8 porciones
TAMAÑO DE LA PORCIÓN: 4 onzas

1 botella (de 750 mL) de vino blanco,
   de preferencia de Chablis

3 onzas de triple seco

3 onzas de ron dorado

1 taza de piña o ananá pelada y cortada
   en cubos (de 1/4 de pulgada)

1 mango mediano, cortado en cubos de
   1/4 de pulgada (1 taza)

2 cdas. de jugo de lima o limón verde

1 cdta. de ralladura de lima o limón
   verde

2 naranjas, exprimidas

1 lima o limón verde, en tajadas delgadas

1 botella (de 750 mL) de agua tónica
   de dieta

1 taza de hojas de menta, lavadas, en
   pedazos, tapadas y refrigeradas

1. En un recipiente grande, echar el vino, triple seco, ron, piña, mango, jugo de limón verde, ralladura de limón verde, jugo de naranja y rebanadas de limón verde. Tapar bien con plástico y refrigerar la mezcla 2 horas.

2. Retirar la sangría del refrigerador, añadir las hojas de menta y agua tónica, y servir.

SELECCIONES/INTERCAMBIOS
1 otro carbohidrato, 1 alcohol

CALORÍAS 170 | **CALORÍAS DE GRASA** 0 | **TOTAL DE GRASA** 0g | **GRASA SATURADA** 0g | **GRASA TRANS** 0g
COLESTEROL 0mg | **SODIO** 15mg | **POTASIO** 210mg | **TOTAL DE CARBOHIDRATOS** 15g
FIBRA ALIMENTARIA 0g | **AZÚCARES** 10g | **PROTEÍNA** 1g | **FÓSFORO** 35mg

CUBA LIBRE

There is a story behind this drink. Legend has it that in 1898 a man named Captain Russell ordered a rum, coke, and lime at a bar in Cuba. He loved the drink so much that he ordered it for his troops and proposed a toast to a "Cuba libre." That's how the drink was born many years ago. I am not much of a drinker, but when I do drink, this is my go-to beverage.

PREP TIME: 5 minutes
STIRRING TIME: 30 seconds
SERVES: 1
SERVING SIZE: 1 drink

2 ounces rum
2 teaspoons lime juice
6 ounces diet cola
1/2 cup ice

1. In a large glass, combine all of the ingredients. Stir gently with a spoon, sit back, and enjoy the history behind this cocktail.

EXCHANGES/CHOICES
1/2 other carbohydrate, 1 alcohol

CALORIES 140 | CALORIES FROM FAT 0 | TOTAL FAT 0g | SATURATED FAT 0g | TRANS FAT 0g
CHOLESTEROL 0mg | SODIUM 15mg | POTASSIUM 50mg | TOTAL CARBOHYDRATE 3g
DIETARY FIBER 0g | SUGARS 1g | PROTEIN 0g | PHOSPHORUS 25mg

CUBA LIBRE

Este trago tiene historia. Según la leyenda, en 1898, el capitán Russell pidió un ron con Coca Cola y limón verde en un bar en Cuba. Le gustó tanto lo que había pedido que lo pidió para sus soldados y propuso un brindis por una "Cuba Libre". Ese es el origen del trago hace muchos años. Yo no bebo mucho, pero cuando lo hago, pido esto.

TIEMPO DE PREPARACIÓN: 5 minutos y medio
RINDE: 1 porción
TAMAÑO DE LA PORCIÓN: 1 trago

2 onzas de ron
2 cdtas. de jugo de lima o limón verde
6 onzas de cola de dieta
1/2 taza de hielo

1. En un vaso grande, mezclar todos los ingredientes. Revolver delicadamente con una cuchara, tomar asiento y disfrutar la historia de este cóctel.

SELECCIONES/INTERCAMBIOS
1/2 otro carbohidrato, 1 alcohol

CALORÍAS 140 | CALORÍAS DE GRASA 0 | TOTAL DE GRASA 0g | GRASA SATURADA 0g | GRASA TRANS 0g
COLESTEROL 0mg | SODIO 15mg | POTASIO 50mg | TOTAL DE CARBOHIDRATOS 3g
FIBRA ALIMENTARIA 0g | AZÚCARES 1g | PROTEÍNA 0g | FÓSFORO 25mg

LADY'S SANGRIA

A few years back, I developed this recipe for a tasting dinner I put together for my amazing wife's birthday. The different fruits used represent the beauty that is my wife, and the dark rum represents yours truly. Enjoy this wonderful cocktail!

PREP TIME: 15 minutes
REFRIGERATION TIME: 2 hours
SERVES: 6
SERVING SIZE: 1 cup

1 (750-mL) bottle white wine
2 peaches, chopped
1 apple, cored and chopped
4 ounces raspberries, lightly muddled
4 ounces triple sec
3 oranges, juiced
1 tablespoon lime juice
4 ounces gold rum
2 cups diet tonic water

1. In a large vessel, add wine, peaches, apple, raspberries, triple sec, orange juice, lime juice, and rum, and stir. Let the sangria sit in the fridge for a couple of hours before serving. Add the tonic water just before serving it to your guests.

EXCHANGES/CHOICES
2 fruit, 1 1/2 alcohol

CALORIES 260 | **CALORIES FROM FAT** 10 | **TOTAL FAT** 1g | **SATURATED FAT** 0g | **TRANS FAT** 0g
CHOLESTEROL 0mg | **SODIUM** 15mg | **POTASSIUM** 400mg | **TOTAL CARBOHYDRATE** 35g
DIETARY FIBER 5g | **SUGARS** 26g | **PROTEIN** 2g | **PHOSPHORUS** 60mg

SANGRÍA DE LADY

Hace unos años inventé esta receta para una cena de degustación que organicé para el cumpleaños de mi maravillosa esposa. Las diversas frutas representan la belleza de mi esposa, y el ron oscuro me representa a mí. ¡Disfruten este excelente coctel!

TIEMPO DE PREPARACIÓN: 15 minutos
TIEMPO DE REFRIGERACIÓN: 2 horas
RINDE: 6 porciones
TAMAÑO DE LA PORCIÓN: 1 taza

1 botella (de 750 mL) de vino blanco

2 duraznos picados

1 manzana sin centro, picada

4 onzas de frambuesas, un poco
    aplastadas

4 onzas de triple seco

3 naranjas, exprimidas

1 cda. de jugo de lima o limón verde

4 onzas de ron dorado

2 tazas de agua tónica de dieta

1. En un recipiente grande, mezclar el vino, los duraznos, la manzana, las frambuesas, el triple seco, el jugo de naranja, el jugo de limón verde y el ron. Refrigerar la sangría un par de horas antes de servir. Agregar el agua tónica justo antes de servirla a los invitados.

SELECCIONES/INTERCAMBIOS
2 frutas, 1 1/2 alcoholes

CALORÍAS 260 | **CALORÍAS DE GRASA** 10 | **TOTAL DE GRASA** 1g | **GRASA SATURADA** 0g | **GRASA TRANS** 0g
COLESTEROL 0mg | **SODIO** 15mg | **POTASIO** 400mg | **TOTAL DE CARBOHIDRATOS** 35g
FIBRA ALIMENTARIA 5g | **AZÚCARES** 26g | **PROTEÍNA** 2g | **FÓSFORO** 60mg

RONALDO'S APPLE PIE

I love apple pie—the smell, the taste of the warm apples, the flaky crust, and the cinnamon. I'm drooling, guys! My version of apple pie does not have the buttery crust, but it does have mucho flavor that your taste buds will enjoy.

PREP TIME: 10 minutes
COOKING TIME: 1 hour
SERVES: 3
SERVING SIZE: 1 apple

---

3 Red Delicious apples
2 tablespoons plus 1/2 teaspoon lime juice, divided
3 tablespoons all-natural almond butter
1/8 teaspoon ground cinnamon
1/8 teaspoon ground nutmeg
1/8 teaspoon vanilla extract
1/8 teaspoon pumpkin spice

1. Preheat oven to 350°F.

2. Core the apples, making sure to leave the bottoms intact. Cut off the top of each apple, about 1/4 inch from the top.

3. In a medium bowl, combine 2 tablespoons lime juice and 2 cups water. Soak the apples in the water for about 5 minutes to prevent browning.

4. In another bowl, add almond butter, cinnamon, nutmeg, vanilla extract, remaining lime juice, and pumpkin spice. Mix together.

5. Remove apples from water and pat dry. Stuff each apple with 1 tablespoon almond butter mixture. Once all apples are stuffed, place them in a deep baking dish. Add about 1/2 inch water to the baking dish, and make sure apples are upright in the water. (The water keeps the apples from drying out.) Bake for 1 hour. While the apples bake, keep an eye on the water level; add more water if needed.

6. Once apples are fork tender, remove from baking dish and serve.

EXCHANGES/CHOICES
1 fruit, 1 1/2 other carbohydrate, 2 fat

CALORIES 250 | CALORIES FROM FAT 90 | TOTAL FAT 10g | SATURATED FAT 1g | TRANS FAT 0g
CHOLESTEROL 0mg | SODIUM 40mg | POTASSIUM 390mg | TOTAL CARBOHYDRATE 40g
DIETARY FIBER 8g | SUGARS 28g | PROTEIN 4g | PHOSPHORUS 115mg

TARTA DE MANZANA DE RONALDO

Me encanta la tarta de manzana: el olor, el sabor de las manzanas calientes, la masa de hojaldre y la canela. ¡Se me hace agua la boca, amigos! Mi versión de la tarta de manzana no tiene la corteza con mantequilla, pero sí mucho sabor que disfrutará.

TIEMPO DE PREPARACIÓN: 10 minutos
TIEMPO DE COCCIÓN: 1 hora
RINDE: 3 porciones
TAMAÑO DE LA PORCIÓN: 1 manzana

---

3 manzanas tipo Red Delicious

2 cdas. más 1/2 cdta. de jugo de lima o limón verde, en partes

3 cdas. de mantequilla natural de almendras

1/8 cdta. de canela molida

1/8 cdta. de nuez moscada molida

1/8 cdta. de extracto de vainilla

1/8 cdta. de especias de tarta de calabaza (*pumpkin spice*)

1. Calentar el horno a 350°F.

2. Sacarles el centro a las manzanas, asegurándose de dejar intacta la parte de abajo. Cortar aproximadamente 1/4 de pulgada de la parte superior de cada manzana.

3. En una vasija mediana, mezclar 2 cdas. de jugo de limón verde y 2 tazas de agua. Remojar las manzanas en el agua aproximadamente 5 minutos para que no se oxiden.

4. En otra vasija, mezclar la mantequilla de almendras, canela, nuez moscada, extracto de vainilla, jugo de limón verde y especias de tarta de calabaza. Mezclar todo.

5. Retirar las manzanas del agua y secarlas con una toalla de papel. Rellenar cada manzana con 1 cda. de la mezcla de mantequilla de almendras. Una vez que todas las manzanas estén rellenas, colocarlas en una asadera profunda. Agregar aproximadamente 1/2 pulgada de agua a la asadera y colocar las manzanas en el agua, paradas. (El agua impide que las manzanas se sequen). Hornear 1 hora. Mientras las manzanas se hornean, fijarse en el nivel del agua; agregar más agua si es necesario.

6. Una vez que las manzanas estén blandas cuando se pinchan con un tenedor, retirar de la asadera y servir.

SELECCIONES/INTERCAMBIOS
1 fruta, 1 1/2 otros carbohidratos, 2 grasas

CALORÍAS 250 | **CALORÍAS DE GRASA** 90 | **TOTAL DE GRASA** 10g | **GRASA SATURADA** 1g | **GRASA TRANS** 0g
COLESTEROL 0mg | **SODIO** 40mg | **POTASIO** 390mg | **TOTAL DE CARBOHIDRATOS** 40g
FIBRA ALIMENTARIA 8g | **AZÚCARES** 28g | **PROTEÍNA** 4g | **FÓSFORO** 115mg

OVEN-BAKED CINNAMON PLANTAINS

I want to be honest with you guys, my baking skills are minimal, and the baked goods I do know how to make are not what you'd call diabetes-friendly. This has been challenging for me. But here is a very nice, healthy dessert that can be enjoyed with a dollop of plain yogurt.

PREP TIME: 10 minutes
COOKING TIME: 20 minutes
SERVES: 8
SERVING SIZE: 6 pieces plantain
and 1 tablespoon yogurt

---

3 ripe plantains (peel should be yellow
with brown freckles), peeled and cut
into 1/4-inch rounds
1 tablespoon avocado oil
1 teaspoon ground cinnamon
1/4 teaspoon ground nutmeg
Parchment paper
8 tablespoons fat-free plain Greek yogurt

1. Preheat oven to 400°F.

2. Place a damp cloth over the plantain slices and set aside.

3. Add avocado oil, cinnamon, and nutmeg to a bowl, and whisk together. (This amplifies the flavor profiles of the cinnamon and nutmeg.) Add the plantains to the bowl and gently fold ingredients together.

4. Line a baking sheet with parchment paper and place the plantain rounds on the pan in uniform lines. Place pan on middle rack of the oven for 20 minutes.

5. Remove from oven and enjoy each serving with 1 tablespoon yogurt.

EXCHANGES/CHOICES
2 1/2 starch, 1/2 fat

CALORIES 200 | **CALORIES FROM FAT** 35 | **TOTAL FAT** 4g | **SATURATED FAT** 0.5g | **TRANS FAT** 0g
CHOLESTEROL 0mg | **SODIUM** 5mg | **POTASSIUM** 680mg | **TOTAL CARBOHYDRATE** 44g
DIETARY FIBER 3g | **SUGARS** 20g | **PROTEIN** 2g | **PHOSPHORUS** 50mg

PLÁTANO CON CANELA AL HORNO

Quiero ser franco con ustedes; mi talento para hacer postres es mínimo, y los productos horneados que sé preparar no son recomendables para las personas con diabetes. Esto ha sido difícil para mí. Pero aquí les presento un delicioso y saludable postre que se puede disfrutar con una cucharada de yogur natural.

TIEMPO DE PREPARACIÓN: 10 minutos
TIEMPO DE COCCIÓN: 20 minutos
RINDE: 8 porciones
TAMAÑO DE LA PORCIÓN: 6 trozos de plátano y 1 cda. de yogur

---

3 plátanos maduros (la cáscara debe estar amarilla, con pecas marrones), pelados y cortados en rodajas de 1/4 de pulgada
1 cda. de aceite de aguacate
1 cdta. de canela molida
1/4 cdta. de nuez moscada molida
Papel mantequilla
8 cdas. de yogur griego de sabor natural, descremado

1. Calentar el horno a 400°F.
2. Colocar un paño húmedo sobre las rodajas de plátano y poner de lado.
3. Echar el aceite de aguacate, la canela y la nuez moscada en una vasija y batir. (Esto aumenta el sabor de la canela y la nuez moscada). Agregar los plátanos a la vasija y mezclar los ingredientes con movimientos suaves.
4. Poner papel mantequilla en una asadera, colocar las rebanadas de plátano en filas uniformes en la asadera. Colocar la asadera en la rejilla del medio del horno durante 20 minutos.
5. Retirar del horno y disfrutar cada porción con 1 cda. de yogur.

SELECCIONES/INTERCAMBIOS
2 1/2 almidones, 1/2 grasa

CALORÍAS 200 | **CALORÍAS DE GRASA** 35 | **TOTAL DE GRASA** 4g | **GRASA SATURADA** 0.5g | **GRASA TRANS** 0g
COLESTEROL 0mg | **SODIO** 5mg | **POTASIO** 680mg | **TOTAL DE CARBOHIDRATOS** 44g
FIBRA ALIMENTARIA 3g | **AZÚCARES** 20g | **PROTEÍNA** 2g | **FÓSFORO** 50mg

LITTLE BROTHER'S PLANTAIN BANANA BREAD

I had to get help from my little brother, Martino, for this recipe. As I said, desserts and I are not amigos, but you guys deserve some great desserts. So my brother said, "I got you." Martino is every bit of 6 feet tall and 200 pounds of a great human being. He has a sweet tooth that led him to create this awesome recipe.

PREP TIME: 15 minutes
COOKING TIME: 45 minutes
SERVES: 16
SERVING SIZE: 1/2-inch slice

---

3 medium ripe plantains, peeled, one cut into 1/8-inch slices, and the other two cut into 4 pieces each, divided

3 eggs

1 tablespoon coconut oil, melted in the microwave

1 teaspoon vanilla extract

1/4 cup all-natural almond butter

1/2 cup fat-free plain Greek yogurt

1/2 cup prunes, frozen for 10 minutes then cut into 1/4-inch cubes

1/2 cup coconut flour

1 teaspoon baking soda

1 teaspoon baking powder

1/4 teaspoon ground cinnamon

1/4 teaspoon ground nutmeg

1. Preheat a nonstick pan over medium heat and brown the plantain slices. Line the bottom of a 4 × 8-inch loaf pan with the slices. Set aside.

2. Preheat oven to 350°F.

3. Place remaining plantain pieces in a bowl and mash with a fork or potato masher. Transfer plantains to bowl of an electric mixer along with the eggs, and mix on medium speed for 1 minute. Mix in melted coconut oil, vanilla, almond butter, yogurt, and prunes, and mix for 1 minute. Add coconut flour, baking soda, baking powder, cinnamon, and nutmeg. Mix on medium speed for an additional 2 minutes.

4. Add batter to the prepped 4 × 8-inch loaf pan. Bake for 45 minutes.

EXCHANGES/CHOICES
1 starch, 1 fat

CALORIES 110 | **CALORIES FROM FAT** 35 | **TOTAL FAT** 4g | **SATURATED FAT** 1.5g | **TRANS FAT** 0g
CHOLESTEROL 35mg | **SODIUM** 140mg | **POTASSIUM** 260mg | **TOTAL CARBOHYDRATE** 17g
DIETARY FIBER 2g | **SUGARS** 8g | **PROTEIN** 4g | **PHOSPHORUS** 70mg

PAN DE PLÁTANO DE MI HERMANO MENOR

Tuve que recibir ayuda de mi hermano menor, Martino, para esta receta. Como dije, los postres y yo no somos amigos, pero ustedes merecen unos cuantos postres fabulosos. Por eso mi hermano me dijo, "Yo me encargo". Martino es todo un hombrón de 6 pies de estatura y 200 libras, un gran ser humano. Le encantan los dulces, lo que lo llevó a crear esta maravillosa receta.

TIEMPO DE PREPARACIÓN: 15 minutos
TIEMPO DE COCCIÓN: 45 minutos
RINDE: 16 porciones
TAMAÑO DE LA PORCIÓN: Rebanada de 1/2 pulgada

---

3 plátanos maduros medianos, pelados, uno de ellos cortado en tajadas de 1/8 de pulgada y los otros dos en 4 trozos cada uno, en partes

3 huevos

1 cda. de aceite de coco, derretido en el microondas

1 cdta. de extracto de vainilla

1/4 taza de mantequilla de almendras natural

1/2 taza de yogur griego de sabor natural, descremado

1/2 taza de ciruelas secas, congelarlas 10 minutos y cortar en cubos de 1/4 de pulgada

1/2 taza de harina de coco

1 cdta. de bicarbonato de soda

1 cdta. de polvo de hornear

1/4 cdta. de canela molida

1/4 cdta. de nuez moscada molida

1. Calentar una sartén antiadherente a fuego medio y dorar las tajadas de plátano. Poner las tajadas en el fondo de un molde de pan de 4 × 8 pulgadas. Poner de lado.

2. Calentar el horno a 350°F.

3. Colocar el resto de los trozos de plátano en una vasija y aplastar con un prensapapas o tenedor. Pasar los plátanos a la vasija de la batidora eléctrica, echar los huevos y mezclar a velocidad media 1 minuto. Agregar el aceite de coco derretido, la vainilla, la mantequilla de almendras, el yogur y las ciruelas, y mezclar 1 minuto. Agregar la harina de coco, el bicarbonato, el polvo de hornear, la canela y la nuez moscada. Mezclar a velocidad media 2 minutos adicionales.

4. Agregar la mezcla al molde de pan preparado de 4 x 8 pulgadas. Hornear 45 minutos.

SELECCIONES/INTERCAMBIOS
1 almidón, 1 grasa

CALORÍAS 110 | **CALORÍAS DE GRASA** 35 | **TOTAL DE GRASA** 4g | **GRASA SATURADA** 1.5g | **GRASA TRANS** 0g
COLESTEROL 35mg | **SODIO** 140mg | **POTASIO** 260mg | **TOTAL DE CARBOHIDRATOS** 17g
FIBRA ALIMENTARIA 2g | **AZÚCARES** 8g | **PROTEÍNA** 4g | **FÓSFORO** 70mg

ANISE-POACHED RED PEARS

There is no easier dessert in my opinion than this dish. It is so simple to put together and cook. All we need for this dessert is some time, patience, and good music. The pear transforms from a juicy, crunchy fruit to a succulent piece of deliciousness. After it is done cooking, just grab a fork and enjoy! Pears contain about 20% of the daily recommended intake of dietary fiber.

PREP TIME: 10 minutes
COOKING TIME: About 2 hours 30 minutes
SERVES: 8
SERVING SIZE: 1/4 pear (about 1/2 cup) and 1 teaspoon liquid

---

2 pounds red pears, cut in half
1 tablespoon anise seeds
1/2 teaspoon ground cinnamon
1/4 teaspoon ground nutmeg
1/2 cup rum
5 cups water

1. Cut each pear into 4 quarters and remove seeds from center. Place pears flesh side down in a Dutch oven or a similar cooking vessel. Add anise seeds, cinnamon, nutmeg, rum, and water.

2. Cover, with lid slightly ajar, and place over medium-low heat to poach for 2 hours. Pears are done when they are fork tender.

3. After 2 hours, turn the heat off and let the pears sit in the liquid until they are cooled. Remove pears from liquid. Turn heat to medium and reduce poaching liquid by half. Strain reduced liquid through a mesh strainer.

4. To serve pears, place a pear quarter on a small plate and drizzle with 1 teaspoon poaching liquid.

RONALDO'S TIP

Mi gente, keep an eye on the pears while cooking to make sure the poaching liquid is at a gentle simmer. It is very important that the water does not evaporate on us!

EXCHANGES/CHOICES
1 fruit, 1/2 fat

CALORIES 100 | **CALORIES FROM FAT** 0 | **TOTAL FAT** 0g | **SATURATED FAT** 0g | **TRANS FAT** 0g
CHOLESTEROL 0mg | **SODIUM** 10mg | **POTASSIUM** 170mg | **TOTAL CARBOHYDRATE** 19g
DIETARY FIBER 4g | **SUGARS** 11g | **PROTEIN** 1g | **PHOSPHORUS** 25mg

PERAS ROJAS ESCALFADAS CON ANÍS

En mi opinión, no hay mejor postre que este. Su preparación es muy fácil. Todo lo que necesitamos para este postre es un poco de tiempo, paciencia y buena música. La pera se transforma de una fruta jugosa y fresca a un suculento y exquisito manjar. Una vez cocida, no tienen sino que agarrar un tenedor y ¡disfrutar! Además, las peras contienen aproximadamente 20% de fibra alimentaria que se recomienda consumir a diario.

TIEMPO DE PREPARACIÓN: 10 minutos
TIEMPO DE COCCIÓN: 2 horas y media
RINDE: 8 porciones
TAMAÑO DE LA PORCIÓN: 1/4 pera
  (aproximadamente 1/2 taza) y 1 cdta.
  de líquido

---

2 libras de peras rojas, cortadas
  por la mitad
1 cda. de semillas de anís
1/2 cdta. de canela molida
1/4 cdta. de nuez moscada molida
1/2 taza de ron
5 tazas de agua

1. Cortar cada pera en cuatro y quitarle las semillas del centro. Colocar las peras con la pulpa hacia abajo en una olla grande con tapa. Agregar las semillas de anís, la canela, la nuez moscada, el ron y el agua.

2. Tapar a medias y escalfarlas a fuego medio bajo 2 horas. Las peras estarán listas cuando al pincharlas con un tenedor estén blandas.

3. Después de 2 horas, apagar el fuego y dejar las peras en su líquido hasta que se enfríen. Retirar las peras del líquido. Bajar la temperatura a media y dejar que se evapore la mitad del líquido. Colar el líquido que quede.

4. Para servir las peras, colocar un cuarto de pera en un plato pequeño y echar encima 1 cdta. del líquido en que se escalfaron.

CONSEJO DE RONALDO

Mi gente, estén atentos a las peras durante la cocción para asegurarse de que el líquido en que se escalfan hierva a fuego lento. ¡Es muy importante que el agua no se evapore!

SELECCIONES/INTERCAMBIOS
1 fruta, 1/2 grasa

CALORÍAS 100 | **CALORÍAS DE GRASA** 0 | **TOTAL DE GRASA** 0g | **GRASA SATURADA** 0g | **GRASA TRANS** 0g
COLESTEROL 0mg | **SODIO** 10mg | **POTASIO** 170mg | **TOTAL DE CARBOHIDRATOS** 19g
FIBRA ALIMENTARIA 4g | **AZÚCARES** 11g | **PROTEÍNA** 1g | **FÓSFORO** 25mg

STEWS
FEEDING THE WHOLE FAMILY

SANCOCHOS
PARA ALIMENTAR A TODA LA FAMILIA

This section covers one of my favorite ways to cook. Learning how to cook one-pot dishes is so essential in today's stressful world. For people who are busy, these recipes will be perfect! Just add your ingredients to a pot or slow cooker in the morning, set a timer, and when you get home there will be something spectacular, flavorful, and healthy waiting for everyone.

It definitely feels like we had some type of stew dish once a week when I was growing up, and it was always a dish I looked forward to. If a stew is prepared properly, there is no better way to experience the deep flavors of yucca, plantains, corn, beef, or chicken. No matter what you put in the stew, the long hours of cooking turn ingredients into something magical. Stew ingredients soak up spices, herbs, and stock like sponges. One-pot dishes are a great way to minimize your salt intake and maximize your spice use. I hope you enjoy this section as much as I enjoyed writing it.

———————————

Esta sección trata sobre una de mis formas preferidas de cocinar. Aprender a cocinar platos de una sola olla ¡es esencial en el estresante mundo de hoy! Para las personas muy ocupadas, ¡estas recetas son perfectas! Simplemente pongan los ingredientes en una olla regular o de cocción lenta por la mañana y prendan el temporizador. Cuando lleguen a casa, algo espectacular, sabroso y saludable los estará esperando.

Creo que durante mi infancia comíamos algún tipo de sancocho una vez por semana, y siempre era un plato que me gustaba. Si el guiso se prepara correctamente, no hay mejor manera de deleitarse con los intensos sabores de la yuca, el plátano, el maíz o la carne de res o pollo. Independientemente de lo que se le ponga, las largas horas de cocción hacen magia con los ingredientes. Estos se empapan de especias, hierbas y caldo, como esponjas. Los platos que se preparan en una sola olla son una gran manera de reducir al mínimo su consumo de sal y maximizar el uso de especias. Espero que disfruten esta sección tanto como yo gocé al escribirla.

—Chef Ronaldo

Vegetable Broth *(Caldo de Vegetales)*

Most of us remember as young kids seeing a big pot on the stove with a bunch of veggies simmering away, eventually becoming an amazing cup of soup or broth for your favorite dishes. This recipe captures my recollection of that experience. Enjoy!

PREP TIME: 20 minutes
COOKING TIME: About 6 hours
SERVES: 5
SERVING SIZE: 1 1/2 cups

---

6 sprigs fresh thyme

6 sprigs fresh cilantro

12 inches butcher's twine

2 stalks celery, washed and cut into
   1/4-inch cubes

3 carrots, washed and cut into
   1/4-inch cubes

2 yellow onions, peeled and cut into
   1/4-inch cubes

1 tablespoon whole peppercorns

2 cloves garlic, peeled

1 teaspoon ground cumin

1 teaspoon dried oregano

3 dried bay leaves

4 quarts water

1. Tie thyme and cilantro sprigs together with butcher's twine and set aside.

2. Add celery, carrots, and yellow onions to a large pot, and sauté over medium heat until ingredients are translucent or shiny.

3. Add peppercorns, garlic, cumin, oregano, and bay leaves to the pot. Tie thyme and cilantro to the handle of the pot and drop in the water. Bring broth to a low simmer, then reduce heat to the lowest setting and cook for 6 hours.

4. After 6 hours, strain the broth and pour in ice cube trays or in a larger container so you can freeze it for later use. You'll have fresh broth ready for any of your favorite dishes or the recipes in my book.

RONALDO'S TIP

Adding fresh herbs to broth creates an amazing, fresh flavor. Tying herb sprigs to the pot allows you to easily remove them from the pot and provides a more concentrated flavor.

EXCHANGES/CHOICES
free food

CALORIES 10 | **CALORIES FROM FAT** 0 | **TOTAL FAT** 0g | **SATURATED FAT** 0g | **TRANS FAT** 0g
CHOLESTEROL 0mg | **SODIUM** 40mg | **POTASSIUM** 70mg | **TOTAL CARBOHYDRATE** 3g
DIETARY FIBER 1g | **SUGARS** 1g | **PROTEIN** 0g | **PHOSPHORUS** 10mg

CALDO DE VEGETALES

La mayoría de nosotros recuerda ver durante nuestra infancia una gran olla en la estufa, en la que hervía una variedad de vegetales, hasta convertirse finalmente en un tazón delicioso de sopa o caldo, uno de nuestros platos favoritos. Esta receta capta mis recuerdos de esa experiencia. ¡A disfrutar!

TIEMPO DE PREPARACIÓN: 20 minutos
TIEMPO DE COCCIÓN: Aproximadamente
   6 horas
RINDE: 5 porciones
TAMAÑO DE LA PORCIÓN: 1 1/2 tazas

6 ramitas de tomillo fresco

6 ramitas de cilantro fresco

12 pulgadas de pita de cocina

2 tallos de apio, lavados y cortados en cubos de 1/4 de pulgada

3 zanahorias, lavadas y cortadas en cubos de 1/4 de pulgada

2 cebollas amarillas, peladas y cortadas en cubos de 1/4 de pulgada

1 cda. de granos de pimienta

2 dientes de ajo, pelados

1 cdta. de comino

1 cdta. de orégano seco

3 hojas de laurel

4 cuartos de galón de agua (4 litros)

1. Atar las ramitas de tomillo y cilantro con pita de cocina y poner de lado.

2. Echar el apio, las zanahorias y las cebollas en una olla grande y sofreír a fuego medio hasta que los ingredientes estén traslúcidos o relucientes.

3. Agregar a la olla los granos de pimienta, el ajo, el comino, el orégano y las hojas de laurel. Atar el tomillo y el cilantro al mango de la olla y dejar caer en el agua. Llevar el caldo a un hervor a fuego lento, luego bajar a la temperatura mínima y cocer 6 horas.

4. Después de las 6 horas, colar el caldo y echarlo en bandejas de hielo o en un recipiente más grande, a fin de congelarlo para usarlo posteriormente. Tendrán caldo fresco y listo para cualquiera de sus platos favoritos o las recetas de mi libro.

CONSEJO DE RONALDO

Agregar hierbas frescas al caldo le da un maravilloso sabor fresco. Atar las ramitas de hierbas a la olla permite retirarlas fácilmente y produce un sabor más concentrado.

SELECCIONES/INTERCAMBIOS
No cuenta

CALORÍAS 10 | **CALORÍAS DE GRASA** 0 | **TOTAL DE GRASA** 0g | **GRASA SATURADA** 0g | **GRASA TRANS** 0g
COLESTEROL 0mg | **SODIO** 40mg | **POTASIO** 70mg | **TOTAL DE CARBOHIDRATOS** 3g
FIBRA ALIMENTARIA 1g | **AZÚCARES** 1g | **PROTEÍNA** 0g | **FÓSFORO** 10mg

MAMI'S CROCK-POT BLACK BEANS

What's so special about Mami's black beans? Just as my abuela's rice could only be made perfectly by her, my mother has a special way to add some deep flavors into her beans. There is no soaking required for these bad boys; my mother always says there's no time for soaking the beans. Her beans go straight into the pot, are brought to a boil, and then brought down to a simmer. Once the beans are tender, the seasoning is added and the beans simmer some more. That first bite...simply amazing! The beans come out tender, creamy, and delicious. This is a food memory I'll always cherish, and now I can share it with you.

PREP TIME: 20 minutes
COOKING TIME: 5 hours 30 minutes
SERVES: 8
SERVING SIZE: 3/4 cup

---

2 cups dried black beans, rinsed and sorted

8 cups water

1 yellow onion, peeled and finely chopped

1 cup finely chopped cilantro

1 cup finely chopped red pepper, washed

1/2 cup finely chopped green onions, washed

1 teaspoon kosher salt

1 teaspoon cracked black pepper

1 teaspoon ground cumin

1 teaspoon ground oregano

1. Add beans and water to slow cooker, set on high, and cook for 5 hours, or until beans are tender. If you can easily squeeze a bean with your fingers, they are done.

2. In a small bowl, combine the remaining ingredients, cover with plastic wrap, and place in the fridge to allow the flavors to marry and intensify.

3. When beans are done, add the mixture from the fridge to the slow cooker and mix well with a spoon. Cook for an additional 30 minutes on low and serve.

EXCHANGES/CHOICES
2 starch, 2 lean protein

CALORIES 240 | **CALORIES FROM FAT** 10 | **TOTAL FAT** 1g | **SATURATED FAT** 0g | **TRANS FAT** 0g | **CHOLESTEROL** 0mg | **SODIUM** 170mg | **POTASSIUM** 1090mg | **TOTAL CARBOHYDRATE** 45g | **DIETARY FIBER** 11g | **SUGARS** 5g | **PROTEIN** 14g | **PHOSPHORUS** 300mg

Cazuela de frijoles negros de mami

¿Qué tienen de especial los frijoles negros de mami? Así como solo mi abuela podía preparar su arroz a la perfección, mi madre tiene una manera especial de darles un sabor exquisito a los frijoles. No es necesario remojarlos; mi madre siempre dice que no hay tiempo para remojar los frijoles. Los frijoles que prepara se echan directamente a la olla, se hacen hervir y luego se baja el fuego. Una vez que los frijoles están blandos, se añaden los condimentos y se cuecen los frijoles a fuego lento un ratito más. Ese primer bocado es... ¡simplemente increíble! Los frijoles salen blandos, cremosos y deliciosos. Este es un recuerdo de comida que siempre atesoraré y ahora puedo compartirlo con ustedes.

TIEMPO DE PREPARACIÓN: 20 minutos
TIEMPO DE COCCIÓN: 5 horas y media
RINDE: 8 porciones
TAMAÑO DE LA PORCIÓN: 3/4 taza

---

2 tazas de frijoles negros secos, limpios y enjuagados

8 tazas de agua

1 cebolla amarilla, pelada y finamente picada

1 taza de cilantro finamente picado

1 taza de pimiento rojo, lavado y finamente picado

1/2 taza de cebollín, lavado y finamente picado

1 cdta. de sal *kosher*

1 cdta. de pimienta negra gruesa

1 cdta. de comino

1 cdta. de orégano en polvo

1. Echar los frijoles y el agua a una olla de cocción lenta, a fuego alto y cocer 5 horas o hasta que estén blandos. Si se puede apretar un frijol fácilmente con los dedos, están listos.

2. En una vasija pequeña, echar y mezclar el resto de los ingredientes, tapar con plástico y colocar en el refrigerador para permitir que los sabores se impregnen e intensifiquen.

3. Cuando los frijoles estén listos, añadir la mezcla refrigerada a la olla y mezclar bien con una cuchara. Cocer 30 minutos adicionales a fuego lento y servir.

SELECCIONES/INTERCAMBIOS
2 almidones, 2 proteínas magras

CALORÍAS 240 | **CALORÍAS DE GRASA** 10 | **TOTAL DE GRASA** 1g | **GRASA SATURADA** 0g | **GRASA TRANS** 0g
COLESTEROL 0mg | **SODIO** 170mg | **POTASIO** 1090mg | **TOTAL DE CARBOHIDRATOS** 45g
FIBRA ALIMENTARIA 11g | **AZÚCARES** 5g | **PROTEÍNA** 14g | **FÓSFORO** 300mg

RIVERSIDE CUBANO VEGETABLE STEW

This recipe is very special to me because it takes me back to when I was 7 years old in Medellín, Colombia. We would go to my aunt's finca (farm) in the beautiful countryside of Colombia in the summers. On one particular visit we went to the river located a few miles west of the farm. This trip was special because we were going to cook at the river, so we carried all of our ingredients, pots, and water with us. It felt like a 5-mile hike. Once we arrived, we set up the pit for our big pot, and the adults began cooking while we took care of having a good time in the river. This recipe definitely brings back the childhood joy that I felt all those years ago.

PREP TIME: 25 minutes
COOKING TIME: About 2 hours
SERVES: 10
SERVING SIZE: 1 cup

2 teaspoons avocado oil

2 stalks celery, washed and cut into 1/8-inch cubes

1/2 cup washed and cubed red pepper (1/8-inch cubes)

1/2 cup washed and cubed green pepper (1/8-inch cubes)

3 stalks green onion, peel away outer layer, wash, and cut into 1/8-inch cubes

1 tablespoon tomato paste

8 cups unsalted vegetable stock

16 ounces yucca, peeled and cut into 1-inch rounds

2 plantains, peeled and cut into 1-inch rounds

12 ounces butternut squash, cut into 1/2-inch cubes

4 dried bay leaves

4 sprigs fresh thyme

1 teaspoon kosher salt

1 teaspoon cracked black pepper

2 teaspoons garlic powder

1/4 teaspoon ground nutmeg

1 teaspoon ground cumin

1. Preheat a large pot over medium heat and add avocado oil. Add celery, red pepper, green pepper, and green onion, and sauté until the vegetables are translucent or shiny. Add tomato paste and mix well with a spoon for about 1 minute; then add vegetable stock.

2. Add the remaining ingredients, bring to a gentle simmer, and cover. Simmer for 2 hours, or until the vegetables are fork tender. Serve.

RONALDO'S TIP

If you have lime hanging around, squeeze a little lime juice into this stew before serving. This little secret is a game changer.

EXCHANGES/CHOICES
3 starch

CALORIES 240 | **CALORIES FROM FAT** 35 | **TOTAL FAT** 4g | **SATURATED FAT** 1g | **TRANS FAT** 0g
CHOLESTEROL 0mg | **SODIUM** 240mg | **POTASSIUM** 940mg | **TOTAL CARBOHYDRATE** 45g
DIETARY FIBER 4g | **SUGARS** 11g | **PROTEIN** 10g | **PHOSPHORUS** 170mg

GUISO CUBANO DE VEGETALES A LA RIBEREÑA

Esta receta es muy especial para mí porque hace que me remonte a cuando tenía 7 años de edad en Medellín, Colombia. En el verano íbamos a la finca de mi tía en la hermosa campiña de Colombia. En una de esas visitas, fuimos a un río ubicado a pocas millas al oeste de la finca. Este paseo fue especial porque planeábamos cocinar al borde del río, por lo que cargamos con todos los ingredientes, las ollas y el agua. Creo que caminamos 5 millas. Una vez que llegamos, hicimos un hoyo para nuestra gran olla, y los adultos comenzaron a cocinar mientras nosotros nos divertíamos en el río. Esta receta sin duda evoca la alegría infantil que sentí hace tantos años.

TIEMPO DE PREPARACIÓN: 25 minutos
TIEMPO DE COCCIÓN: Aproximadamente
   2 horas
RINDE: 10 porciones
TAMAÑO DE LA PORCIÓN: 1 taza

2 cdtas. de aceite de aguacate

2 tallos de apio, lavados y cortados en cubos de 1/8 de pulgada

1/2 taza de pimiento rojo, lavado y cortado en cubos de 1/8 de pulgada

1/2 taza de pimiento verde, lavado y cortado en cubos de 1/8 de pulgada

3 cebollines, sin la capa exterior, lavados y cortados en trozos de 1/8 de pulgada

1 cda. de pasta de tomate

8 tazas de caldo vegetal sin sal

16 onzas de yuca, pelada y cortada en rodajas de 1 pulgada

2 plátanos, pelados y cortados en tajadas de 1 pulgada

12 onzas de calabaza (tipo butternut), cortada en cubos de 1/2 pulgada

4 hojas de laurel

Hojas de 4 ramitas de tomillo fresco, descartar tallos

1 cdta. de sal *kosher*

1 cdta. de pimienta negra gruesa

2 cdtas. de ajo en polvo

1/4 cdta. de nuez moscada molida

1 cdta. de comino

1. Calentar una olla grande a fuego medio y echar el aceite de aguacate. Agregar el apio, pimiento rojo, pimiento verde y cebollines, y sofreír hasta que los vegetales estén traslúcidos o relucientes. Agregar la pasta de tomate y mezclar bien con un cucharón, aproximadamente 1 minuto. Luego agregar el caldo vegetal.

2. Agregar el resto de los ingredientes, hacer hervir a fuego lento y tapar. Cocer a fuego lento 2 horas o hasta que los vegetales estén blandos cuando se pinchen con un tenedor. Servir.

CONSEJO DE RONALDO

Si tienen una lima o limón verde a la mano, expriman un poco de jugo en este guiso antes de servir. Este secretito es fenomenal.

SELECCIONES/INTERCAMBIOS
3 almidones

CALORÍAS 240 | **CALORÍAS DE GRASA** 35 | **TOTAL DE GRASA** 4g | **GRASA SATURADA** 1g | **GRASA TRANS** 0g
COLESTEROL 0mg | **SODIO** 240mg | **POTASIO** 940mg | **TOTAL DE CARBOHIDRATOS** 45g
FIBRA ALIMENTARIA 4g | **AZÚCARES** 11g | **PROTEÍNA** 10g | **FÓSFORO** 170mg

Cubed Beef Fall Stew

This dish is great to cook ahead of time for that evening or for the week. The stew reheats well, and I think it tastes better each time you reheat it. When reheating this stew, don't use high heat. I suggest medium heat; it heats gently so the meat and vegetables don't become mushy.

PREP TIME: 20 minutes
COOKING TIME: 4 hours 45 minutes
SERVES: 8
SERVING SIZE: 1 1/4 cups

2 teaspoons avocado oil
3 carrots, washed and cut into 1/2-inch cubes
1 celery stick, washed and cut into 1/2-inch cubes
1 yellow onion, peeled and cut into 1/2-inch cubes
2 pounds eye-of-round beef roast, cut into 3/4-inch cubes
1 tablespoon tomato paste
1 cup red wine
6 1/2 cups water
4 cups peeled, seeded, cubed butternut squash (1-inch cubes)
2 cups peeled, seeded, cubed pumpkin (1-inch cubes)
2 cups peeled, seeded, cubed acorn squash (1-inch cubes)
3 dried bay leaves
4 teaspoons kosher salt
1 teaspoon cracked black pepper
2 teaspoons garlic powder
1 teaspoon ground cumin
2 teaspoons dried oregano
1/4 teaspoon ground nutmeg

1. Preheat a Dutch oven or large pot on the stove and add avocado oil. Add carrots, celery, and onion, and sauté until translucent or shiny. Add beef, and brown. Add tomato paste and mix with the meat and vegetables. Add red wine and mix with a wooden spoon for about 1 minute. Add water.

2. Add butternut squash, pumpkin, acorn squash, bay leaves, salt, pepper, garlic powder, cumin, oregano, and nutmeg, and mix well. When liquid comes to a simmer, reduce heat to low and cook for 4 hours 30 minutes. You want to see bubbles barely breaking the surface so you know everything is cooking low and slow.

3. After about 4 hours 30 minutes, beef should be almost falling apart and vegetables should be fork tender. Remove from heat and serve. *Toma!*

EXCHANGES/CHOICES
1 1/2 starch, 5 lean protein

CALORIES 360 | **CALORIES FROM FAT** 90 | **TOTAL FAT** 10g | **SATURATED FAT** 3g | **TRANS FAT** 0g
CHOLESTEROL 105mg | **SODIUM** 390mg | **POTASSIUM** 1230mg | **TOTAL CARBOHYDRATE** 22g
DIETARY FIBER 4g | **SUGARS** 6g | **PROTEIN** 40g | **PHOSPHORUS** 440mg

GUISO OTOÑAL DE CARNE DE RES

Este plato es ideal para prepararlo con anticipación para la noche o el resto de la semana. El guiso recalentado sabe muy bien, y creo que cada vez que se vuelve a calentar, sabe mejor. Cuando lo recaliente, no lo haga a fuego alto. Sugiero que use fuego medio; se calienta lentamente para que la carne y los vegetales no se pongan demasiado blandos.

TIEMPO DE PREPARACIÓN: 20 minutos
TIEMPO DE COCCIÓN: 4 horas y 45 minutos
RINDE: 8 porciones
TAMAÑO DE LA PORCIÓN: 1 1/4 tazas

2 cdtas. de aceite de aguacate

3 zanahorias, lavadas y cortadas en cubos de 1/2 pulgada

1 tallo de apio, lavado y cortado en cubos de 1/2 pulgada

1 cebolla amarilla, pelada y cortada en cubos de 1/2 pulgada

2 libras de asado redondo o peceto de res (*eye of the round*), cortado en cubos de 3/4 de pulgada

1 cda. de pasta de tomate

1 taza de vino tinto

6 1/2 tazas de agua

4 tazas de calabaza (tipo *butternut*), pelada, sin semillas y cortada en cubos de 1 pulgada

2 tazas de calabaza, pelada, sin semillas y cortada en cubos de 1 pulgada

2 tazas de calabaza (tipo *acorn*), pelada, sin semillas y cortada en cubos de 1 pulgada

3 hojas de laurel

4 cdtas. de sal *kosher*

1 cdta. de pimienta negra gruesa

2 cdtas. de ajo en polvo

1 cdta. de comino

2 cdtas. de orégano seco

1/4 cdta. de nuez moscada molida

1. Calentar una olla grande con tapa en la estufa y echar el aceite de aguacate. Agregar las zanahorias, apio y cebolla, y sofreír hasta que estén traslúcidos o relucientes. Agregar la carne y dorar. Agregar la pasta de tomate y mezclar con la carne y los vegetales. Agregar el vino tinto y mezclar con un cucharón de madera aproximadamente 1 minuto. Agregar el agua.

2. Añadir los diferentes tipos de calabaza, hojas de laurel, sal, pimienta, ajo en polvo, comino, orégano y nuez moscada, y mezclar bien. Cuando el líquido empiece a hervir, bajar a fuego lento y cocer 4 horas y media. Lo ideal es ver apenas un poco de borboteo en la superficie para saber que todo se está cocinando lentamente.

3. Después de 4 horas y media, la carne de res, prácticamente, se debe desmenuzar sola, y los vegetales deben estar blandos cuando se pinchen con un tenedor. Retirar del fuego y servir. ¡Toma!

SELECCIONES/INTERCAMBIOS
1 1/2 almidones, 5 proteínas magras

CALORÍAS 360 | **CALORÍAS DE GRASA** 90 | **TOTAL DE GRASA** 10g | **GRASA SATURADA** 3g | **GRASA TRANS** 0g
COLESTEROL 105mg | **SODIO** 390mg | **POTASIO** 1230mg | **TOTAL DE CARBOHIDRATOS** 22g
FIBRA ALIMENTARIA 4g | **AZÚCARES** 6g | **PROTEÍNA** 40g | **FÓSFORO** 440mg

Slow-Cooker Red Beans and Pork Chop Stew

PREP TIME: 25 minutes
COOKING TIME: 6 hours 40 minutes
SERVES: 8
SERVING SIZE: 1 pork chop and
    1/2 cup red beans

---

3 cups dried red kidney beans, sorted
   and rinsed
8 cups water
2 dried bay leaves
1 teaspoon ground cumin
2 teaspoons dried oregano
1/2 cup finely chopped red peppers
1/2 cup finely chopped green peppers
1 cup finely chopped yellow onion
1 cup finely chopped cilantro
2 teaspoons cracked black pepper
1/2 teaspoon kosher salt
1 tablespoon finely chopped fresh garlic
1 teaspoon garlic powder
8 (4-ounce) center-cut pork chops

1. Add beans and water to slow cooker and set on high for 5 hours. (You will know the red beans are done when you place one of them between your fingers and gently press it together. There should be a little give, which indicates that beans are ready.)

2. In a mixing bowl, add bay leaves, cumin, oregano, red peppers, green peppers, onion, cilantro, pepper, salt, garlic, and garlic powder, and mix ingredients with a spoon. Place bowl in refrigerator to let flavors marry.

3. Using a nonstick pan, sear pork chops on both sides, creating a nice brown color. Once browned, place pork chops in the slow cooker along with the ingredients from the refrigerator. Mix well and set the slow cooker on low. Bring to a gentle simmer, cover with lid slightly ajar (trust me, guys, it's okay), then cook for about 1 hour 30 minutes.

4. After 1 hour 30 minutes, check that the meat and vegetables are tender, stir, and cook for an additional 5 minutes. Serve and enjoy. *Toma!*

EXCHANGES/CHOICES
2 starch, 5 lean protein

CALORIES 370 | **CALORIES FROM FAT** 25 | **TOTAL FAT** 3g | **SATURATED FAT** 1g | **TRANS FAT** 0g | **CHOLESTEROL** 55mg | **SODIUM** 400mg | **POTASSIUM** 1680mg | **TOTAL CARBOHYDRATE** 45g | **DIETARY FIBER** 18g | **SUGARS** 2g | **PROTEIN** 42g | **PHOSPHORUS** 630mg

Guiso de frijoles colorados y chuleta de cerdo

TIEMPO DE PREPARACIÓN: 25 minutos
TIEMPO DE COCCIÓN: 6 horas y 40 minutos
RINDE: 8 porciones
TAMAÑO DE LA PORCIÓN: 1 chuleta de cerdo
  y 1/2 taza de frijoles colorados

---

3 tazas de frijoles colorados secos,
  limpios y enjuagados

8 tazas de agua

2 hojas de laurel

1 cdta. de comino

2 cdtas. de orégano seco

1/2 taza de pimiento rojo, finamente
  picado

1/2 taza de pimiento verde, finamente
  picado

1 taza de cebolla amarilla, finamente
  picada

1 taza de cilantro, finamente picado

2 cdtas. de pimienta negra gruesa

1/2 cdta. de sal *kosher*

1 cda. de ajo fresco, finamente picado

1 cdta. de ajo en polvo

8 chuletas de cerdo de corte del centro
  (de 4 onzas)

1. Poner el agua y los frijoles en la olla de cocción lenta y cocer a temperatura alta 5 horas. (Se sabe que los frijoles colorados están listos tras apretar uno de ellos con los dedos suavemente. Debe ceder un poco, lo que indica que los frijoles están listos).

2. En una vasija, poner las hojas de laurel, comino, orégano, pimientos rojos, pimientos verdes, cebolla, cilantro, pimienta, sal, ajo y ajo en polvo, y mezclar los ingredientes con un cucharón. Colocar la vasija en el refrigerador para que los sabores se impregnen.

3. Usando una sartén antiadherente, dorar las chuletas de cerdo por ambos lados, hasta que tengan un agradable color marrón. Colocar las chuletas doradas en una olla de cocción lenta con los ingredientes en el refrigerador. Mezclar bien y bajar la temperatura. Hacer hervir a fuego lento, con la tapa entreabierta (confíen en mí, amigos, no pasará nada), y cocer 1 hora y media.

4. Unos 90 minutos más tarde, comprobar que la carne y los vegetales estén blandos, revolver y cocer 5 minutos adicionales. Servir y disfrutar ¡Toma!

SELECCIONES/INTERCAMBIOS
2 almidones, 5 proteínas magras

CALORÍAS 370 | **CALORÍAS DE GRASA** 25 | **TOTAL DE GRASA** 3g | **GRASA SATURADA** 1g | **GRASA TRANS** 0g
COLESTEROL 55mg | **SODIO** 400mg | **POTASIO** 1680mg | **TOTAL DE CARBOHIDRATOS** 45g
FIBRA ALIMENTARIA 18g | **AZÚCARES** 2g | **PROTEÍNA** 42g | **FÓSFORO** 630mg

BARLEY AND BEEF STEW

PREP TIME: 20 minutes
COOKING TIME: 3 hours 30 minutes
SERVES: 8
SERVING SIZE: 1 cup

2 teaspoons avocado oil

2 1/2 pounds beef bottom round steak, cut into 1-inch cubes

1 pound Roma tomatoes, quartered

1/2 cup finely chopped Spanish onion

1 teaspoon ground cumin

1 tablespoon dried oregano

1 teaspoon Chinese five-spice powder

1/2 teaspoon onion powder

1 teaspoon kosher salt

3 dried bay leaves

48 ounces unsalted chicken stock

12 ounces uncooked barley

1. Preheat Dutch oven or similar pot over medium heat and add avocado oil. Brown beef on all sides, remove from Dutch oven, and set aside.

2. Place tomatoes and onions in the Dutch oven and stir until they are cooked through. Turn off the heat.

3. In a small bowl, combine cumin, oregano, five-spice powder, onion powder, and salt, and stir.

4. Turn the stove back on to the same temperature and add beef and spice mixture to the Dutch oven. Mix well. Add chicken stock and stir; place bay leaves inside the pot.

5. Reduce heat to low, place lid on the Dutch oven, and cook for 2 hours.

6. After 2 hours, add barley and stir. Cover again and cook for 1 additional hour, or until barley is tender. (There should be a little give when barley is pressed between the fingers.) Remove bay leaves and serve immediately.

RONALDO'S TIP

Serve this stew with
a squeeze of lime and
some cilantro if you
are feeling bold.

EXCHANGES/CHOICES
2 starch, 5 lean protein

CALORIES 390 | **CALORIES FROM FAT** 70 | **TOTAL FAT** 8g | **SATURATED FAT** 2.5g | **TRANS FAT** 0g
CHOLESTEROL 85mg | **SODIUM** 380mg | **POTASSIUM** 950mg | **TOTAL CARBOHYDRATE** 40g
DIETARY FIBER 8g | **SUGARS** 3g | **PROTEIN** 40g | **PHOSPHORUS** 475mg

GUISO DE CARNE Y CEBADA

TIEMPO DE PREPARACIÓN: 20 minutos
TIEMPO DE COCCIÓN: 3 horas y media
RINDE: 8 porciones
TAMAÑO DE LA PORCIÓN: 1 taza

2 cdtas. de aceite de aguacate

2 1/2 libras de punta de anca *(bottom round steak)*, cortada en cubos de 1 pulgada

1 libra de tomates Roma, en cuartos

1/2 taza de cebolla española, finamente picada

1 cdta. de comino

1 cda. de orégano

1 cdta. de 5 especias chinas, en polvo

1/2 cdta. de cebolla en polvo

1 cdta. de sal *kosher*

3 hojas de laurel

48 onzas de caldo de pollo sin sal

12 onzas de cebada cruda

1. Calentar una olla grande con tapa a fuego medio y echar el aceite de aguacate. Dorar toda la superficie de la carne, retirar de la olla y poner de lado.

2. Colocar los tomates y cebollas en la olla, y revolver hasta que se cuezan. Apagar el fuego.

3. En una vasija pequeña, mezclar el comino, orégano, especias chinas, cebolla en polvo y sal, y revolver.

4. Volver a prender la estufa a la misma temperatura y agregar a la olla la carne y la mezcla de especias. Mezclar bien. Agregar el caldo de pollo y revolver. Agregar las hojas de laurel a la olla.

5. Poner a fuego lento, tapar la olla y cocer 2 horas.

6. Después de 2 horas, agregar la cebada y revolver. Volver a tapar y cocer 1 hora adicional o hasta que la cebada esté blanda. (La cebada debe ceder un poco cuando se apriete). Retirar las hojas de laurel y servir inmediatamente.

CONSEJO DE RONALDO

Si se sienten audaces, sirvan este guiso con un chorrito de limón y un poco de cilantro.

SELECCIONES/INTERCAMBIOS
2 almidones, 5 proteínas magras

CALORÍAS 390 | **CALORÍAS DE GRASA** 70 | **TOTAL DE GRASA** 8g | **GRASA SATURADA** 2.5g | **GRASA TRANS** 0g
COLESTEROL 85mg | **SODIO** 380mg | **POTASIO** 950mg | **TOTAL DE CARBOHIDRATOS** 40g
FIBRA ALIMENTARIA 8g | **AZÚCARES** 3g | **PROTEÍNA** 40g | **FÓSFORO** 475mg

SIDE DISHES & CONDIMENTS
ACOMPAÑANTES Y SALSAS

This chapter covers an essential part of any great dinner: the sides. I always have trouble finding the right healthy side to pair with a main dish. In my experience, many American side dishes seem unhealthy. So this chapter is dedicated to making some incredible sides that are healthy and easy to make and that the whole family will love.

———————

Este capítulo trata sobre un aspecto esencial de cualquier gran cena: los acompañantes o guarniciones. Siempre tengo dificultad para encontrar el acompañamiento adecuado y saludable de los platos principales. He notado que en Estados Unidos muchas guarniciones parecen ser poco saludables. Así que este capítulo se dedica a fabulosas guarniciones que son saludables y fáciles de preparar. Le encantarán a toda la familia.

—Chef Ronaldo

Cilantro Mango Brown Rice

PREP TIME: 10 minutes
COOKING TIME: 20 minutes
SERVES: 10
SERVING SIZE: 1/2 cup

1 1/2 cups uncooked brown rice
2 1/2 cups water
1 teaspoon kosher salt
4 ounces mango, peeled and diced
2 teaspoons avocado oil
2 tablespoons minced cilantro

1. Add rice, water, salt, mango, and oil to a rice cooker. Mix with a spoon, and follow rice-cooker instructions. (This is the easiest way to make this dish.) If you don't have a rice cooker, add rice, water, salt, mango, and oil to a small pot. Mix with a spoon and bring to a boil. Then reduce heat to low, cover pot tightly with foil or with a tight-fitting lid, and cook for about 15–20 minutes, or until rice is fluffy and tender.

2. Once rice is done, fold in the cilantro and serve.

EXCHANGES/CHOICES
2 starch

CALORIES 150 | CALORIES FROM FAT 20 | TOTAL FAT 2g | SATURATED FAT 0g | TRANS FAT 0g
CHOLESTEROL 0mg | SODIUM 200mg | POTASSIUM 120mg | TOTAL CARBOHYDRATE 30g
DIETARY FIBER 1g | SUGARS 2g | PROTEIN 3g | PHOSPHORUS 100mg

ARROZ INTEGRAL CON CILANTRO Y MANGO

TIEMPO DE PREPARACIÓN: 10 minutos
TIEMPO DE COCCIÓN: 20 minutos
RINDE: 10 porciones
TAMAÑO DE LA PORCIÓN: 1/2 taza

1 1/2 tazas de arroz integral sin cocer

2 1/2 tazas de agua

1 cdta. de sal *kosher*

4 onzas de mango pelado y picado en cuadrados

2 cdtas. de aceite de aguacate

2 cdas. de cilantro finamente picado

1. Poner el arroz, agua, sal, mango y aceite en una arrocera. Revolver con un cucharón y seguir las instrucciones de la arrocera. (Esta es la manera más fácil de hacer este plato). Si no tiene arrocera, poner el arroz, agua, sal, mango y aceite en una olla pequeña. Mezclar con un cucharón y hacer hervir. Luego poner a fuego lento, tapar bien la olla con papel de aluminio o una tapa que cierre bien y cocer aproximadamente 15-20 minutos o hasta que el arroz esté graneado y blando.

2. Una vez que el arroz esté listo, mezclar con el cilantro y servir.

SELECCIONES/INTERCAMBIOS
2 almidones

CALORÍAS 150 | **CALORÍAS DE GRASA** 20 | **TOTAL DE GRASA** 2g | **GRASA SATURADA** 0g | **GRASA TRANS** 0g
COLESTEROL 0mg | **SODIO** 200mg | **POTASIO** 120mg | **TOTAL DE CARBOHIDRATOS** 30g
FIBRA ALIMENTARIA 1g | **AZÚCARES** 2g | **PROTEÍNA** 3g | **FÓSFORO** 100mg

BRAISED DUTCH-OVEN LENTILS

Who doesn't love lentils? They taste delicious on their own or as a side dish. They warm you up and fill you with great nutrition. I used to eat lentils with rice (arroz con lentejas), but that dish is high in carbohydrate. So I went ahead and tried lentils on their own, and I've loved them ever since. Did you know kids like lentils? Just ask my son, Liam!

PREP TIME: 20 minutes
COOKING TIME: 1 hour 15 minutes
SERVES: 10
SERVING SIZE: 1/2 cup

2 teaspoons canola oil
1/2 cup finely chopped yellow onions
1 stalk celery, washed and finely chopped
1 clove garlic, peeled and finely chopped
4 sprigs thyme, leaves removed
1 tablespoon tomato paste
1 teaspoon Spanish smoked paprika
1 cup washed and finely chopped plum tomatoes
1 teaspoon cracked black pepper
2 1/2 cups lentils
2 quarts water
2 teaspoons kosher salt, divided
2 dried bay leaves

1. Preheat Dutch oven or similar pot over low heat and add canola oil. Add onions, celery, garlic, thyme, tomato paste, paprika, tomatoes, and pepper, and sauté on low until vegetables are translucent. This is the base of the dish (the *sofrito*).

2. Add lentils, water, 1 teaspoon salt, and bay leaves, and mix well with a spoon. Bring to a gentle simmer and cover with lid left slightly ajar. Cook on low heat until lentils are tender, about 1 hour.

3. Once lentils are tender, add remaining salt and mix. Cook for an additional 5 minutes. Remove bay leaves. Serve and enjoy.

EXCHANGES/CHOICES
2 starch, 1 lean protein

CALORIES 180 | CALORIES FROM FAT 20 | TOTAL FAT 2g | SATURATED FAT 0g | TRANS FAT 0g
CHOLESTEROL 0mg | SODIUM 410mg | POTASSIUM 550mg | TOTAL CARBOHYDRATE 30g
DIETARY FIBER 15g | SUGARS 2g | PROTEIN 13g | PHOSPHORUS 230mg

LENTEJAS GUISADAS A FUEGO LENTO

¿A quién no le gustan las lentejas? Saben deliciosas por sí solas o como guarnición. Te calientan y te nutren mucho. Solía comer arroz con lentejas, pero es un platillo con muchos carbohidratos. Así que probé comer las lentejas solas y, desde entonces, me encantan. ¿Sabían que a los niños les gustan las lentejas? ¡Pregúntenle a mi hijo, Liam!

TIEMPO DE PREPARACIÓN: 20 minutos
TIEMPO DE COCCIÓN: 1 hora, 15 minutos
RINDE: 10 porciones
TAMAÑO DE LA PORCIÓN: 1/2 taza

2 cdtas. de aceite de canola

1/2 taza de cebolla amarilla, finamente picada

1 tallo de apio, lavado y finamente picado

1 diente de ajo, pelado y finamente picado

Hojas de 4 ramitas de tomillo fresco, descartar tallos

1 cda. de pasta de tomate

1 cdta. de pimentón español ahumado (*paprika*)

1 taza de tomates ciruelos, lavados y finamente picados

1 cdta. de pimienta negra gruesa

2 1/2 tazas de lentejas

2 cuartos de galón de agua

2 cdtas. de sal *kosher*, en partes

2 hojas de laurel

1. Calentar una olla con tapa a fuego lento y echar el aceite de canola. Agregar la cebolla, apio, ajo, tomillo, pasta de tomate, pimentón, tomates y pimienta, y sofreír hasta que los vegetales estén traslúcidos. Este es el sofrito del plato.

2. Agregar las lentejas, agua, 1 cdta. sal y hojas de laurel, y mezclar bien con un cucharón. Hervir a fuego lento y tapar a medias. Cocer a fuego lento hasta que las lentejas estén blandas, aproximadamente 1 hora.

3. Una vez que las lentejas estén blandas, echarles la sal restante y mezclar. Cocer 5 minutos adicionales. Sacar las hojas de laurel. Servir y disfrutar.

SELECCIONES/INTERCAMBIOS
2 almidones, 1 proteína magra

CALORÍAS 180 | **CALORÍAS DE GRASA** 20 | **TOTAL DE GRASA** 2g | **GRASA SATURADA** 0g | **GRASA TRANS** 0g
COLESTEROL 0mg | **SODIO** 410mg | **POTASIO** 550mg | **TOTAL DE CARBOHIDRATOS** 30g
FIBRA ALIMENTARIA 15g | **AZÚCARES** 2g | **PROTEÍNA** 13g | **FÓSFORO** 230mg

LATIN SPAGHETTI SQUASH

PREP TIME: 15 minutes
COOKING TIME: 45 minutes
SERVES: 4
SERVING SIZE: 1 cup

1 large (about 1 1/2-pound) spaghetti squash
2 large sheets foil (large enough to wrap squash half)
1/4 teaspoon kosher salt
1 teaspoon cracked black pepper
4 sprigs thyme, leaves removed
4 cloves garlic, peeled and minced
1 tablespoon reduced-fat margarine
1/2 cup thinly sliced Spanish onion
1 cup unsalted chicken stock
3 tablespoons grated queso fresco
2 tablespoons minced cilantro

1. Preheat oven to 400°F.

2. Split spaghetti squash into 2 equal parts with a large chef's knife. Scoop out the seeds with a spoon. Place squash halves on 2 separate large pieces of foil. Season each squash half with salt and pepper. On each half, place leaves from 2 sprigs thyme, 2 garlic cloves, and 1/2 tablespoon reduced-fat margarine, and wrap with foil, creating 2 pouches. Cook in oven for 35 minutes, or until squash are tender.

3. Remove squash from foil and reserve liquid to make a sauce. Use a fork to scrape the meat out of the squash, and set aside. (This is the fun part of this dish.)

4. Preheat sauté pan over medium heat and add reserved squash-cooking liquid and onions. Sauté until translucent.

5. Add chicken stock and spaghetti squash, and toss for 2 minutes. Add queso fresco and cook for an additional 5 minutes to allow flavors to develop.

6. Fold in cilantro and serve.

RONALDO'S TIP

To make cleanup easier, reserve the spaghetti squash shells and use them as plates.

EXCHANGES/CHOICES
3 vegetable, 1/2 fat

CALORIES 100 | **CALORIES FROM FAT** 25 | **TOTAL FAT** 3g | **SATURATED FAT** 1g | **TRANS FAT** 0g
CHOLESTEROL 0mg | **SODIUM** 200mg | **POTASSIUM** 290mg | **TOTAL CARBOHYDRATE** 15g
DIETARY FIBER 3g | **SUGARS** 5g | **PROTEIN** 3g | **PHOSPHORUS** 60mg

Espagueti de Calabaza a la Latina

TIEMPO DE PREPARACIÓN: 15 minutos
TIEMPO DE COCCIÓN: 45 minutos
RINDE: 4 porciones
TAMAÑO DE LA PORCIÓN: 1 taza

---

1 calabaza grande tipo espagueti (aproximadamente 1 libra y media)

2 láminas grandes de papel de aluminio (lo suficientemente grandes para envolver media calabaza)

1/4 cdta. de sal *kosher*

1 cdta. de pimienta negra gruesa

Hojas de 4 ramitas de tomillo, sin tallos

4 dientes de ajo, pelados y picados

1 cda. de margarina con poca grasa

1/2 taza de cebolla española en rodajas delgadas

1 taza de caldo de pollo sin sal

3 cdas. de queso fresco, rallado

2 cdas. de cilantro finamente picado

1. Calentar el horno a 400°F.

2. Cortar la calabaza tipo espagueti en 2 partes iguales con un cuchillo grande. Quitar las semillas con una cuchara. Colocar cada mitad de la calabaza en una lámina de papel de aluminio y envolver la calabaza formando un tazón. Sazonar cada media calabaza con sal y pimienta. En cada mitad, colocar las hojas de 2 ramitas de tomillo, 2 dientes de ajo y 1/2 cda. de margarina con poca grasa. Hornear 35 minutos o hasta que la calabaza esté blanda.

3. Sacar la calabaza del papel de aluminio y guardar el líquido para hacer una salsa. Usar un tenedor para raspar y sacar la pulpa de la calabaza, y poner de lado. (Esta es la gracia de este plato).

4. Calentar la sartén a fuego medio y echar la cebolla y el líquido de la calabaza que se guardó. Sofreír hasta que esté traslúcida.

5. Agregar el caldo de pollo y la calabaza, y revolver 2 minutos. Agregar el queso fresco y cocer 5 minutos adicionales para permitir que los sabores afloren.

6. Incorporar el cilantro y servir.

CONSEJO DE RONALDO

Para que sea más fácil limpiar después, se puede guardar la cáscara de la calabaza y usarla como platos.

SELECCIONES/INTERCAMBIOS
3 vegetales, 1/2 grasa

CALORÍAS 100 | **CALORÍAS DE GRASA** 25 | **TOTAL DE GRASA** 3g | **GRASA SATURADA** 1g | **GRASA TRANS** 0g
COLESTEROL 0mg | **SODIO** 200mg | **POTASIO** 290mg | **TOTAL DE CARBOHIDRATOS** 15g
FIBRA ALIMENTARIA 3g | **AZÚCARES** 5g | **PROTEÍNA** 3g | **FÓSFORO** 60mg

Roasted Plantains and Poblano Pepper with Guava Sauce

PREP TIME: 10 minutes
COOKING TIME: 45 minutes
SERVES: 8
SERVING SIZE: 1 piece plantain and 1
  tablespoon sauce

2 ripe plantains
2 large sheets foil (large enough to
  wrap plantain)
1 poblano pepper, cut into
  1/4-inch cubes
1 teaspoon avocado oil
3/4 cup unsalted chicken stock
1/4 cup finely chopped shallots
1 clove garlic, peeled and finely chopped
1/4 cup guava cubes (1/4-inch cubes)
1/4 cup rice vinegar
1/2 teaspoon kosher salt
1 teaspoon cracked black pepper
1/2 cup crumbled queso fresco
2 tablespoons finely chopped cilantro

1. Preheat oven to 400°F.

2. Cut the tips off the plantains. Insert the tip of a paring knife about 1/2 inch into each plantain and run it from top to bottom. Wrap each plantain in a foil sheet. Roast in oven for 30 minutes, then remove from oven and set aside. Leave oven on.

3. Wash and dry poblano pepper. Rub avocado oil on the outside of pepper and (carefully) place over a flame or in oven until the outside is charred. Once pepper is charred, place in a bowl and cover until steam loosens the skin. Run pepper under cold water to remove the char, then dice pepper.

4. In small saucepan add stock, shallots, garlic, poblano pepper, guava, and bring up to a rolling simmer. Cook until a smooth paste forms, about 5 minutes. Add rice vinegar, salt, and pepper, and whisk well to make sure you don't have any lumps in the sauce. Reduce heat to low and continue cooking for 2 minutes. Pour sauce in blender and purée until sauce is smooth.

5. Remove foil from plantains and cut each into 4 equal quarters. Carefully split open the plantain along the cut. Add 1 tablespoon guava sauce, top with queso fresco, and garnish with cilantro. Enjoy!

EXCHANGES/CHOICES
1 starch

CALORIES 80 | **CALORIES FROM FAT** 10 | **TOTAL FAT** 1g | **SATURATED FAT** 0g | **TRANS FAT** 0g
CHOLESTEROL 0mg | **SODIUM** 135mg | **POTASSIUM** 300mg | **TOTAL CARBOHYDRATE** 17g
DIETARY FIBER 2g | **SUGARS** 8g | **PROTEIN** 2g | **PHOSPHORUS** 35mg

PLÁTANOS Y CHILES POBLANOS ASADOS CON SALSA DE GUAYABA

TIEMPO DE PREPARACIÓN: 10 minutos
TIEMPO DE COCCIÓN: 45 minutos
RINDE: 8 porciones
TAMAÑO DE LA PORCIÓN: 1 trozo de plátano y 1 cda. de salsa

---

2 plátanos maduros

2 láminas grandes de papel de aluminio (lo suficientemente grandes para envolver un plátano)

1 chile poblano, cortado en cubos de 1/4 de pulgada

1 cdta. de aceite de aguacate

3/4 taza de caldo de pollo sin sal

1/4 taza de cebolla escalonia (*shallots*), finamente picada

1 diente de ajo, pelado y finamente picado

1/4 taza de guayaba en cubos (de 1/4 de pulgada)

1/4 de taza de vinagre de arroz

1/2 cdta. de sal *kosher*

1 cdta. de pimienta negra gruesa

1/2 taza de queso fresco desmenuzado

2 cdas. de cilantro finamente picado

1. Calentar el horno a 400°F.

2. Cortar las puntas de los plátanos. Meter la punta de un cuchillo de pelar hasta aproximadamente 1/2 pulgada de profundidad en cada plátano y cortar de arriba a abajo. Envolver cada plátano con papel de aluminio. Asar en el horno 30 minutos y luego retirar y poner de lado. Dejar el horno prendido.

3. Lavar y secar el chile poblano seco. Frotar aceite de aguacate en la parte exterior del chile y colocar (con cuidado) sobre una llama o en el horno hasta que el exterior se carbonice. Una vez que el chile esté chamuscado, colocar en una vasija y cubrir hasta que el vapor afloje la piel. Enjuagar el chile con agua fría para eliminar las partes chamuscadas, luego cortar el chile en cubos.

4. En una olla pequeña echar el caldo, cebolla escalonia, ajo, chile poblano, guayaba y hacer hervir a fuego lento. Cocer hasta que se forme una pasta suave, unos 5 minutos. Agregar el vinagre de arroz, sal y pimienta, y mezclar bien para asegurarse de que no haya grumos en la salsa. Poner a fuego lento y seguir cociendo 2 minutos. Licuar la salsa hasta que tenga consistencia uniforme.

5. Retirar el papel de aluminio de los plátanos y cortar cada uno en 4 partes iguales. Abrir el plátano a lo largo del corte, con cuidado. Agregar 1 cda. de la salsa de guayaba, poner encima el queso fresco y decorar con cilantro. ¡A disfrutar!

SELECCIONES/INTERCAMBIOS
1 almidón

CALORÍAS 80 | **CALORÍAS DE GRASA** 10 | **TOTAL DE GRASA** 1g | **GRASA SATURADA** 0g | **GRASA TRANS** 0g | **COLESTEROL** 0mg | **SODIO** 135mg | **POTASIO** 300mg | **TOTAL DE CARBOHIDRATOS** 17g | **FIBRA ALIMENTARIA** 2g | **AZÚCARES** 8g | **PROTEÍNA** 2g | **FÓSFORO** 35mg

Rum-Infused Yucca *con Mojo*

PREP TIME: 15 minutes
COOKING TIME: 40 minutes
SERVES: 4
SERVING SIZE: 3 ounces

9 ounces yucca, peeled

1/2 teaspoon kosher salt, divided

2 teaspoons avocado oil

1 cup sliced Spanish onion

1/2 jalapeño, washed and finely chopped

1 clove garlic, peeled and finely chopped

1 teaspoon cracked black pepper

1 ounce white rum

1 tablespoon white vinegar

1. Fill saucepan 3/4 of the way full with water. Add peeled yucca and 1/4 teaspoon salt, and simmer for 20 minutes, or until the yucca can be easily pierced with a fork. Turn off heat, carefully remove yucca from water, reserving water. Extract the tough root in the middle of the yucca with a knife and discard. Set yucca aside.

2. Preheat sauté pan over medium heat and add avocado oil. Reduce heat to low, add onions, jalapeño, and garlic, and sauté until onions are translucent. Add remaining salt and pepper.

3. Add white rum to deglaze the pan. (Warning: Rum is flammable, so be careful.) Wait until flames die out, then add 2 cups reserved yucca water and white vinegar. Simmer for 10 minutes over low heat. Add the yucca and let it warm up in the sauce for about 2 minutes. Serve.

RONALDO'S TIP

To peel yucca, cut into 3 pieces and place flat side down on a cutting surface. Run knife down the root to reveal the white flesh and remove the peel. This is a little tough, but be patient.

EXCHANGES/CHOICES
2 starch

CALORIES 160 | **CALORIES FROM FAT** 25 | **TOTAL FAT** 3g | **SATURATED FAT** 0g | **TRANS FAT** 0g | **CHOLESTEROL** 0mg | **SODIUM** 250mg | **POTASSIUM** 250mg | **TOTAL CARBOHYDRATE** 29g | **DIETARY FIBER** 2g | **SUGARS** 3g | **PROTEIN** 1g | **PHOSPHORUS** 30mg

YUCA INFUNDIDA CON RON Y MOJO

TIEMPO DE PREPARACIÓN: 15 minutos
TIEMPO DE COCCIÓN: 40 minutos
RINDE: 4 porciones
TAMAÑO DE LA PORCIÓN: 3 onzas

9 onzas de yuca, pelada

1/2 cdta. de sal *kosher*, en partes

2 cdtas. de aceite de aguacate

1 taza de cebolla española en rodajas

1/2 jalapeño, lavado y finamente picado

1 diente de ajo, pelado y finamente picado

1 cdta. de pimienta negra gruesa

1 onza de ron blanco

1 cda. de vinagre blanco

1. Llenar 3/4 de una olla con agua. Agregar la yuca pelada y 1/4 cdta. de sal, y cocer a fuego lento 20 minutos o hasta que la yuca se pueda pinchar fácilmente con un tenedor. Apagar el fuego, retirar la yuca del agua con cuidado y guardar el agua. Cortar la raíz dura del centro de la yuca con un cuchillo y desechar. Poner la yuca de lado.

2. Calentar la sartén a fuego medio y echar el aceite de aguacate. Bajar el fuego, agregar la cebolla, jalapeño y ajo, y sofreír hasta que la cebolla esté traslúcida. Echar el resto de la sal y pimienta.

3. Agregar el ron blanco para desglasar la sartén. (ADVERTENCIA: El ron es inflamable, así que tengan cuidado.) Esperar hasta que la llama se extinga y luego añadir 2 tazas del agua en que se hirvió la yuca y el vinagre blanco. Hervir a fuego lento 10 minutos. Agregar la yuca y dejar que se caliente en la salsa 2 minutos. Servir.

CONSEJO DE RONALDO

Para pelar la yuca, cortar en 3 trozos y colocar el lado plano hacia abajo sobre una superficie para cortar. Pasar el cuchillo a lo largo de la raíz para que se vea la pulpa blanca y pelar. Es un poco difícil, pero hay que ser paciente.

SELECCIONES/INTERCAMBIOS
2 almidones

CALORÍAS 160 | **CALORÍAS DE GRASA** 25 | **TOTAL DE GRASA** 3g | **GRASA SATURADA** 0g | **GRASA TRANS** 0g
COLESTEROL 0mg | **SODIO** 250mg | **POTASIO** 250mg | **TOTAL DE CARBOHIDRATOS** 29g
FIBRA ALIMENTARIA 2g | **AZÚCARES** 3g | **PROTEÍNA** 1g | **FÓSFORO** 30mg

CHIPOTLE SAUCE

I love this chipotle sauce! I know it's not a typical side dish, but it can be a great accompaniment to any meal. This sauce is universal; it can be used as a marinade for your proteins, as a dip for chips, or as a topping for lunch or dinner. It is a great way to add flavor without adding more salt. The sauce can be stored for 7 days in the refrigerator, but you can also freeze it for up to 3 months.

PREP TIME: 10 minutes
COOKING TIME: 1 hour 10 minutes
SERVES: 60
SERVING SIZE: 2 tablespoons

10 dehydrated chipotle pods, stems removed
1 quart water (to rehydrate chipotle pods)
3 tablespoons lime juice
1 tablespoon canola oil
1 cup diced Spanish onion
1 roasted red pepper, diced
1 cup diced green pepper
3 cloves garlic, peeled and minced
1 tablespoon Spanish smoked paprika
1 teaspoon curry powder
1 teaspoon ground cumin
2 dried bay leaves
1 teaspoon kosher salt
1 teaspoon cracked black pepper
1 quart unsalted vegetable stock

1. In a large stock pot, add chipotle pods, water, and lime juice. Cover and bring to a simmer. Cook until chipotles are tender, about 30 minutes.

2. Meanwhile, add canola oil, onion, roasted red pepper, green pepper, and garlic to a large sauté pan, and sauté over low heat for 10 minutes, or until tender. (Sautéing over low heat allows the flavors to develop.) Season with smoked paprika, curry, cumin, bay leaves, salt, and pepper.

3. Check your chipotles; they should be tender enough to purée. Drain chipotles. Working in 3 batches, add 1/3 of the chipotles and 1/3 of the vegetable stock to a blender and purée until smooth. Repeat until all of the chipotles and stock have been puréed.

4. Add chipotle sauce to the pan with the vegetables and stir to combine. Once all the ingredients are mixed, simmer for 20 minutes over low heat.

5. Purée the mixture once more to create a smooth consistency. Pour sauce into a large container and cool in an ice bath. Then store or serve. Enjoy this delicious sauce!

EXCHANGES/CHOICES
free food

CALORIES 10 | **CALORIES FROM FAT** 0 | **TOTAL FAT** 0g | **SATURATED FAT** 0g | **TRANS FAT** 0g
CHOLESTEROL 0mg | **SODIUM** 70mg | **POTASSIUM** 25mg | **TOTAL CARBOHYDRATE** 1g
DIETARY FIBER 0g | **SUGARS** 1g | **PROTEIN** 0g | **PHOSPHORUS** 0mg

SALSA DE CHIPOTLE

¡Me encanta esta salsa de chipotle! Sé que no es una guarnición típica, pero va muy bien con cualquier comida. Esta salsa es universal; puede utilizarse como adobo para sus proteínas, como salsa o pico de gallo para chips o totopos, o para echarle encima al almuerzo o la cena. Es una gran manera de añadir sabor sin agregar sal. La salsa se puede guardar 7 días en el refrigerador, pero también se puede congelar hasta 3 meses.

TIEMPO DE PREPARACIÓN: 10 minutos
TIEMPO DE COCCIÓN: 1 hora y 10 minutos
RINDE: 60 porciones
TAMAÑO DE LA PORCIÓN: 2 cdas.

---

10 vainas de chipotle deshidratados, sin tallos

1 cuarto de galón de agua (para rehidratar las vainas de chipotle)

3 cdas. de jugo de lima o limón verde

1 cda. de aceite de canola

1 taza de cebolla española picada

1 pimiento rojo asado, cortado en cubos

1 taza de pimiento verde, cortado en cubos

3 dientes de ajo, pelados y picados

1 cda. de pimentón español ahumado (*paprika*)

1 cdta. de polvo de curry

1 cdta. de comino

2 hojas de laurel

1 cdta. de sal *kosher*

1 cdta. de pimienta negra gruesa

1 cuarto de galón de caldo vegetal sin sal

1. En una olla grande de sopa, echar las vainas de chipotle y jugo de limón verde. Tapar y hacer hervir a fuego lento. Cocer hasta que los chipotles se pongan blandos, unos 30 minutos.

2. Mientras tanto, echar el aceite de canola, cebolla, pimiento rojo, pimiento verde y ajo a una sartén grande, y saltear a fuego bajo 10 minutos o hasta que estén blandos. (Saltear a fuego lento permite que afloren los sabores). Sazonar con pimentón, curry, comino, hojas de laurel, sal y pimienta.

3. Probar los chipotles; deben estar suficientemente blandos como para licuarlos. Escurrir los chipotles. En tres tandas, echar 1/3 de los chipotles y 1/3 del caldo de verduras a una licuadora y licuar hasta que tenga consistencia uniforme. Repetir hasta licuar todos los chipotles y el caldo.

4. Echar la salsa de chipotle a la sartén con los vegetales y mezclar. Una vez que se mezclan todos los ingredientes, cocer a fuego lento 20 minutos.

5. Licuar la mezcla una vez más para que tenga consistencia cremosa. Echar la salsa en un recipiente grande y dejar enfriar sobre hielo. Luego guardar o servir. ¡Disfruten esta deliciosa salsa!

SELECCIONES/INTERCAMBIOS
No cuenta

CALORÍAS 10 | **CALORÍAS DE GRASA** 0 | **TOTAL DE GRASA** 0g | **GRASA SATURADA** 0g | **GRASA TRANS** 0g
COLESTEROL 0mg | **SODIO** 70mg | **POTASIO** 25mg | **TOTAL DE CARBOHIDRATOS** 1g
FIBRA ALIMENTARIA 0g | **AZÚCARES** 1g | **PROTEÍNA** 0g | **FÓSFORO** 0mg

Red and Yellow Cherry Tomato Salsa

PREP TIME: 15 minutes
REFRIGERATION TIME: 40 minutes
SERVES: 8
SERVING SIZE: 1/4 cup

---

1 poblano pepper
1 teaspoon avocado oil
1 cup washed and chopped red cherry
   tomatoes
1 cup washed and chopped yellow cherry
   tomatoes
1/2 cup cubed yellow onion
   (1/4-inch cubes)
1 ounce lime juice
1/2 cup finely chopped cilantro
1 teaspoon kosher salt
1 teaspoon cracked black pepper
1/4 teaspoon ground cumin
1 cup unsalted chicken stock

1. Rub poblano pepper with avocado oil and place directly over a flame to roast. Rotate poblano pepper once the side in contact with fire has charred, making sure to char all sides. Once all sides are charred, removed from flame and cover with a bowl for about 3 minutes, creating a steam lock to loosen the pepper skin. Remove bowl and run pepper under water, using a paper towel to gently remove the char from pepper.

2. In a mixing bowl combine poblano pepper and all remaining ingredients. Mix well with your hands (it adds love to the dish).

3. Place mixture in food processor or blender and pulsate a few times until a chunky salsa forms.

4. Refrigerate for 30 minutes before serving so flavors have time to marry.

EXCHANGES/CHOICES
1 vegetable

CALORIES 25 | **CALORIES FROM FAT** 10 | **TOTAL FAT** 1g | **SATURATED FAT** 0g | **TRANS FAT** 0g
CHOLESTEROL 0mg | **SODIUM** 250mg | **POTASSIUM** 170mg | **TOTAL CARBOHYDRATE** 4g
DIETARY FIBER 1g | **SUGARS** 2g | **PROTEIN** 1g | **PHOSPHORUS** 25mg

SALSA DE TOMATES CEREZOS ROJOS Y AMARILLOS

TIEMPO DE PREPARACIÓN: 15 minutos
TIEMPO DE IGERACIGERACIÓN: 40 minutos
RINDE: 8 porciones
TAMAÑO DE LA PORCIÓN: 1/4 taza

1 chile poblano

1 cdta. de aceite de aguacate

1 taza de tomates cerezos rojos, lavados y picados

1 taza de tomates cerezos amarillos, lavados y picados

1/2 taza de cebolla amarilla (en cubos de 1/4 de pulgada)

1 onza de jugo de lima o limón verde

1/2 taza de cilantro finamente picado

1 cdta. de sal *kosher*

1 cdta. de pimienta negra gruesa

1/4 cdta. de comino

1 taza de caldo de pollo sin sal

1. Echarle aceite de aguacate al chile poblano y colocarlo directamente sobre una llama para asarlo. Girar hasta que todo el chile se chamusque en contacto con el fuego. Cuando esté completamente chamuscado, sacarlo del fuego y ponerlo en una vasija con tapa unos 3 minutos, sin dejar que se escape el vapor para que la cáscara del chile se afloje. Sacar el chile de la vasija, enjuagarlo con agua fría y usar una toalla de papel para eliminar con cuidado la cáscara chamuscada.

2. Echar el chile poblano y todos los demás ingredientes en una vasija y mezclar. Mezclar bien con las manos (le da un toque de amor al plato).

3. Colocar la mezcla en el procesador de alimentos o licuadora y prender y apagar varias veces, dejando que la salsa tenga trozos sin licuar.

4. Refrigerar 30 minutos antes de servir, para dar tiempo a que se impregnen los sabores.

SELECCIONES/INTERCAMBIOS
1 vegetal

CALORÍAS 25 | **CALORÍAS DE GRASA** 10 | **TOTAL DE GRASA** 1g | **GRASA SATURADA** 0g | **GRASA TRANS** 0g
COLESTEROL 0mg | **SODIO** 250mg | **POTASIO** 170mg | **TOTAL DE CARBOHIDRATOS** 4g
FIBRA ALIMENTARIA 1g | **AZÚCARES** 2g | **PROTEÍNA** 1g | **FÓSFORO** 25mg

THYME-ROASTED SHALLOTS

This is a great recipe, guys! It's simple but delicious. Who knew an ingredient that is usually added to dishes as a "supporting character" could become a star?

PREP TIME: 10 minutes
COOKING TIME: 30 minutes
SERVES: 8
SERVING SIZE: About 4 shallots (2 ounces)

1 pound shallots, peeled
1/4 teaspoon ground thyme
1/2 teaspoon kosher salt
1/4 teaspoon cracked black pepper
2 teaspoons avocado oil

1. Preheat oven to 400°F.

2. Place shallots in a bowl, add all remaining ingredients, and toss. Make sure to toss with a little passion to make sure the seasoning spreads evenly.

3. Roast in the oven for 30 minutes.

4. Remove from oven and let shallots rest for several minutes before serving.

EXCHANGES/CHOICES
2 vegetable

CALORIES 50 | **CALORIES FROM FAT** 10 | **TOTAL FAT** 1g | **SATURATED FAT** 0g | **TRANS FAT** 0g
CHOLESTEROL 0mg | **SODIUM** 130mg | **POTASSIUM** 190mg | **TOTAL CARBOHYDRATE** 10g
DIETARY FIBER 2g | **SUGARS** 5g | **PROTEIN** 1g | **PHOSPHORUS** 35mg

CEBOLLAS ESCALONIAS ASADAS CON TOMILLO

¡Esta es una receta fabulosa, amigos! Es simple pero deliciosa. ¿Quién habría pensado que este ingrediente que por lo general se agrega a los platos como "actor de reparto", podría ser una estrella?

TIEMPO DE PREPARACIÓN: 10 minutos
TIEMPO DE COCCIÓN: 30 minutos
RINDE: 8 porciones
TAMAÑO DE LA PORCIÓN: 4 cebollas escalonias (2 onzas)

---

1 libra de cebollas escalonias (shallots), peladas
1/4 cdta. de tomillo en polvo
1/2 cdta. de sal *kosher*
1/4 cdta. de pimienta negra gruesa
2 cdtas. de aceite de aguacate

1. Calentar el horno a 400°F.

2. Colocar las cebollas escalonias en una vasija, agregar todos los demás ingredientes y mezclar con pasión para asegurarse de que las especias se distribuyan por todas partes.

3. Asar en el horno 30 minutos.

4. Retirar del horno y poner las cebollas de lado varios minutos antes de servir.

SELECCIONES/INTERCAMBIOS
2 vegetales

CALORÍAS 50 | **CALORÍAS DE GRASA** 10 | **TOTAL DE GRASA** 1g | **GRASA SATURADA** 0g | **GRASA TRANS** 0g
COLESTEROL 0mg | **SODIO** 130mg | **POTASIO** 190mg | **TOTAL DE CARBOHIDRATOS** 10g
FIBRA ALIMENTARIA 2g | **AZÚCARES** 5g | **PROTEÍNA** 1g | **FÓSFORO** 35mg

Rosemary-Roasted Brussels Sprouts

PREP TIME: 10 minutes
COOKING TIME: 30 minutes
SERVES: 4
SERVING SIZE: 1 cup

1 pound Brussels sprouts, washed, dried and cut in half
1/4 teaspoon kosher salt
1/4 teaspoon cracked black pepper
1 tablespoon finely chopped fresh rosemary
1 1/2 teaspoons avocado oil
Parchment paper

1. Preheat oven to 400°F.

2. Place all ingredients into a mixing bowl and toss together. Place Brussels sprouts on a parchment paper–lined baking sheet and roast for 30 minutes.

3. Remove from oven and serve.

RONALDO'S TIP

When tossing these ingredients, use a little hip. They mix better that way. Enjoy these Brussels sprouts with any meat, fish, or pork dish, or just enjoy them alone.

EXCHANGES/CHOICES
2 vegetable

CALORIES 70 | CALORIES FROM FAT 20 | TOTAL FAT 2g | SATURATED FAT 0g | TRANS FAT 0g
CHOLESTEROL 0mg | SODIUM 150mg | POTASSIUM 450mg | TOTAL CARBOHYDRATE 10g
DIETARY FIBER 4g | SUGARS 3g | PROTEIN 4g | PHOSPHORUS 80mg

COLES DE BRUSELAS ASADAS CON ROMERO

TIEMPO DE PREPARACIÓN: 10 minutos
TIEMPO DE COCCIÓN: 30 minutos
RINDE: 4 porciones
TAMAÑO DE LA PORCIÓN: 1 taza

1 libra de coles de Bruselas, lavadas,
secadas y cortadas por la mitad
1/4 cdta. de sal *kosher*
1/4 cdta. de pimienta negra gruesa
1 cda. de romero fresco, finamente
picado
1 1/2 cdtas. de aceite de aguacate
Papel mantequilla

1. Calentar el horno a 400°F.

2. Colocar todos los ingredientes en una vasija y mezclar bien. Colocar las coles de Bruselas en una lata con papel mantequilla y asar 30 minutos.

3. Retirar del horno y servir.

CONSEJO DE RONALDO

Al echar los ingredientes, hay que usar un poco la cadera. Así se mezclan mejor. Disfruten las coles de Bruselas con cualquier plato de carne, pescado o cerdo, o simplemente solas.

SELECCIONES/INTERCAMBIOS
2 vegetales

CALORÍAS 70 | CALORÍAS DE GRASA 20 | TOTAL DE GRASA 2g | GRASA SATURADA 0g | GRASA TRANS 0g
COLESTEROL 0mg | SODIO 150mg | POTASIO 450mg | TOTAL DE CARBOHIDRATOS 10g
FIBRA ALIMENTARIA 4g | AZÚCARES 3g | PROTEÍNA 4g | FÓSFORO 80mg

CUBANO ROASTED BROCCOLI FLORETS

PREP TIME: 10 minutes
COOKING TIME: 25 minutes
SERVES: 4
SERVING SIZE: 1 cup

3 cloves garlic, peeled and thinly sliced
1/4 teaspoon ground cumin
1 teaspoon lime juice
1/8 teaspoon cracked black pepper
1/2 cup thinly sliced Spanish onion
2 teaspoons avocado oil
16 ounces broccoli florets
Parchment paper

1. Preheat oven to 350°F.

2. In a bowl combine the garlic, cumin, lime juice, pepper, and onion. Toss ingredients well so the seasoning spreads evenly. Add avocado oil and broccoli florets to bowl and toss again.

3. Place all ingredients on a parchment paper-lined baking sheet and roast for 25 minutes.

4. Remove from oven, and grab a fork so you can enjoy this delicious dish.

EXCHANGES/CHOICES
2 vegetable, 1/2 fat

CALORIES 70 | **CALORIES FROM FAT** 25 | **TOTAL FAT** 3g | **SATURATED FAT** 0g | **TRANS FAT** 0g
CHOLESTEROL 0mg | **SODIUM** 40mg | **POTASSIUM** 400mg | **TOTAL CARBOHYDRATE** 10g
DIETARY FIBER 3g | **SUGARS** 3g | **PROTEIN** 4g | **PHOSPHORUS** 85mg

BRÓCOLI ASADO A LA CUBANA

TIEMPO DE PREPARACIÓN: 10 minutos
TIEMPO DE COCCIÓN: 25 minutos
RINDE: 4 porciones
TAMAÑO DE LA PORCIÓN: 1 taza

3 dientes de ajo, pelados y picados en tajadas delgadas

1/4 cdta. de comino

1 cdta. de jugo de lima o limón verde

1/8 cdta. de pimienta negra gruesa

1/2 taza de cebolla española en rodajas finas

2 cdtas. de aceite de aguacate

16 onzas de brócoli

Papel mantequilla

1. Calentar el horno a 350°F.

2. Echar en una vasija el ajo, comino, jugo de limón verde, pimienta y cebolla. Mezclar los ingredientes bien para que las especias se distribuyan uniformemente. Agregar el aceite de aguacate y el brócoli a la vasija y revolver.

3. Colocar todos los ingredientes en una lata con papel mantequilla y asar 25 minutos.

4. Retirar del horno y agarrar un tenedor para disfrutar este delicioso platillo.

SELECCIONES/INTERCAMBIOS
2 vegetales, 1/2 grasa

CALORÍAS 70 | **CALORÍAS DE GRASA** 25 | **TOTAL DE GRASA** 3g | **GRASA SATURADA** 0g | **GRASA TRANS** 0g
COLESTEROL 0mg | **SODIO** 40mg | **POTASIO** 400mg | **TOTAL DE CARBOHIDRATOS** 10g
FIBRA ALIMENTARIA 3g | **AZÚCARES** 3g | **PROTEÍNA** 4g | **FÓSFORO** 85mg

GARDEN WHOLE-ROASTED HERBED CARROTS

When I was a young, handsome, crazy little kid in Medellín, Colombia, we would take trips to the countryside where my aunt lived. She had a huge finca (farm) that had cattle, pigs, chickens, and a huge garden. One of my favorite things to do was dig up the carrots and enjoy their crisp, sweet flavor. This recipe honors that memory. The marjoram adds that finca aroma, the onions have that special sweetness that only roasted onions can, and these flavors bring back my childhood memories once more.

PREP TIME: 10 minutes
COOKING TIME: 25 minutes
SERVES: 6
SERVING SIZE: 3 ounces (about 1 carrot)

1 1/2 pounds whole carrots, washed
2 teaspoons avocado oil
2 tablespoons marjoram leaves
2 cloves garlic, thinly sliced
1/2 cup sliced Spanish onion
1/4 teaspoon kosher salt
1/2 teaspoon cracked black pepper
Parchment paper

1. Preheat oven to 350°F.

2. Remove carrot tops and wash carrots thoroughly. In a large bowl, add oil, marjoram, garlic, onion, salt, and pepper. Mix ingredients together, and rub mixture on the carrots. Do this with love, guys! Massage in that flavor, because it is always about the *sazón*.

3. Place the carrots cushioned against each other on a baking sheet lined with parchment paper, set timer to 25 minutes, and place carrots in the oven. You know the drill here: remove from oven and enjoy.

EXCHANGES/CHOICES
2 1/2 vegetable, 1/2 fat

CALORIES 70 | **CALORIES FROM FAT** 20 | **TOTAL FAT** 2g | **SATURATED FAT** 0g | **TRANS FAT** 0g
CHOLESTEROL 0mg | **SODIUM** 160mg | **POTASSIUM** 400mg | **TOTAL CARBOHYDRATE** 13g
DIETARY FIBER 4g | **SUGARS** 6g | **PROTEIN** 1g | **PHOSPHORUS** 45mg

ZANAHORIAS ASADAS ENTERAS CON HIERBAS

Cuando era un chico guapo y loco en Medellín, Colombia, con frecuencia íbamos al campo, donde vivía mi tía en una enorme finca con vacas, cerdos, pollos y un gran huerto. Una de las cosas que más me gustaba hacer era desenterrar zanahorias y disfrutar su sabor crocante y dulce. Esta receta es un homenaje a esos recuerdos. La mejorana le da aroma a finca, las cebollas resaltan esa dulzura especial de una manera que solo pueden hacerlo las cebollas asadas, y el sabor evoca una vez más esos recuerdos de mi niñez.

TIEMPO DE PREPARACIÓN: 10 minutos
TIEMPO DE COCCIÓN: 25 minutos
RINDE: 6 porciones
TAMAÑO DE LA PORCIÓN: 3 onzas
(aproximadamente 1 zanahoria)

1 1/2 libras de zanahorias enteras, lavadas

2 cdtas. de aceite de aguacate

2 cdas. de hojas de mejorana

2 dientes de ajo, en rodajas delgadas

1/2 taza de cebolla española en rodajas

1/4 cdta. de sal *kosher*

1/2 cdta. de pimienta negra gruesa

Papel mantequilla

1. Calentar el horno a 350°F.

2. Recortar la parte superior de las zanahorias y lavarlas bien. En una vasija grande, mezclar el aceite, mejorana, ajo, cebolla, sal y pimienta. Echar la mezcla en las zanahorias. ¡Hay que hacerlo con amor! Masajear para que se impregnen de sabor porque todo es cuestión de sazón.

3. Colocar las zanahorias unas pegadas a las otras en una lata para hornear con papel mantequilla, poner la alarma para 25 minutos y meter las zanahorias en el horno. Y el resto es obvio: se sacan del horno y se disfrutan.

SELECCIONES/INTERCAMBIOS
2 1/2 vegetales, 1/2 grasa

CALORÍAS 70 | **CALORÍAS DE GRASA** 20 | **TOTAL DE GRASA** 2g | **GRASA SATURADA** 0g | **GRASA TRANS** 0g
COLESTEROL 0mg | **SODIO** 160mg | **POTASIO** 400mg | **TOTAL DE CARBOHIDRATOS** 13g
FIBRA ALIMENTARIA 4g | **AZÚCARES** 6g | **PROTEÍNA** 1g | **FÓSFORO** 45mg

ROSEMARY-ROASTED ASPARAGUS

PREP TIME: 10 minutes
COOKING TIME: 20 minutes
SERVES: 4
SERVING SIZE: About 4 spears (1/2 cup)

---

1 pound fresh asparagus
5 ounces baby bella mushrooms, sliced
1 cup sliced Spanish onion
1/2 teaspoon kosher salt
1/4 teaspoon cracked black pepper
1 1/2 tablespoons finely chopped fresh
    rosemary
2 teaspoons avocado oil
Parchment paper

1. Preheat oven to 350°F.

2. Remove tough ends of asparagus and place spears in a large bowl. Add mushrooms, onion, salt, pepper, rosemary, and oil to bowl. Toss ingredients to make sure the asparagus gets coated with flavor.

3. Place asparagus first on a baking sheet lined with parchment paper, then add the onions and mushrooms. Place tray in the oven for 20 minutes.

4. Remove from oven and enjoy some wonderful crunch and a lot of *sazón*.

EXCHANGES/CHOICES
2 vegetable, 1/2 fat

CALORIES 70 | **CALORIES FROM FAT** 25 | **TOTAL FAT** 3g | **SATURATED FAT** 0g | **TRANS FAT** 0g
CHOLESTEROL 0mg | **SODIUM** 250mg | **POTASSIUM** 450mg | **TOTAL CARBOHYDRATE** 10g
DIETARY FIBER 3g | **SUGARS** 4g | **PROTEIN** 4g | **PHOSPHORUS** 115mg

ESPÁRRAGOS ASADOS CON ROMERO

TIEMPO DE PREPARACIÓN: 10 minutos
TIEMPO DE COCCIÓN: 20 minutos
RINDE: 4 porciones
TAMAÑO DE LA PORCIÓN: Unos 4 espárragos
    (1/2 taza)

---

1 libra de espárragos frescos

5 onzas de champiñones Portobello pequeños, en rodajas

1 taza de cebolla española en rodajas

1/2 cdta. de sal *kosher*

1/4 cdta. de pimienta negra gruesa

1 1/2 cdas. de romero fresco, finamente picado

2 cdtas. de aceite de aguacate

Papel mantequilla

1. Calentar el horno a 350°F.

2. Cortar y descartar los extremos duros de los espárragos y colocar estos en una vasija grande. Agregar los champiñones, cebolla, sal, pimienta, romero y aceite a la vasija. Mezclar los ingredientes para asegurarse de que los espárragos estén recubiertos de sabor.

3. Colocar los espárragos primero en una lata con papel mantequilla, luego agregar las cebollas y champiñones. Colocar la lata en el horno 20 minutos.

4. Retirar del horno y disfrutar el crujido maravilloso y mucha sazón.

SELECCIONES/INTERCAMBIOS
2 vegetales, 1/2 grasa

CALORÍAS 70 | **CALORÍAS DE GRASA** 25 | **TOTAL DE GRASA** 3g | **GRASA SATURADA** 0g | **GRASA TRANS** 0g
COLESTEROL 0mg | **SODIO** 250mg | **POTASIO** 450mg | **TOTAL DE CARBOHIDRATOS** 10g
FIBRA ALIMENTARIA 3g | **AZÚCARES** 4g | **PROTEÍNA** 4g | **FÓSFORO** 115mg

Rosemary Cauliflower Steaks

PREP TIME: 15 minutes
COOKING TIME: 25 minutes
SERVES: 8
SERVING SIZE: 4 ounces

1/2 teaspoon kosher salt, divided
1 cauliflower head (about 2 pounds)
2 teaspoons avocado oil
2 cloves garlic, peeled and thinly sliced
1 tablespoon minced fresh rosemary
1/8 teaspoon cracked black pepper
1/8 teaspoon ground nutmeg
1 cup unsalted chicken stock

1. Fill a large pot 3/4 of the way full with water and add 1/4 teaspoon salt to it. Bring water to a boil. Turn off heat.

2. Remove any green stems from the cauliflower, then place cauliflower head in water for 7 minutes. Remove from water and let cool on a rack so excess water drips off.

3. Remove the stalk of the cauliflower (the really hard part at the bottom of the cauliflower) and slice cauliflower head into 1-inch-thick steaks with a knife.

4. Preheat nonstick pan over high heat and sear cauliflower steaks for 1 minute on each side.

5. Once steaks have been seared, turn stove down to medium heat and add avocado oil to the pan. Insert garlic, rosemary, remaining salt, pepper, and nutmeg, and cook for 1 minute. Add chicken stock and let it simmer for 2 minutes to create a nice broth for the cauliflower.

6. Serve cauliflower steaks on a plate and drizzle sauce on top.

EXCHANGES/CHOICES
2 vegetable, 1/2 fat

CALORIES 70 | **CALORIES FROM FAT** 20 | **TOTAL FAT** 2g | **SATURATED FAT** 0g | **TRANS FAT** 0g
CHOLESTEROL 0mg | **SODIUM** 220mg | **POTASSIUM** 540mg | **TOTAL CARBOHYDRATE** 11g
DIETARY FIBER 4g | **SUGARS** 5g | **PROTEIN** 4g | **PHOSPHORUS** 90mg

FILETES DE COLIFLOR CON ROMERO

TIEMPO DE PREPARACIÓN: 15 minutos
TIEMPO DE COCCIÓN: 25 minutos
RINDE: 8 porciones
TAMAÑO DE LA PORCIÓN: 4 onzas

1/2 cdta. de sal *kosher*, en partes

1 coliflor entera (aproximadamente 2 libras)

2 cdtas. de aceite de aguacate

2 dientes de ajo, pelados y picados en tajadas delgadas

1 cda. de romero fresco, picado

1/8 cdta. de pimienta negra gruesa

1/8 cdta. de nuez moscada molida

1 taza de caldo de pollo sin sal

1. Llenar 3/4 de una olla grande con agua y agregar 1/4 cdta. de sal. Hacer hervir. Apagar el fuego.

2. Eliminar los tallos verdes de la coliflor, luego meter la coliflor en el agua 7 minutos. Retirar del agua y dejar enfriar sobre una rejilla para que se escurra el exceso de agua.

3. Cortar el tallo de la coliflor (la parte realmente dura debajo de la cabeza) y con un cuchillo cortar la coliflor en filetes de 1 pulgada de espesor.

4. Calentar una olla antiadherente a fuego alto y dorar las rebanadas de coliflor 1 minuto por lado.

5. Una vez que las rebanadas se doren, bajar el fuego a medio y agregar el aceite de aguacate a la sartén. Añadir el ajo, romero, sal restante, pimienta y nuez moscada, y cocer 1 minuto. Agregar el caldo de pollo y cocer a fuego lento 2 minutos para crear un buen caldo para la coliflor.

6. Servir las rebanadas de coliflor en un plato y echar la salsa encima.

SELECCIONES/INTERCAMBIOS
2 vegetales, 1/2 grasa

CALORÍAS 70 | **CALORÍAS DE GRASA** 20 | **TOTAL DE GRASA** 2g | **GRASA SATURADA** 0g | **GRASA TRANS** 0g
COLESTEROL 0mg | **SODIO** 220mg | **POTASIO** 540mg | **TOTAL DE CARBOHIDRATOS** 11g
FIBRA ALIMENTARIA 4g | **AZÚCARES** 5g | **PROTEÍNA** 4g | **FÓSFORO** 90mg

LA ESQUINA LIME MANGO SLICES

This is one of my all-time favorite snacks and mango dishes. It packs a whole lot of flavor. La esquina translates to "the corner"; the corner was the spot to get mangoes when I was a child. I used to buy mangoes from a lad who would cut them with the precision of a ninja and sprinkle salt and squeeze lime on top. Who knew something so simple would be so delicious? The sweetness from the mango, the tartness from the lime, and the salt seem to come together in perfect harmony. I hope you enjoy this dish as much as I do.

PREP TIME: 5 minutes
REFRIGERATION TIME: 10 minutes
SERVES: 3
SERVING SIZE: 4 ounces

1 large (12-ounce) ripe mango, peeled and cut into 10 slices
1 lime, juiced
1/4 teaspoon kosher salt
1/8 teaspoon chili powder

1. Add mango slices to a bowl.

2. To a separate bowl, add lime juice, salt, and chili powder. Whisk briskly for 30 seconds to bring the *sazón* together. Add the mango slices and toss well.

3. You can serve this right away, but if you place it in the fridge for 10 minutes, magical things will happen to the flavors.

EXCHANGES/CHOICES
1 fruit

CALORIES 60 | CALORIES FROM FAT 0 | TOTAL FAT 0g | SATURATED FAT 0g | TRANS FAT 0g
CHOLESTEROL 0mg | SODIUM 170mg | POTASSIUM 180mg | TOTAL CARBOHYDRATE 15g
DIETARY FIBER 2g | SUGARS 13g | PROTEIN 1g | PHOSPHORUS 15mg

RONALDO'S CUBAN SANDWICH, p. 248
SÁNDWICH CUBANO DE RONALDO, p. 249

Mojo-Marinated Pork Tenderloin (Pernil), p. 48
Lomo de cerdo adobado con mojo, p. 49

GREEN VEGETABLE EGG TORTILLA, p. 182
OMELET DE VERDURAS, p. 183

SEARED SCALLOPS WITH ROASTED GRAPE TOMATOES, p. 238
CONCHAS DORADAS CON TOMATES CEREZOS ASADOS, p. 239

Summer Peach and Corn Salad, p. 222
Ensalada veraniega de maíz y durazno, p. 223

ROASTED PLANTAINS AND POBLANO PEPPER WITH GUAVA SAUCE, p. 102
PLÁTANOS Y CHILES POBLANOS ASADOS CON SALSA DE GUAYABA, p. 103

LADY'S SANGRIA, p. 70
SANGRÍA DE LADY, p. 71

RONALDO'S APPLE PIE, p. 72
TARTA DE MANZANA DE RONALDO, p. 73

TAJADAS DE MANGO CON LIMÓN VERDE DE LA ESQUINA

Este es uno de mis platillos preferidos con mango. Me encanta como bocadillo por la intensidad de su sabor. Solía comprárselos a un muchacho en la calle que los cortaba con la precisión de un ninja y les echaba sal y les exprimía limón verde. ¿Quién hubiese pensado que algo tan simple pudiera ser tan delicioso? La dulzura del mango, la acidez del limón verde y la sal parecen combinarse en perfecta armonía. Espero que disfruten este plato tanto como yo.

TIEMPO DE PREPARACIÓN: 5 minutos
TIEMPO DE REFRIGERACIÓN: 10 minutos
RINDE: 3 porciones
TAMAÑO DE LA PORCIÓN: 4 onzas

1 mango maduro grande (de 12 onzas),
   pelado y cortado en 10 rodajas
1 lima o limón verde, exprimido
1/4 cdta. de sal *kosher*
1/8 cdta. de chile en polvo

1. Poner el mango en tajadas en una vasija.

2. En una vasija aparte, echar el jugo de limón verde, sal y chile en polvo. Batir enérgicamente 30 segundos para mezclar bien la sazón. Agregar las tajadas de mango y mezclar bien.

3. Se puede servir de inmediato, pero si se mete al refrigerador 10 minutos, los sabores se trasforman por arte de magia.

SELECCIONES/INTERCAMBIOS
1 fruta

CALORÍAS 60 | CALORÍAS DE GRASA 0 | TOTAL DE GRASA 0g | GRASA SATURADA 0g | GRASA TRANS 0g
COLESTEROL 0mg | SODIO 170mg | POTASIO 180mg | TOTAL DE CARBOHIDRATOS 15g
FIBRA ALIMENTARIA 2g | AZÚCARES 13g | PROTEÍNA 1g | FÓSFORO 15mg

MANGO SALSA

I love mangoes...a lot! This has to be my second favorite mango dish. (My first favorite is La Esquina Lime Mango Slices on page 124.) Mango salsa is great because it's so versatile. I love to put it on grilled fish or pork. The tartness of the lime and the sweetness of the mango are such a good combination. This salsa is always good with some multigrain chips if you are in the mood to snack.

PREP TIME: 10 minutes
REFRIGERATION TIME: 1 hour
SERVES: 16
SERVING SIZE: 2 tablespoons

8 ounces mango, peeled and cut into
    1/2-inch cubes
1/2 cup cubed Spanish onion
    (1/4-inch cubes)
2 tablespoons finely chopped cilantro
2 tablespoons lime juice
1/4 teaspoon Chinese ginger powder
1 teaspoon kosher salt

1. Grab a large bowl and add all ingredients. Mix with a plastic spatula and cover with plastic wrap. Place bowl in the fridge for 1 hour before serving so flavors can marry.

EXCHANGES/CHOICES
free food

CALORIES 10 | **CALORIES FROM FAT** 0 | **TOTAL FAT** 0g | **SATURATED FAT** 0g | **TRANS FAT** 0g
CHOLESTEROL 0mg | **SODIUM** 120mg | **POTASSIUM** 35mg | **TOTAL CARBOHYDRATE** 3g
DIETARY FIBER 0g | **SUGARS** 2g | **PROTEIN** 0g | **PHOSPHORUS** 0mg

SALSA DE MANGO

¡Me encanta el mango... me fascina! Este es mi segundo plato preferido de mango. El primero es Tajadas de mango con limón verde de la esquina de la pág. 125). La salsa de mango es ideal porque es muy versátil. Me encanta echárselo al pescado o carne de cerdo a la parrilla. La acidez del limón verde y la dulzura del mango son una buena combinación. Esta salsa siempre va bien con chips o totopos de granos integrales, si les provoca un bocadillo.

TIEMPO DE PREPARACIÓN: 10 minutos
TIEMPO DE REFRIGERACIÓN: 1 hora
RINDE: 16 porciones
TAMAÑO DE LA PORCIÓN: 2 cdas.

8 onzas de mango, pelado y cortado en cubos de 1/2 pulgada

1/2 taza de cebolla española (en cubos de 1/4 de pulgada)

2 cdas. de cilantro finamente picado

2 cdas. de jugo de lima o limón verde

1/4 cdta. de jengibre chino en polvo

1 cdta. de sal *kosher*

1. Poner todos los ingredientes en una vasija grande. Mezclar con una espátula de plástico y cubrir con envoltura plástica. Colocar la vasija en el refrigerador 1 hora antes de servir para que los sabores se impregnen.

SELECCIONES/INTERCAMBIOS
No cuenta

CALORÍAS 10 | **CALORÍAS DE GRASA** 0 | **TOTAL DE GRASA** 0g | **GRASA SATURADA** 0g | **GRASA TRANS** 0g
COLESTEROL 0mg | **SODIO** 120mg | **POTASIO** 35mg | **TOTAL DE CARBOHIDRATOS** 3g
FIBRA ALIMENTARIA 0g | **AZÚCARES** 2g | **PROTEÍNA** 0g | **FÓSFORO** 0mg

TOMATILLO-AVOCADO SALSA

Salsas are really fun (and I am not talking about the dance)! Salsas have a great, chunky texture, and you can control the flavors. What?! Yes, you control the level of heat and how much salsa you put on a chip or a piece of chicken, meat, or fish. I think that's pretty cool. And this recipe packs a good punch.

PREP TIME: 10 minutes
REFRIGERATION TIME: 2 hours
SERVES: 20
SERVING SIZE: 2 tablespoons

12 ounces tomatillos, husks removed, tomatillos washed and cut in half
4 ounces cubed red pepper, washed
4 tablespoons finely chopped cilantro
2 tablespoons distilled vinegar
6 tablespoons lime juice
6 ounces Hass avocado flesh
1 teaspoon kosher salt
1/4 teaspoon cracked black pepper
1/2 cup cold unsalted vegetable stock
1/2 cup sliced Spanish onion
1/2 teaspoon ground cumin
10 ounces plum tomatoes, washed and chopped

1. Add all ingredients to a blender. Pulsate 5 times for 1 second each time. Blend on the purée setting for 1 minute.

2. To store salsa, pour it into mason jars or other containers and place in the refrigerator. Allow salsa to cool completely before serving, about 2 hours.

EXCHANGES/CHOICES
1 vegetable

CALORIES 30 | **CALORIES FROM FAT** 10 | **TOTAL FAT** 1g | **SATURATED FAT** 0g | **TRANS FAT** 0g
CHOLESTEROL 0mg | **SODIUM** 110mg | **POTASSIUM** 140mg | **TOTAL CARBOHYDRATE** 3g
DIETARY FIBER 1g | **SUGARS** 2g | **PROTEIN** 1g | **PHOSPHORUS** 20mg

SALSA DE TOMATILLO Y AGUACATE

Las salsas son realmente divertidas (y no estoy hablando de bailar). Tienen una gran textura en la que se notan los trozos y se pueden controlar los sabores. ¡¿Qué?! Sí, pueden controlar cuán picantes son y cuánta salsa poner en un chip o pedazo de pollo, carne o pescado. Me parece genial. Y esta receta es muy sabrosa.

TIEMPO DE PREPARACIÓN: 10 minutos
TIEMPO DE REFRIGERACIÓN: 2 horas
RINDE: 20 porciones
TAMAÑO DE LA PORCIÓN: 2 cdas.

---

12 onzas de tomatillos pelados, lavados y cortados por la mitad

4 onzas de pimiento rojo, lavado y en cubos

4 cdas. de cilantro finamente picado

2 cdas. de vinagre destilado

6 cdas. de jugo de lima o limón verde

6 onzas de pulpa de aguacate

1 cdta. de sal *kosher*

1/4 cdta. de pimienta negra gruesa

1/2 taza de caldo de vegetales sin sal y frío

1/2 taza de cebolla española en rodajas

1/2 cdta. de comino

10 onzas de tomates ciruelos, lavados y picados

1. Meter todos los ingredientes en una licuadora. Prender y apagar 5 veces, 1 segundo a la vez. Licuar 1 minuto.

2. Para guardar la salsa, echar en frascos de conserva u otros recipientes y refrigerar. Dejar que la salsa se enfríe del todo antes de servir, unas 2 horas.

SELECCIONES/INTERCAMBIOS
1 vegetal

CALORÍAS 30 | **CALORÍAS DE GRASA** 10 | **TOTAL DE GRASA** 1g | **GRASA SATURADA** 0g | **GRASA TRANS** 0g
COLESTEROL 0mg | **SODIO** 110mg | **POTASIO** 140mg | **TOTAL DE CARBOHIDRATOS** 3g
FIBRA ALIMENTARIA 1g | **AZÚCARES** 2g | **PROTEÍNA** 1g | **FÓSFORO** 20mg

TURKEY BACON CHUNKY GUACAMOLE

PREP TIME: 15 minutes
COOKING TIME: 5 minutes
SERVES: 10
SERVING SIZE: 1/4 cup

3 Hass avocados (12 ounces), pitted (pits reserved), skin removed, and cut into 1/4-inch cubes

6 tomatillos, husks removed, finely chopped

1 cup finely chopped Spanish onion

1 cup finely chopped cilantro

1 poblano pepper, finely chopped

4 limes, juiced

1 teaspoon lime zest

1 teaspoon kosher salt

1 teaspoon fennel seed

1/4 teaspoon cracked black pepper

2 ounces turkey bacon, finely chopped

1. Place pits of the avocado in a large bowl. Add avocado cubes, tomatillos, onion, cilantro, poblano pepper, lime juice, lime zest, salt, fennel seed, and pepper, and mix with a plastic spatula. (Make sure you mix gently—remember, it's a chunky guacamole.)

2. Preheat a nonstick pan over medium heat. Add turkey bacon and cook for about 5 minutes, stirring constantly so bacon doesn't burn. Remove turkey bacon from pan and place on a paper towel to remove any excess fat.

3. Fold turkey bacon into the guacamole. Serve.

RONALDO'S TIP

Adding the avocado pits to the guacamole will keep it from turning brown.

EXCHANGES/CHOICES
1 vegetable, 1 1/2 fat

CALORIES 100 | **CALORIES FROM FAT** 60 | **TOTAL FAT** 7g | **SATURATED FAT** 1g | **TRANS FAT** 0g
CHOLESTEROL 5mg | **SODIUM** 130mg | **POTASSIUM** 310mg | **TOTAL CARBOHYDRATE** 8g
DIETARY FIBER 4g | **SUGARS** 2g | **PROTEIN** 3g | **PHOSPHORUS** 60mg

GUACAMOLE EN TROZOS GRANDES CON TOCINO DE PAVO

TIEMPO DE PREPARACIÓN: 15 minutos
TIEMPO DE COCCIÓN: 5 minutos
RINDE: 10 porciones
TAMAÑO DE LA PORCIÓN: 1/4 taza

3 aguacates Hass (de 12 onzas) sin pepa (guardar la pepa), pelados y cortados en cubos de 1/4 pulgada

6 tomatillos, pelados y finamente picados

1 taza de cebolla española, finamente picada

1 taza de cilantro finamente picado

1 chile poblano, finamente picado

4 limas o limones verdes, exprimidos

1 cdta. de ralladura de lima o limón verde

1 cdta. de sal *kosher*

1 cdta. de semillas de hinojo

1/4 cdta. de pimienta negra gruesa

2 onzas de tocino de pavo, finamente picado

1. Colocar la pepa del aguacate en una vasija grande. Agregar el aguacate en cubos, los tomates, cebolla, cilantro, chile poblano, jugo de limón verde, ralladura de limón verde, sal, semillas de hinojo y pimienta, y mezclar con una espátula de plástico. (Asegúrese de mezclar con movimientos suaves; recuerde que el guacamole debe tener trozos grandes).

2. Calentar una sartén antiadherente a fuego medio. Echar el tocino de pavo y freírlo 5 minutos, revolviendo constantemente para que no se queme. Retirar el tocino de pavo de la sartén y colocarlo sobre papel absorbente para que absorba el exceso de grasa.

3. Echar el tocino de pavo en el guacamole. Servir.

CONSEJO DE RONALDO

Poner la pepa de aguacate en el guacamole evitará que se oxide (se ponga oscuro).

SELECCIONES/INTERCAMBIOS
1 vegetal, 1 1/2 grasas

CALORÍAS 100 | **CALORÍAS DE GRASA** 60 | **TOTAL DE GRASA** 7g | **GRASA SATURADA** 1g | **GRASA TRANS** 0g
COLESTEROL 5mg | **SODIO** 130mg | **POTASIO** 310mg | **TOTAL DE CARBOHIDRATOS** 8g
FIBRA ALIMENTARIA 4g | **AZÚCARES** 2g | **PROTEÍNA** 3g | **FÓSFORO** 60mg

CURRIED KALE CHIPS

Kale chips are a great lower-carbohydrate alternative to regular corn chips. And they taste delicious.

PREP TIME: 5 minutes
COOKING TIME: 20 minutes
SERVES: 6
SERVING SIZE: 1 cup

1 (16-ounce) bag kale
1 1/2 teaspoons curry powder
1/2 teaspoon kosher salt
1 teaspoon avocado oil

1. Preheat oven to 325°F.

2. Remove kale from bag and wash and dry it. Place kale, curry powder, salt, and oil into a large bowl, and toss well.

3. Place kale in a single layer on 3 baking sheets and bake for 20 minutes, or until kale chips are lightly brown. Serve.

EXCHANGES/CHOICES
2 vegetable

CALORIES 50 | CALORIES FROM FAT 20 | TOTAL FAT 2g | SATURATED FAT 0g | TRANS FAT 0g
CHOLESTEROL 0mg | SODIUM 190mg | POTASSIUM 380mg | TOTAL CARBOHYDRATE 7g
DIETARY FIBER 3g | SUGARS 2g | PROTEIN 3g | PHOSPHORUS 70mg

CHIPS DE COL RIZADA CON CURRY

Los chips de col rizada son una excelente alternativa a los chips o tostones regulares de maíz. Tienen pocos carbohidratos y saben delicioso.

TIEMPO DE PREPARACIÓN: 5 minutos
TIEMPO DE COCCIÓN: 20 minutos
RINDE: 6 porciones
TAMAÑO DE LA PORCIÓN: 1 taza

1 bolsa (de 16 onzas) de col rizada
1 1/2 cdtas. de curry en polvo
1/2 cdta. de sal *kosher*
1 cdta. de aceite de aguacate

1. Calentar el horno a 325°F.

2. Sacar la col rizada de la bolsa, lavarla y secarla. Echar la col rizada, el curry en polvo, la sal y el aceite en una vasija grande, y mezclar bien.

3. Colocar la col en una sola capa en 3 latas y hornear 20 minutos o hasta que los chips se doren ligeramente. Servir.

SELECCIONES/INTERCAMBIOS
2 vegetales

CALORÍAS 50 | **CALORÍAS DE GRASA** 20 | **TOTAL DE GRASA** 2g | **GRASA SATURADA** 0g | **GRASA TRANS** 0g
COLESTEROL 0mg | **SODIO** 190mg | **POTASIO** 380mg | **TOTAL DE CARBOHIDRATOS** 7g
FIBRA ALIMENTARIA 3g | **AZÚCARES** 2g | **PROTEÍNA** 3g | **FÓSFORO** 70mg

Coconut-Raisin Rice

PREP TIME: 15 minutes
COOKING TIME: 20–25 minutes
SERVES: 12
SERVING SIZE: 1/2 cup

1 tablespoon plus 1 teaspoon avocado oil, divided
1/2 medium Spanish onion, peeled and finely chopped (about 1/2 cup)
1/2 cup raisins, finely chopped
2 cups parboiled rice
1 cup light coconut milk
1 1/2 cups water
1 teaspoon kosher salt

1. Preheat a medium nonstick pan over medium-high heat. Add 1 teaspoon oil and wait 10 seconds for the oil to heat up. Add onions and raisins, and cook for about 2 minutes until onions are cooked through. Turn off heat and set aside.

2. Transfer mixture from pan to a large saucepot and add rice, coconut milk, water, salt, and remaining oil.

3. Place saucepot over medium heat and bring mixture to a simmer. Reduce heat to low and place lid on the pot or cover tightly with foil. Cook for about 20 minutes, or until rice is tender. Fluff rice with fork before serving.

EXCHANGES/CHOICES
2 starch

CALORIES 160 | CALORIES FROM FAT 35 | TOTAL FAT 4g | SATURATED FAT 1.5g | TRANS FAT 0g
CHOLESTEROL 0mg | SODIUM 160mg | POTASSIUM 180mg | TOTAL CARBOHYDRATE 30g
DIETARY FIBER 1g | SUGARS 4g | PROTEIN 3g | PHOSPHORUS 110mg

ARROZ CON COCO Y PASAS

TIEMPO DE PREPARACIÓN: 15 minutos
TIEMPO DE COCCIÓN: 20-25 minutos
RINDE: 12 porciones
TAMAÑO DE LA PORCIÓN: 1/2 taza

1 cda. más 1 cdta. de aceite de aguacate, en partes

1/2 cebolla española, pelada y finamente picada (aproximadamente 1/2 taza)

1/2 taza de pasas picadas

2 tazas de arroz precocido

1 taza de leche de coco *light*

1 1/2 tazas de agua

1 cdta. de sal *kosher*

1. Calentar una sartén antiadherente mediana a fuego medio alto. Agregar 1 cdta. de aceite y esperar 10 segundos hasta que se caliente. Agregar la cebolla y las pasas, y cocer 2 minutos hasta que la cebolla esté completamente cocida. Apagar el fuego y poner de lado.

2. Pasar la mezcla de la sartén a una olla grande y agregar el arroz, la leche de coco, el agua, la sal y el resto del aceite.

3. Colocar la olla a fuego medio y hervir la mezcla a fuego lento. Bajar el fuego y tapar la olla o cubrirla bien con papel de aluminio. Cocer unos 20 minutos o hasta que el arroz esté blando. Con un tenedor, granear el arroz antes de servir.

SELECCIONES/INTERCAMBIOS
2 almidones

CALORÍAS 160 | **CALORÍAS DE GRASA** 35 | **TOTAL DE GRASA** 4g | **GRASA SATURADA** 1.5g | **GRASA TRANS** 0g
COLESTEROL 0mg | **SODIO** 160mg | **POTASIO** 180mg | **TOTAL DE CARBOHIDRATOS** 30g
FIBRA ALIMENTARIA 1g | **AZÚCARES** 4g | **PROTEÍNA** 3g | **FÓSFORO** 110mg

NOT YOUR *ABUELA'S TOSTONES*

"How can this be, mijo?" That is probably what my grandma would have said about this recipe. Many people think tostones (fried plantains) are not tostones if you don't fry them. Fried plantains are amazing, it's true. But I'm trying to stick around for a long time. This recipe is a great, healthy alternative to classic tostones.

PREP TIME: 15 minutes
COOKING TIME: 20 minutes
SERVES: 4
SERVING SIZE: 3 pieces

2 green plantains
Parchment paper
2 teaspoons avocado oil
1/2 teaspoon sea salt
1 teaspoon cracked black pepper

1. Preheat oven to 400°F.

2. Cut both ends off plantains with a chef's knife. Insert tip of knife into the plantain slightly and run from top to bottom with curved part of the plantain facing you. (Repeat 5 times per plantain to make peeling easier.) Once you've made the slits, place plantains in a pot filled with hot water for about 5 minutes, until the water loosens the shell from the plantains. Working on one plantain at a time, remove from water and peel the shell with your thumb. Cut each plantain on the bias into 6 equal pieces and place back in the water. Set aside.

3. Fill a large saucepan 3/4 of the way full with water and bring to a boil. Add plantain pieces to boiling water and cook for 5 minutes. Using a small strainer, remove plantains from water to a plate lined with a paper towel.

4. Line the bottom of small pot with plastic wrap. To make *tostones,* use the bottom of the small pot and press down gently on plantain piece. Repeat with all plantain pieces. Place all 12 pieces on a parchment paper–lined baking sheet in a uniform manner. Brush *tostones* with oil.

5. Bake for 10–15 minutes, or until plantains are crisp on the outside and a little soft in the middle. Remove from oven, place in a bowl, sprinkle in salt and pepper, and toss the *tostones.* Now they're ready to serve!

EXCHANGES/CHOICES
1 1/2 starch, 1/2 fat

CALORIES 130 | **CALORIES FROM FAT** 25 | **TOTAL FAT** 3g | **SATURATED FAT** 0g | **TRANS FAT** 0g
CHOLESTEROL 0mg | **SODIUM** 240mg | **POTASSIUM** 460mg | **TOTAL CARBOHYDRATE** 29g
DIETARY FIBER 2g | **SUGARS** 13g | **PROTEIN** 1g | **PHOSPHORUS** 30mg

TOSTONES QUE NO SON LOS DE TU ABUELA

"¿Cómo puede ser esto, mijo?" Eso es probablemente lo que mi abuela habría dicho sobre esta receta. Muchas personas piensan que los tostones (plátanos fritos) no son tostones si no se fríen. El plátano frito es maravilloso, es cierto. Pero estoy tratando de hacer que mi vida sea larga. Esta receta es una gran alternativa saludable a los clásicos tostones.

TIEMPO DE PREPARACIÓN: 15 minutos
TIEMPO DE COCCIÓN: 20 minutos
RINDE: 4 porciones
TAMAÑO DE LA PORCIÓN: 3 tostones

2 plátanos verdes
Papel mantequilla
2 cdtas. de aceite de aguacate
1/2 cdta. de sal marina
1 cdta. de pimienta negra gruesa

1. Calentar el horno a 400°F.

2. Cortar ambos extremos de los plátanos con un cuchillo de chef. Meter la punta de un cuchillo en el plátano y cortar de arriba a abajo (con la parte encorvada hacia la persona). (Repetir 5 veces por plátano para poder pelarlos más fácilmente). Una vez que se hagan los cortes, colocar los plátanos en una olla llena de agua caliente unos 5 minutos, hasta que el agua afloje la cáscara de los plátanos. Sacar los plátanos del agua, uno por uno, y pelar la cáscara con el pulgar. Cortar cada plátano en diagonal en 6 trozos iguales y volver a meter al agua. Poner de lado.

3. Llenar 3/4 de una olla grande de agua y hervir. Agregar los trozos de plátano en el agua hirviendo y cocer 5 minutos. Usando un colador pequeño, retirar los plátanos del agua, a un plato cubierto con una toalla de papel.

4. Cubrir la base de una olla pequeña con plástico. Para hacer los tostones, utilizar la parte inferior de la ollita para presionar con cuidado el trozo de plátano. Repetir con cada trozo de plátano. Colocar los 12 trozos de manera uniforme en una lata forrada de papel mantequilla. Untar los tostones con aceite.

5. Hornear 10-15 minutos o hasta que el interior del plátano se ponga un poco suave y el exterior esté crujiente. Sacar los tostones del horno, poner en una vasija, echarles sal y pimienta, y mezclar. ¡Ya están listos para servir!

SELECCIONES/INTERCAMBIOS
1 1/2 almidones, 1/2 grasa

CALORÍAS 130 | **CALORÍAS DE GRASA** 25 | **TOTAL DE GRASA** 3g | **GRASA SATURADA** 0g | **GRASA TRANS** 0g
COLESTEROL 0mg | **SODIO** 240mg | **POTASIO** 460mg | **TOTAL DE CARBOHIDRATOS** 29g
FIBRA ALIMENTARIA 2g | **AZÚCARES** 13g | **PROTEÍNA** 1g | **FÓSFORO** 30mg

SMOOTHIES

BATIDOS

This chapter is geared toward making smoothies. Nothing is better than a refreshing smoothie, especially when it's filled with vitamins and minerals. The smoothies in this chapter will definitely take you to a tropical place. And trust me when I tell you they are not just for summertime.

Este capítulo se centra en la preparación de batidos. No hay nada mejor que un refrescante batido de frutas, especialmente cuando está repleto de vitaminas y minerales. Los batidos de este capítulo definitivamente los llevarán a un lugar tropical. Y créanme cuando les digo que no son solo para el verano.

—Chef Ronaldo

Avo-Berrie Smoothie

Don't have time to make a hot breakfast? Here is a great shake that will fill you up for the morning. The key to this recipe is the combination of avocado and banana. The good fat in the avocado will help slow down the digestion of the sugars in the banana, which will help with blood glucose maintenance.

PREP TIME: 5 minutes
BLENDING TIME: 1 minute 30 seconds
SERVES: 2
SERVING SIZE: 1 cup

1/2 cup raspberries, washed

1 cup unsweetened almond milk

1 banana, peeled

1/2 lime, juiced

3 ounces Hass avocado flesh (about 1/2 avocado)

1 cup ice

1. Add all ingredients to a blender and blend for 1 minute 30 seconds. Enjoy this great morning shake!

EXCHANGES/CHOICES
1 1/2 fruit, 1 1/2 fat

CALORIES 150 | **CALORIES FROM FAT** 70 | **TOTAL FAT** 8g | **SATURATED FAT** 1g | **TRANS FAT** 0g
CHOLESTEROL 0mg | **SODIUM** 80mg | **POTASSIUM** 540mg | **TOTAL CARBOHYDRATE** 23g
DIETARY FIBER 7g | **SUGARS** 9g | **PROTEIN** 2g | **PHOSPHORUS** 55mg

BATIDO DE AGUACATE Y BAYAS

¿No tienen tiempo para preparar un desayuno caliente? Este es un gran batido que los llenará por la mañana. La clave de esta receta es la combinación de plátano y aguacate. La grasa beneficiosa del aguacate ayuda a retrasar la digestión de las azúcares en el plátano, lo que los ayudará con el control de la glucosa.

TIEMPO DE PREPARACIÓN: 5 minutos
TIEMPO DE LICUADO: 1 minuto y medio
RINDE: 2 porciones
TAMAÑO DE LA PORCIÓN: 1 taza

1/2 taza de frambuesas, lavadas

1 taza de leche de almendras sin azúcar

1 plátano pelado

1/2 lima o limón verde, exprimido

3 onzas de pulpa de aguacate Hass
  (1/2 aguacate)

1 taza de hielo

1. Licuar todos los ingredientes 1 minuto y 30 segundos. ¡Disfruten este fabuloso batido matutino!

SELECCIONES/INTERCAMBIOS
1 1/2 frutas, 1 1/2 grasas

CALORÍAS 150 | **CALORÍAS DE GRASA** 70 | **TOTAL DE GRASA** 8g | **GRASA SATURADA** 1g | **GRASA TRANS** 0g
COLESTEROL 0mg | **SODIO** 80mg | **POTASIO** 540mg | **TOTAL DE CARBOHIDRATOS** 23g
FIBRA ALIMENTARIA 7g | **AZÚCARES** 9g | **PROTEÍNA** 2g | **FÓSFORO** 55mg

CUBANO GREEN SMOOTHIE

I'm not going to lie, the idea of blending greens together did not set my taste buds on fire. But this recipe makes a shake so delicious that I shook my head and said, "No way!" The way the spinach and cilantro flavors awaken once the blender blades hit is truly awesome. The greens become more vibrant, especially when blended with the lime juice. This shake will turn you into a greens lover.

PREP TIME: 10 minutes
BLENDING TIME: 2 minutes
SERVES: 2
SERVING SIZE: 1 cup

2 cups spinach, washed
1 cup cilantro, washed
3 ounces Hass avocado flesh
   (about 1/2 avocado)
1 tablespoon lime juice
1 1/2 cups fat-free plain Greek yogurt
1/4 teaspoon ground ginger
1 cup ice

1. Add all ingredients to a blender. Pulsate 5 times to incorporate ingredients. Blend for 2 minutes and serve.

EXCHANGES/CHOICES
1 fat-free milk, 1 vegetable, 1 1/2 fat

CALORIES 190 | CALORIES FROM FAT 60 | TOTAL FAT 7g | SATURATED FAT 1g | TRANS FAT 0g
CHOLESTEROL 0mg | SODIUM 170mg | POTASSIUM 920mg | TOTAL CARBOHYDRATE 22g
DIETARY FIBER 4g | SUGARS 15g | PROTEIN 13g | PHOSPHORUS 335mg

BATIDO VERDE A LA CUBANA

No les voy a mentir; no se me hace agua la boca con la idea de licuar varias verduras. Pero esta receta produce un batido tan delicioso que me hizo sacudir la cabeza y decir: "¡Increíble!" Los sabores de la espinaca y el cilantro se elevan a otra dimensión tras el proceso de licuado, lo que es realmente impresionante. Se realza el sabor de las verduras, especialmente cuando se licúan con el jugo de limón verde. Este batido hará que se vuelvan aficionados a las verduras.

TIEMPO DE PREPARACIÓN: 10 minutos
TIEMPO DE LICUADO: 2 minutos
RINDE: 2 porciones
TAMAÑO DE LA PORCIÓN: 1 taza

---

2 tazas de espinaca, lavada

1 taza de cilantro, lavado

3 onzas de pulpa de aguacate Hass
(1/2 aguacate)

1 cda. de jugo de lima o limón verde

1 1/2 tazas de yogur griego de sabor
natural, descremado

1/4 cdta. de jengibre en polvo

1 taza de hielo

1. Poner todos los ingredientes en la licuadora. Prender y apagar 5 veces para mezclar bien los ingredientes. Licuar 2 minutos y servir.

SELECCIONES/INTERCAMBIOS
1 leche descremada, 1 vegetal, 1 1/2 grasas

CALORÍAS 190 | **CALORÍAS DE GRASA** 60 | **TOTAL DE GRASA** 7g | **GRASA SATURADA** 1g | **GRASA TRANS** 0g
COLESTEROL 0mg | **SODIO** 170mg | **POTASIO** 920mg | **TOTAL DE CARBOHIDRATOS** 22g
FIBRA ALIMENTARIA 4g | **AZÚCARES** 15g | **PROTEÍNA** 13g | **FÓSFORO** 335mg

MORNING DANCING SMOOTHIE

Get the pleasure without the guilt; this health-boosting shake will get your day started on the right foot. Berries are amazing, with lots of antioxidants and fiber. They are good for heart health too. Those are some pretty cool benefits for such great-tasting fruits.

PREP TIME: 10 minutes
BLENDING TIME: 2 minutes
SERVES: 2
SERVING SIZE: 1 cup

1/2 cup raspberries, washed
1/2 cup blackberries, washed
1 cup strawberries, washed
1/2 banana
1 cup fat-free plain Greek yogurt
1 cup ice

1. Add all ingredients to a blender and blend for 2 minutes. It doesn't get easier than that, *mi gente.* Have a great day!

EXCHANGES/CHOICES
1 1/2 fruit, 1 1/2 lean protein

CALORIES 150 | CALORIES FROM FAT 10 | TOTAL FAT 1g | SATURATED FAT 0g | TRANS FAT 0g
CHOLESTEROL 0mg | SODIUM 40mg | POTASSIUM 490mg | TOTAL CARBOHYDRATE 24g
DIETARY FIBER 6g | SUGARS 14g | PROTEIN 13g | PHOSPHORUS 195mg

BATIDO DE BAILE MATUTINO

Dense un gusto sin sentirse culpables; este batido es bueno para la salud y hará que comiencen el día con el pie derecho. Las bayas son fabulosas, pues tienen muchos antioxidantes y fibra. Además, son buenas para el corazón. Son estupendos beneficios para frutas de tan buen sabor.

1. Licuar todos los ingredientes 2 minutos. No hay nada más fácil, mi gente. ¡Que tengan un día maravilloso!

TIEMPO DE PREPARACIÓN: 10 minutos
TIEMPO DE LICUADO: 2 minutos
RINDE: 2 porciones
TAMAÑO DE LA PORCIÓN: 1 taza

1/2 taza de frambuesas, lavadas
1/2 taza de moras, lavadas
1 taza de fresas, lavadas
1/2 plátano
1 taza de yogur griego de sabor natural, descremado
1 taza de hielo

SELECCIONES/INTERCAMBIOS
1 1/2 frutas, 1 1/2 proteínas magras

CALORÍAS 150 | **CALORÍAS DE GRASA** 10 | **TOTAL DE GRASA** 1g | **GRASA SATURADA** 0g | **GRASA TRANS** 0g
COLESTEROL 0mg | **SODIO** 40mg | **POTASIO** 490mg | **TOTAL DE CARBOHIDRATOS** 24g
FIBRA ALIMENTARIA 6g | **AZÚCARES** 14g | **PROTEÍNA** 13g | **FÓSFORO** 195mg

MORNING MANGO SURPRISE

Packed with flavor, vitamin C, dietary fiber, minerals, and many other healthy goodies, this smoothie is a great way to start off that early morning grind. It's easy to make and even better to drink.

PREP TIME: 5 minutes
BLENDING TIME: 1 minute 30 seconds
SERVES: 4
SERVING SIZE: 1 cup

1 large ripe mango (8 ounces), peeled
1 (6-ounce) navel orange, peeled
16 ounces water
1 cup ice

1. Add all ingredients to a blender and blend for 1 minute 30 seconds. Yes, that's it! Now enjoy.

EXCHANGES/CHOICES
1 fruit

CALORIES 60 | **CALORIES FROM FAT** 0 | **TOTAL FAT** 0g | **SATURATED FAT** 0g | **TRANS FAT** 0g
CHOLESTEROL 0mg | **SODIUM** 5mg | **POTASSIUM** 170mg | **TOTAL CARBOHYDRATE** 14g
DIETARY FIBER 2g | **SUGARS** 11g | **PROTEIN** 1g | **PHOSPHORUS** 20mg

SORPRESA MATUTINA DE MANGO

Este batido está repleto de sabor, vitamina C, fibra alimentaria, minerales y muchas otras delicias saludables; además es una excelente manera de empezar la rutina diaria temprano de mañana. Es fácil de hacer y una excelente bebida.

TIEMPO DE PREPARACIÓN: 5 minutos
TIEMPO DE LICUADO: 1 minuto y medio
RINDE: 4 porciones
TAMAÑO DE LA PORCIÓN: 1 taza

---

1 mango maduro grande (de 8 onzas), pelado
1 naranja (de 6 onzas), pelada
16 onzas de agua
1 taza de hielo

1. Licuar todos los ingredientes 1 minuto y 30 segundos. Sí, ¡eso es todo! Ahora disfruten.

SELECCIONES/INTERCAMBIOS
1 fruta

CALORÍAS 60 | **CALORÍAS DE GRASA** 0 | **TOTAL DE GRASA** 0g | **GRASA SATURADA** 0g | **GRASA TRANS** 0g
COLESTEROL 0mg | **SODIO** 5mg | **POTASIO** 170mg | **TOTAL DE CARBOHIDRATOS** 14g
FIBRA ALIMENTARIA 2g | **AZÚCARES** 11g | **PROTEÍNA** 1g | **FÓSFORO** 20mg

PAPAYA-RAMA

Papaya is one of the best fruits that you could possibly consume. Papaya is high in vitamins and antioxidants that nourish your body. I love the refreshing taste of papaya on a hot summer day. This recipe is simple and delicious.

PREP TIME: 5 minutes
BLENDING TIME: 2 minutes
SERVES: 4
SERVING SIZE: 8 ounces

16 ounces papaya meat, seeds removed
16 ounces water
1 cup ice
1 tablespoon lime juice

1. Add all ingredients to a blender and pulsate 5 times. Blend for 2 minutes. If you would like to chill the smoothie, transfer it to a large container and place in the refrigerator before serving. Enjoy!

EXCHANGES/CHOICES
1 fruit

CALORIES 45 | CALORIES FROM FAT 0 | TOTAL FAT 0g | SATURATED FAT 0g | TRANS FAT 0g
CHOLESTEROL 0mg | SODIUM 10mg | POTASSIUM 300mg | TOTAL CARBOHYDRATE 12g
DIETARY FIBER 2g | SUGARS 7g | PROTEIN 1g | PHOSPHORUS 5mg

PAPAYA-RAMA

La papaya o fruta bomba es una de las frutas más saludables que pueden consumir. Es rica en vitaminas y antioxidantes que nutren el cuerpo. Me encanta el sabor refrescante de la papaya los calurosos días de verano. Esta receta es sencilla y deliciosa.

TIEMPO DE PREPARACIÓN: 5 minutos
TIEMPO DE LICUADO: 2 minutos
RINDE: 4 porciones
TAMAÑO DE LA PORCIÓN: 8 onzas

16 onzas de pulpa de papaya, sin semillas

16 onzas de agua

1 taza de hielo

1 cda. de jugo de lima o limón verde

1. Poner todos los ingredientes en la licuadora y prender y apagar 5 veces. Licuar 2 minutos. Si quieren que el batido esté bien frío, échenlo en un envase grande y pónganlo en el refrigerador antes de servir. ¡A disfrutar!

SELECCIONES/INTERCAMBIOS
1 fruta

CALORÍAS 45 | **CALORÍAS DE GRASA** 0 | **TOTAL DE GRASA** 0g | **GRASA SATURADA** 0g | **GRASA TRANS** 0g
COLESTEROL 0mg | **SODIO** 10mg | **POTASIO** 300mg | **TOTAL DE CARBOHIDRATOS** 12g
FIBRA ALIMENTARIA 2g | **AZÚCARES** 7g | **PROTEÍNA** 1g | **FÓSFORO** 5mg

Summertime Strawberry Fiesta

Strawberries seem like the perfect fruit; they're shaped like a heart, sweet, and refreshing. This is a great strawberry smoothie that tastes like a wonderful treat.

PREP TIME: 5 minutes
BLENDING TIME: 1 minute 30 seconds
SERVES: 3
SERVING SIZE: 1 cup

1 1/2 cups ripe strawberries, tops removed
16 ounces unsweetened almond milk
4 ounces water
1 cup ice

1. Add strawberries, almond milk, water, and ice to a blender and pulsate 5 times. Blend for 1 minute 30 seconds or until smooth. Enjoy!

EXCHANGES/CHOICES
1/2 other carbohydrate, 1/2 fat

CALORIES 70 | **CALORIES FROM FAT** 35 | **TOTAL FAT** 4g | **SATURATED FAT** 0g | **TRANS FAT** 0g
CHOLESTEROL 0mg | **SODIUM** 230mg | **POTASSIUM** 300mg | **TOTAL CARBOHYDRATE** 9g
DIETARY FIBER 3g | **SUGARS** 4g | **PROTEIN** 2g | **PHOSPHORUS** 45mg

FIESTA VERANIEGA DE FRESAS

Las fresas parecen ser la fruta perfecta; tienen forma de corazón, y son dulces y refrescantes. Este es un genial batido de fresa que sabe de maravilla.

TIEMPO DE PREPARACIÓN: 5 minutos
TIEMPO DE LICUADO: 1 minuto y medio
RINDE: 3 porciones
TAMAÑO DE LA PORCIÓN: 1 taza

---

1 1/2 tazas de fresas maduras, sin la parte superior

16 onzas de leche de almendra sin endulzar

4 onzas de agua

1 taza de hielo

1. Poner las fresas, leche de almendras, agua y hielo en la licuadora y prender y apagar 5 veces. Licuar 1 minuto y 30 segundos o hasta que tenga consistencia uniforme. ¡A disfrutar!

SELECCIONES/INTERCAMBIOS
1/2 otro carbohidrato, 1/2 grasa

CALORÍAS 70 | **CALORÍAS DE GRASA** 35 | **TOTAL DE GRASA** 4g | **GRASA SATURADA** 0g | **GRASA TRANS** 0g
COLESTEROL 0mg | **SODIO** 230mg | **POTASIO** 300mg | **TOTAL DE CARBOHIDRATOS** 9g
FIBRA ALIMENTARIA 3g | **AZÚCARES** 4g | **PROTEÍNA** 2g | **FÓSFORO** 45mg

MAMI'S BANANA AND OATS SMOOTHIE

When I was a young kid, my mom would make avena (oatmeal) shakes for us all the time. They were so delicious, and my favorite was the one she made with banana. This recipe is a healthy alternative.

PREP TIME: 2 minutes
BLENDING TIME: 1 minute 30 seconds
SERVES: 2
SERVING SIZE: 1 cup

1 cup unsweetened almond milk

1/2 cup fat-free plain Greek yogurt

1/2 teaspoon ground cinnamon

1/8 teaspoon ground nutmeg

1/3 cup old-fashioned rolled oats

1 small ripe banana, cut into 1-inch rounds

1 cup ice

1. Add all ingredients to a blender and pulsate 5 times. Blend for 1 minute 30 seconds or until smooth.

EXCHANGES/CHOICES
1 fruit, 1/2 fat-free milk, 1 protein

CALORIES 150 | **CALORIES FROM FAT** 25 | **TOTAL FAT** 3g | **SATURATED FAT** 0g | **TRANS FAT** 0g | **CHOLESTEROL** 0mg | **SODIUM** 100mg | **POTASSIUM** 380mg | **TOTAL CARBOHYDRATE** 24g | **DIETARY FIBER** 4g | **SUGARS** 8g | **PROTEIN** 9g | **PHOSPHORUS** 155mg

BATIDO DE PLÁTANO Y AVENA DE MAMI

Cuando era niño, mami nos preparaba batidos de avena todo el tiempo. Eran deliciosos, y mi preferido era el de plátano. Esta receta es una alternativa saludable.

TIEMPO DE PREPARACIÓN: 2 minutos
TIEMPO DE LICUADO: 1 minuto y medio
RINDE: 2 porciones
TAMAÑO DE LA PORCIÓN: 1 taza

1 taza de leche de almendras sin azúcar

1/2 taza de yogur griego de sabor natural, descremado

1/2 cdta. de canela molida

1/8 cdta. de nuez moscada molida

1/3 taza de avena entera tradicional

1 plátano maduro pequeño, cortado en tajadas de 1 pulgada

1. Poner todos los ingredientes en la licuadora y prender y apagar 5 veces. Licuar 1 minuto y medio o hasta que tenga consistencia uniforme.

SELECCIONES/INTERCAMBIOS
1 fruta, 1/2 leche descremada, 1 proteína

CALORÍAS 150 | **CALORÍAS DE GRASA** 25 | **TOTAL DE GRASA** 3g | **GRASA SATURADA** 0g | **GRASA TRANS** 0g
COLESTEROL 0mg | **SODIO** 100mg | **POTASIO** 380mg | **TOTAL DE CARBOHIDRATOS** 24g
FIBRA ALIMENTARIA 4g | **AZÚCARES** 8g | **PROTEÍNA** 9g | **FÓSFORO** 155mg

ALL-SEASONS BERRY SMOOTHIE

During the summertime I freeze a lot of different berries so I can make this shake whenever I'm in a hurry. Berries freeze well in resealable plastic bags and don't lose their flavor. They are full of dietary fiber, antioxidants, vitamins, and minerals. Those are some powerful little berries in this tasty smoothie!

PREP TIME: 5 minutes
BLENDING TIME: 2 minutes
SERVES: 2
SERVING SIZE: 8 ounces

1/2 cup blackberries
1/2 cup blueberries
1/2 cup raspberries
1 cup spinach (you may substitute a different green)
16 ounces unsweetened almond milk
1 cup ice

1. Add all ingredients to a blender and pulsate 5 times. Blend for 2 minutes or until smooth. Enjoy!

EXCHANGES/CHOICES
1 fruit, 1/2 fat

CALORIES 90 | **CALORIES FROM FAT** 25 | **TOTAL FAT** 3g | **SATURATED FAT** 0g | **TRANS FAT** 0g
CHOLESTEROL 0mg | **SODIUM** 160mg | **POTASSIUM** 340mg | **TOTAL CARBOHYDRATE** 15g
DIETARY FIBER 6g | **SUGARS** 7g | **PROTEIN** 3g | **PHOSPHORUS** 50mg

BATIDO DE BAYAS DE TODA ESTACIÓN

Durante el verano congelo muchas bayas diferentes para poder preparar este batido cuando estoy apurado. Congelo las bayas en bolsas de plástico con cierre y así no pierden sabor. Están repletas de minerales, antioxidantes, vitaminas y fibra alimentaria. Las pequeñas bayas de este sabroso licuado ¡son potentes!

TIEMPO DE PREPARACIÓN: 5 minutos
TIEMPO DE LICUADO: 2 minutos
RINDE: 2 porciones
TAMAÑO DE LA PORCIÓN: 8 onzas

1/2 taza de moras

1/2 taza de arándanos (*blueberries*)

1/2 taza de frambuesas

1 taza de espinaca (se puede sustituir por otra verdura)

16 onzas de leche de almendra sin endulzar

1 taza de hielo

1. Poner todos los ingredientes en la licuadora y prender y apagar 5 veces. Licuar 2 minutos o hasta que tenga consistencia uniforme. ¡A disfrutar!

SELECCIONES/INTERCAMBIOS
1 fruta, 1/2 grasa

CALORÍAS 90 | **CALORÍAS DE GRASA** 25 | **TOTAL DE GRASA** 3g | **GRASA SATURADA** 0g | **GRASA TRANS** 0g
COLESTEROL 0mg | **SODIO** 160mg | **POTASIO** 340mg | **TOTAL DE CARBOHIDRATOS** 15g
FIBRA ALIMENTARIA 6g | **AZÚCARES** 7g | **PROTEÍNA** 3g | **FÓSFORO** 50mg

GUANÁBANA (SOURSOP) SHAKE

The guanábana (soursop) fruit is very large with a round shape. The fruit inside is white with large black seeds. When I was a child we would come across soursops in the mountains of Colombia, and I saw them once again years later in Puerto Rico. Their flavor is mild, lightly sweet, and refreshing. Unfortunately, I have never been able to locate this fruit in New Jersey, where I currently live. Since we don't have guanábanas on hand, I have substituted frozen guanábana pulp.

PREP TIME: 5 minutes
BLENDING TIME: 1 minute 30 seconds
SERVES: 5
SERVING SIZE: 1 cup

1 (14-ounce) packet frozen *guanábana* pulp (Goya)
5 mint leaves
1 tablespoon lime juice (about 1 lime)
1 cup ice
4 cups water

1. Let *guanábana* pulp defrost a little before cutting to make the process easier. Cut *guanábana* pulp into 8 pieces and add to a blender.

2. Add mint, lime juice, ice, and water, and blend for 1 minute 30 seconds. Make sure to stir before drinking. Place any unused shake in the refrigerator; the juice will be good for about 5 days. Enjoy!

EXCHANGES/CHOICES
1 fruit

CALORIES 60 | **CALORIES FROM FAT** 0 | **TOTAL FAT** 0g | **SATURATED FAT** 0g | **TRANS FAT** 0g
CHOLESTEROL 0mg | **SODIUM** 20mg | **POTASSIUM** 240mg | **TOTAL CARBOHYDRATE** 14g
DIETARY FIBER 3g | **SUGARS** 11g | **PROTEIN** 1g | **PHOSPHORUS** 25mg

BATIDO DE GUANÁBANA

La guanábana es una fruta muy grande de forma redonda, con pulpa blanca y grandes semillas negras. De niño encontrábamos guanábanas en las montañas de Colombia. Las volví a ver años más tarde en Puerto Rico. Tienen sabor suave, ligeramente dulce y refrescante. Desafortunadamente, no he podido encontrar esta fruta en Nueva Jersey, donde vivo. Ya que no tenemos guanábanas a la mano, las sustituyo por pulpa congelada.

TIEMPO DE PREPARACIÓN: 5 minutos
TIEMPO DE LICUADO: 1 minuto y medio
RINDE: 5 porciones
TAMAÑO DE LA PORCIÓN: 1 taza

---

1 paquete (de 14 onzas) de pulpa congelada de guanábana (Goya)

5 hojas de menta

1 cda. de jugo de lima o limón verde (aproximadamente 1 limón)

1 taza de hielo

4 tazas de agua

1. Descongelar un poco la pulpa de guanábana antes de cortar para que el proceso sea más fácil. Cortar la guanábana en 8 trozos y poner a la licuadora.

2. Agregar la menta, el jugo de limón verde, hielo y agua, y mezclar 1 minuto y medio. Asegúrense de agitarlo antes de beber. Colocar el batido que sobre en el refrigerador; el jugo dura unos 5 días. ¡A disfrutar!

SELECCIONES/INTERCAMBIOS
1 fruta

CALORÍAS 60 | **CALORÍAS DE GRASA** 0 | **TOTAL DE GRASA** 0g | **GRASA SATURADA** 0g | **GRASA TRANS** 0g
COLESTEROL 0mg | **SODIO** 20mg | **POTASIO** 240mg | **TOTAL DE CARBOHIDRATOS** 14g
FIBRA ALIMENTARIA 3g | **AZÚCARES** 11g | **PROTEÍNA** 1g | **FÓSFORO** 25mg

GUAVALIME FRESCA

Rich in dietary fiber and vitamin C, guava packs a punch if you need a pick-me-up during the afternoon grind. Guava is semi-sweet with a creamy texture; it's ideal for a refreshing drink. Guava can be found in the States, but you have to go to a specialty market, and they can be expensive. Frozen guava pulp (used in this recipe) is a great solution!

PREP TIME: 10 minutes
BLENDING TIME: 1 minute 30 seconds
SERVES: 6 cups
SERVING SIZE: 1 cup

1 (14-ounce) packet frozen guava pulp
  (Goya)
2 tablespoons lime juice
  (about 1 1/2 limes)
2 1/2 cups sparkling water
1 1/2 cups water
1 cup ice

1. Let guava defrost a little before cutting to make the process easier. Cut guava into 8 pieces.

2. Add all ingredients to a blender and pulsate 5 times. Blend for 1 minute 30 seconds or until smooth. Make sure to stir before drinking. Place any unused smoothie in the refrigerator; the juice will be good for about 5 days.

EXCHANGES/CHOICES
1 fruit

CALORIES 50 | **CALORIES FROM FAT** 10 | **TOTAL FAT** 1g | **SATURATED FAT** 0g | **TRANS FAT** 0g
CHOLESTEROL 0mg | **SODIUM** 25mg | **POTASSIUM** 290mg | **TOTAL CARBOHYDRATE** 10g
DIETARY FIBER 4g | **SUGARS** 6g | **PROTEIN** 2g | **PHOSPHORUS** 30mg

AGUA FRESCA DE GUAYABA Y LIMÓN VERDE

La guayaba es muy rica en fibra alimentaria y vitamina C, si necesitan algo que les dé energía durante el día. La guayaba es semidulce y tiene una textura cremosa; es ideal para una bebida refrescante. Se puede encontrar guayaba en Estados Unidos, pero es necesario ir a un mercado especializado, y puede ser cara. La pulpa congelada de guayaba (que se usa en esta receta) ¡es una gran solución!

TIEMPO DE PREPARACIÓN: 10 minutos
TIEMPO DE LICUADO: 1 minuto y medio
RINDE: 6 tazas
TAMAÑO DE LA PORCIÓN: 1 taza

1 paquete (de 14 onzas) de pulpa congelada de guayaba (Goya)

2 cdas. de jugo de lima o limón verde (aproximadamente 1 limón y medio)

2 1/2 tazas de agua con gas

1 1/2 tazas de agua

1 taza de hielo

1. Descongelar un poco la guayaba antes de cortar para que el proceso sea más fácil. Cortar la guayaba en 8 trozos.

2. Poner todos los ingredientes en la licuadora y prender y apagar 5 veces. Licuar 1 minuto y medio o hasta que tenga consistencia uniforme. Asegúrense de agitarlo antes de beber. Colocar el batido que sobre en el refrigerador; el jugo dura unos 5 días.

SELECCIONES/INTERCAMBIOS
1 fruta

CALORÍAS 50 | **CALORÍAS DE GRASA** 10 | **TOTAL DE GRASA** 1g | **GRASA SATURADA** 0g | **GRASA TRANS** 0g
COLESTEROL 0mg | **SODIO** 25mg | **POTASIO** 290mg | **TOTAL DE CARBOHIDRATOS** 10g
FIBRA ALIMENTARIA 4g | **AZÚCARES** 6g | **PROTEÍNA** 2g | **FÓSFORO** 30mg

ALMOND MILK, COCONUT, AND MANGO SHAKE

Mangoes are one of my top three favorite fruits. I remember the mango tree farm my father had behind his restaurant in Colombia; those mangoes were the size of coconuts, let me tell you. Life is made of food memories, and this memory is one that I cherish.

1. Add all ingredients to a blender and pulsate 5 times. Blend for 1 minute or until smooth. Enjoy!

PREP TIME: 5–7 minutes
BLENDING TIME: 1 minute
SERVES: 4
SERVING SIZE: 1 cup

2 medium ripe mangoes
   (about 8 ounces), peeled and
   cut into 1/2-inch cubes
1 cup coconut water
1 cup unsweetened almond milk
1 tablespoon lime juice
1 cup ice

EXCHANGES/CHOICES
1 fruit

CALORIES 50 | CALORIES FROM FAT 10 | TOTAL FAT 1g | SATURATED FAT 0g | TRANS FAT 0g
CHOLESTEROL 0mg | SODIUM 55mg | POTASSIUM 230mg | TOTAL CARBOHYDRATE 12g
DIETARY FIBER 1g | SUGARS 10g | PROTEIN 1g | PHOSPHORUS 20mg

BATIDO DE LECHE DE ALMENDRAS, COCO Y MANGO

El mango es una de mis tres frutas preferidas. Recuerdo el huerto de mangos que mi padre tenía detrás de su restaurante en Colombia; ¡los mangos eran del tamaño de cocos! La vida está llena de recuerdos de comida, y este es uno que atesoro.

TIEMPO DE PREPARACIÓN: 5-7 minutos
TIEMPO DE LICUADO: 1 minuto
RINDE: 4 porciones
TAMAÑO DE LA PORCIÓN: 1 taza

2 mangos medianos (de aproximadamente 8 onzas), pelados y cortados en cubos de 1/2 pulgada

1 taza de agua de coco

1 taza de leche de almendras sin azúcar

1 cda. de jugo de lima o limón verde

1 taza de hielo

1. Poner todos los ingredientes en la licuadora y prender y apagar 5 veces. Licuar 1 minuto o hasta que tenga consistencia uniforme. ¡A disfrutar!

SELECCIONES/INTERCAMBIOS
1 fruta

CALORÍAS 50 | **CALORÍAS DE GRASA** 10 | **TOTAL DE GRASA** 1g | **GRASA SATURADA** 0g | **GRASA TRANS** 0g
COLESTEROL 0mg | **SODIO** 55mg | **POTASIO** 230mg | **TOTAL DE CARBOHIDRATOS** 12g
FIBRA ALIMENTARIA 1g | **AZÚCARES** 10g | **PROTEÍNA** 1g | **FÓSFORO** 20mg

"BB" SHAKE

The "BB" in the recipe title stands for the blueberries and bananas in this delicious shake. This is a great shake to have in the morning after a good workout. It contains antioxidants, potassium, and a little protein to fuel your body perfectly.

PREP TIME: 5–10 minutes
BLENDING TIME: 1 minute 30 seconds
SERVES: 3
SERVING SIZE: 1 cup

1 cup blueberries, washed
1 medium banana, peeled and cut into 3 pieces
1/2 cup fat-free plain Greek yogurt
1 cup 2% milk
1 tablespoon all-natural almond butter
1/4 teaspoon ground cinnamon
1 teaspoon lime juice
1 cup ice

1. Add all ingredients to a blender and pulsate 5 times. Blend for 1 minute 30 seconds or until smooth. Enjoy!

EXCHANGES/CHOICES
1 fruit, 1/2 fat-free milk, 1 fat

CALORIES 160 | CALORIES FROM FAT 45 | TOTAL FAT 5g | SATURATED FAT 1.5g | TRANS FAT 0g
CHOLESTEROL 0mg | SODIUM 80mg | POTASSIUM 400mg | TOTAL CARBOHYDRATE 24g
DIETARY FIBER 3g | SUGARS 16g | PROTEIN 8g | PHOSPHORUS 170mg

BATIDO DE ARÁNDANOS Y PLÁTANO

Este un batido fabuloso para la mañana, después de una buena sesión de ejercicio. Contiene antioxidantes, potasio y un poco de proteína para nutrir el cuerpo perfectamente.

TIEMPO DE PREPARACIÓN: 5-10 minutos
TIEMPO DE LICUADO: 1 minuto y medio
RINDE: 3 porciones
TAMAÑO DE LA PORCIÓN: 1 taza

1 taza de arándanos *(blueberries)*, lavados

1 plátano mediano, pelado y cortado en 3 trozos

1/2 taza de yogur griego de sabor natural, descremado

1 taza de leche con 2% de grasa

1 cda. de mantequilla natural de almendras

1/4 cdta. de canela molida

1 cdta. de jugo de lima o limón verde

1 taza de hielo

1. Poner todos los ingredientes en la licuadora y prender y apagar 5 veces. Licuar 1 minuto y medio o hasta que tenga consistencia uniforme. ¡A disfrutar!

SELECCIONES/INTERCAMBIOS
1 fruta, 1/2 leche sin grasa, 1 grasa

CALORÍAS 160 | **CALORÍAS DE GRASA** 45 | **TOTAL DE GRASA** 5g | **GRASA SATURADA** 1.5g | **GRASA TRANS** 0g
COLESTEROL 0mg | **SODIO** 80mg | **POTASIO** 400mg | **TOTAL DE CARBOHIDRATOS** 24g
FIBRA ALIMENTARIA 3g | **AZÚCARES** 16g | **PROTEÍNA** 8g | **FÓSFORO** 170mg

Avocado on the Beach

PREP TIME: 5–10 minutes
BLENDING TIME: 1 minute 30 seconds
SERVES: 3
SERVING SIZE: 1 cup

4 ounces Hass avocado flesh
1 medium mango (about 4 ounces),
   peeled and cut into 1/2-inch cubes
1 orange, peeled and seeded
1 tablespoon lime juice
1 1/2 cups water
1 cup ice

1. Add all ingredients to a blender and pulsate 5 times. Blend for 1 minute 30 seconds. Enjoy!

EXCHANGES/CHOICES
1 1/2 fruit, 2 fat

CALORIES 160 | **CALORIES FROM FAT** 80 | **TOTAL FAT** 9g | **SATURATED FAT** 1.5g | **TRANS FAT** 0g
CHOLESTEROL 0mg | **SODIUM** 5mg | **POTASSIUM** 510mg | **TOTAL CARBOHYDRATE** 22g
DIETARY FIBER 6g | **SUGARS** 15g | **PROTEIN** 2g | **PHOSPHORUS** 50mg

AGUACATE PLAYERO

TIEMPO DE PREPARACIÓN: 5-10 minutos
TIEMPO DE LICUADO: 1 minuto y medio
RINDE: 3 porciones
TAMAÑO DE LA PORCIÓN: 1 taza

4 onzas de pulpa de aguacate Hass

1 mango mediano (de aproximadamente 4 onzas), pelado y cortado en cubos de 1/2 pulgada

1 naranja, pelada y sin semillas

1 cda. de jugo de lima o limón verde

1 1/2 tazas de agua

1 taza de hielo

1. Poner todos los ingredientes en la licuadora y prender y apagar 5 veces. Licuar 1 minuto y medio. ¡A disfrutar!

SELECCIONES/INTERCAMBIOS
1 1/2 fruta, 2 grasas

CALORÍAS 160 | **CALORÍAS DE GRASA** 80 | **TOTAL DE GRASA** 9g | **GRASA SATURADA** 1.5g | **GRASA TRANS** 0g
COLESTEROL 0mg | **SODIO** 5mg | **POTASIO** 510mg | **TOTAL DE CARBOHIDRATOS** 22g
FIBRA ALIMENTARIA 6g | **AZÚCARES** 15g | **PROTEÍNA** 2g | **FÓSFORO** 50mg

TRIPLE L SHAKE

This recipe is dedicated to my wife. She is one of the reasons I began drinking this shake. Ever since I met my wife, she's always had some type of fruit shake in her hand. This is my take on one of her favorites: the avocado shake.

PREP TIME: 5 minutes
BLENDING TIME: 1 minute 30 seconds
SERVES: 2
SERVING SIZE: 1 cup

4 ounces Hass avocado flesh
4 ounces papaya
1 teaspoon ground ginger
1 tablespoon lime juice
1 cup fat-free plain Greek yogurt
1 cup ice

1. Add all ingredients to a blender and pulsate 5 times. Blend for 1 minute 30 seconds or until smooth. Enjoy!

EXCHANGES/CHOICES
1 fruit, 2 lean protein, 1 fat

CALORIES 190 | CALORIES FROM FAT 80 | TOTAL FAT 9g | SATURATED FAT 1.5g | TRANS FAT 0g
CHOLESTEROL 0mg | SODIUM 50mg | POTASSIUM 610mg | TOTAL CARBOHYDRATE 16g
DIETARY FIBER 5g | SUGARS 8g | PROTEIN 13g | PHOSPHORUS 190mg

BATIDO TRIPLE L

Esta receta se la dedico a mi esposa. Es una de las razones por las que empecé a tomar este batido. Desde que la conocí, ella siempre ha tenido algún tipo de batido en la mano. Esta es mi versión de uno de sus favoritos: el batido de aguacate.

1. Poner todos los ingredientes en la licuadora y prender y apagar 5 veces. Licuar 1 minuto y medio o hasta que tenga consistencia uniforme. ¡A disfrutar!

TIEMPO DE PREPARACIÓN: 5 minutos
TIEMPO DE LICUADO: 1 minuto y medio
RINDE: 2 porciones
TAMAÑO DE LA PORCIÓN: 1 taza

4 onzas de pulpa de aguacate Hass
4 onzas de papaya
1 cdta. de jengibre en polvo
1 cda. de jugo de lima o limón verde
1 taza de yogur griego de sabor natural, descremado
1 taza de hielo

SELECCIONES/INTERCAMBIOS
1 fruta, 2 proteínas magras, 1 grasa

CALORÍAS 190 | **CALORÍAS DE GRASA** 80 | **TOTAL DE GRASA** 9g | **GRASA SATURADA** 1.5g | **GRASA TRANS** 0g
COLESTEROL 0mg | **SODIO** 50mg | **POTASIO** 610mg | **TOTAL DE CARBOHIDRATOS** 16g
FIBRA ALIMENTARIA 5g | **AZÚCARES** 8g | **PROTEÍNA** 13g | **FÓSFORO** 190mg

BREAKFAST
DESAYUNO

This chapter covers my favorite (and a very important) meal. Breakfast sets the tone for the day, and these easy-to-prepare recipes will make your morning even better. Breakfast was always a family meal when I was growing up. Why not keep that tradition going in your own home?

Este capítulo se lo dedico a mi comida preferida (y una que es muy importante). El desayuno marca la pauta para el día, y estas recetas fáciles de preparar harán su mañana incluso mejor. Siempre tomábamos el desayuno en familia cuando era chico. ¿Por qué no continuar esa tradición en su propia casa?

—Chef Ronaldo

OPEN-FACED EGG SANDWICH

This is a quick sandwich you can make if you are on the run in the morning. It contains protein, and good fats and carbohydrate that will be sure to wake you up.

PREP TIME: 5 minutes
COOKING TIME: 5 minutes
SERVES: 2
SERVING SIZE: 1 sandwich

1/4 teaspoon avocado oil
2 eggs
1 multigrain sandwich thin, split open
2 slices tomato
1 (1/4-inch) slice low-sodium deli turkey, cut in half
1 (1/4-inch) slice low-sodium deli ham, cut in half
1 slice 2% reduced-fat gouda cheese, cut in half

1. Preheat a nonstick skillet over medium-high heat and add oil.

2. Crack the eggs into separate bowls then add to the skillet. Fry the eggs for about 1 minute 30 seconds, then turn off the stove. Residual heat will finish cooking the eggs.

3. Toast sandwich thin halves. Create your sandwiches by layering 1 slice tomato, 1/2 slice turkey, 1/2 slice ham, 1/2 slice cheese, and 1 egg on each piece of bread.

EXCHANGES/CHOICES
1 starch, 1 1/2 lean protein

CALORIES 150 | CALORIES FROM FAT 45 | TOTAL FAT 5g | SATURATED FAT 2g | TRANS FAT 0g
CHOLESTEROL 25mg | SODIUM 430mg | POTASSIUM 220mg | TOTAL CARBOHYDRATE 12g
DIETARY FIBER 2g | SUGARS 3g | PROTEIN 13g | PHOSPHORUS 185mg

SÁNDWICH ABIERTO DE HUEVO

Se trata de un sándwich rápido que pueden preparar si están apurados por la mañana. Contiene proteínas y también grasas y carbohidratos buenos que sin duda los despertarán.

TIEMPO DE PREPARACIÓN: 5 minutos
TIEMPO DE COCCIÓN: 5 minutos
RINDE: 2 porciones
TAMAÑO DE LA PORCIÓN: 1 sándwich

1/4 cdta. de aceite de aguacate

2 huevos

1 panecillo delgado de sándwich de cereales múltiples, cortado por la mitad

2 tajadas de tomate

1 tajada (de 1/4 de pulgada) de pavo embutido, con poco sodio, cortada por la mitad

1 tajada (de 1/4 de pulgada) de jamón embutido, con poco sodio, cortada por la mitad

1 tajada de queso gouda con la grasa reducida al 2%, cortada por la mitad

1. Calentar una olla antiadherente a fuego medio-alto y agregar el aceite.

2. Partir los huevos en una vasija aparte y echarlos a la sartén. Freír los huevos aproximadamente 1 minuto y medio, y apagar la estufa. El calor residual terminará de cocinar el huevo.

3. Tostar el pan. Crear los sándwiches poniendo en capas sobre cada mitad de pan 1 tajada de tomate, 1/2 tajada de pavo, 1/2 tajada de jamón, 1/2 tajada de queso y 1 huevo.

SELECCIONES/INTERCAMBIOS
1 almidón, 1 1/2 proteínas magras

CALORÍAS 150 | **CALORÍAS DE GRASA** 45 | **TOTAL DE GRASA** 5g | **GRASA SATURADA** 2g | **GRASA TRANS** 0g
COLESTEROL 25mg | **SODIO** 430mg | **POTASIO** 220mg | **TOTAL DE CARBOHYDRATOS** 12g
FIBRA ALIMENTARIA 2g | **AZÚCARES** 3g | **PROTEÍNA** 13g | **FÓSFORO** 185mg

MORNING POWER OATS

PREP TIME: 10 minutes
COOKING TIME: 10 minutes
SERVES: 4
SERVING SIZE: 1/2 cup oats and
  1/4 cup fruit

3 1/2 cups unsweetened almond milk
1 teaspoon ground cinnamon
1 3/4 cups old-fashioned oats
1/2 cup blueberries, cut in half
1/2 cup cubed strawberries
  (1/4-inch cubes)

1. To a large saucepan, add milk and cinnamon, and bring milk to a simmer. Add oats, reduce heat to low, and stir oats for about 5 minutes. (I know stirring isn't fun, but it is the trick to some great oats.)

2. Once the oats are tender, transfer to a bowl and top with blueberries and strawberries.

EXCHANGES/CHOICES
1 starch, 1 fat-free milk

CALORIES 180 | **CALORIES FROM FAT** 45 | **TOTAL FAT** 5g | **SATURATED FAT** 0g | **TRANS FAT** 0g
CHOLESTEROL 0mg | **SODIUM** 130mg | **POTASSIUM** 280mg | **TOTAL CARBOHYDRATE** 30g
DIETARY FIBER 6g | **SUGARS** 3g | **PROTEIN** 6g | **PHOSPHORUS** 170mg

AVENA PARA LA ENERGÍA MATUTINA

TIEMPO DE PREPARACIÓN: 10 minutos
TIEMPO DE COCCIÓN: 10 minutos
RINDE: 4 porciones
TAMAÑO DE LA PORCIÓN: 1/2 taza de avena
y 1/4 taza de fruta

---

3 1/2 tazas de leche de almendras sin azúcar

1 cdta. de canela molida

1 3/4 tazas de avena entera tradicional

1/2 taza de arándanos *(blueberries)*, cortados por la mitad

1/2 taza de fresas, cortadas en cubos de 1/4 de pulgada

1. Echar en una olla grande la leche y la canela, y hervir a fuego lento. Agregar la avena, poner a fuego lento, y cocer revolviendo por unos 5 minutos. (Sé que revolver no es divertido, pero el truco para preparar avena excelente es ese).

2. Una vez que la avena esté blanda, pasar a una vasija y echar encima los arándanos y las fresas.

SELECCIONES/INTERCAMBIOS
1 almidón, 1 leche descremada

CALORÍAS 180 | **CALORÍAS DE GRASA** 45 | **TOTAL DE GRASA** 5g | **GRASA SATURADA** 0g | **GRASA TRANS** 0g
COLESTEROL 0mg | **SODIO** 130mg | **POTASIO** 280mg | **TOTAL DE CARBOHYDRATOS** 30g
FIBRA ALIMENTARIA 6g | **AZÚCARES** 3g | **PROTEÍNA** 6g | **FÓSFORO** 170mg

Baked Egg with Avocado, Tomato, and Citrus Salad

PREP TIME: 15 minutes
COOKING TIME: 2–5 minutes
SERVES: 2
SERVING SIZE: 1 egg and 1/2 salad

2 eggs
2 teaspoons canola oil, divided
1 fluid ounce lime juice
1 teaspoon kosher salt
1/2 teaspoon cracked black pepper
2 ounces Hass avocado, cubed
1 large tomato, thinly sliced
2 ounces red onion, peeled and thinly
  sliced
1/4 cup finely chopped cilantro

1. Preheat oven to 400°F.

2. Crack each egg into a separate bowl without breaking the yolks. Set aside.

3. Preheat small ovenproof pan and add 1 teaspoon canola oil. Add eggs, and immediately transfer pan to the oven. Cook for about 2–5 minutes, or until eggs reach desired doneness.

4. In a small bowl add remaining canola oil, lime juice, salt, and pepper, and whisk ingredients together to create the dressing. Add avocado, tomato, red onion, and cilantro to the dressing, and toss.

5. Remove eggs from oven. Plate salad ingredients first and top with the eggs. Serve.

EXCHANGES/CHOICES
2 vegetable, 1 medium-fat protein, 2 fat

CALORIES 190 | **CALORIES FROM FAT** 130 | **TOTAL FAT** 14g | **SATURATED FAT** 2.5g | **TRANS FAT** 0g
CHOLESTEROL 185mg | **SODIUM** 80mg | **POTASSIUM** 500mg | **TOTAL CARBOHYDRATE** 11g
DIETARY FIBER 4g | **SUGARS** 4g | **PROTEIN** 8g | **PHOSPHORUS** 150mg

HUEVOS AL HORNO CON ENSALADA DE AGUACATE, TOMATE Y CÍTRICOS

TIEMPO DE PREPARACIÓN: 15 minutos
TIEMPO DE COCCIÓN: 2-5 minutos
RINDE: 2 porciones
TAMAÑO DE LA PORCIÓN: 1 huevo
   y 1/2 ensalada

---

2 huevos
2 cdtas. de aceite de canola, en partes
1 onza líquida de jugo de lima o limón
   verde
1 cdta. de sal *kosher*
1/2 cdta. de pimienta negra gruesa
2 onzas de aguacate Hass, en cubos
1 tomate grande, en tajadas finas
2 onzas de cebolla roja, pelada y en
   tajadas finas
1/4 taza de cilantro finamente picado

1. Calentar el horno a 400°F.

2. Partir los huevos en un recipiente separado, sin romper la yema. Poner de lado.

3. Calentar una sartén pequeña que se pueda meter al horno y agregar 1 cdta. de aceite de canola. Agregar los huevos y meter la sartén al horno de inmediato. Hornear unos 2-5 minutos o hasta que los huevos lleguen al punto de cocción deseado.

4. En una vasija pequeña echar el resto del aceite de canola, el jugo de limón verde, sal y pimienta, y batir los ingredientes para crear la salsa. Agregar el aguacate, tomate, cebolla roja y cilantro al aliño, y revolver.

5. Retirar los huevos del horno. Poner en el plato los ingredientes de la ensalada primero y luego poner los huevos encima. Servir.

SELECCIONES/INTERCAMBIOS
2 vegetales, 1 proteína con grasa moderada, 2 grasas

CALORÍAS 190 | **CALORÍAS DE GRASA** 130 | **TOTAL DE GRASA** 14g | **GRASA SATURADA** 2.5g | **GRASA TRANS** 0g
COLESTEROL 185mg | **SODIO** 80mg | **POTASIO** 500mg | **TOTAL DE CARBOHYDRATOS** 11g
FIBRA ALIMENTARIA 4g | **AZÚCARES** 4g | **PROTEÍNA** 8g | **FÓSFORO** 150mg

TIA MARIA'S *PAPAS CRIOLLAS*

Who is Maria? She is my aunt. When I was growing up in Colombia, she would sell fried baby yellow potatoes sprinkled with salt. They were buttery, soft, and delicious. This is my version of her dish with an added touch of Cuban sazón.

PREP TIME: 15 minutes
COOKING TIME: 55 minutes
SERVES: 4
SERVING SIZE: 4 ounces

1 pound baby yellow potatoes, washed and halved
1/2 cup finely chopped yellow onion
1/2 cup finely chopped red pepper
1/4 teaspoon dried oregano
4 sprigs fresh thyme leaves
1 clove garlic, peeled and finely chopped
1/4 teaspoon sea salt
1 teaspoon cracked black pepper
1/4 teaspoon ground cumin
2 teaspoons avocado oil
2 cups canned crushed tomatoes
1 cup unsalted chicken stock

1. Preheat oven to 400°F.

2. Place potatoes on a baking sheet and cook in the oven for 30 minutes.

3. While potatoes cook, add onion, red pepper, oregano, thyme, garlic, salt, pepper, and cumin to a mixing bowl. Toss ingredients well.

4. Preheat skillet over medium heat. Once pan is hot, add oil and wait 10 seconds for oil to heat up. Add mixture from the bowl and sauté over medium heat until ingredients are translucent or shiny, about 5 minutes.

5. Add crushed tomatoes and chicken stock to the skillet. Reduce heat to low and simmer gently for 15 minutes.

6. Once potatoes are done cooking, add to the skillet and simmer for about 5 minutes. Serve.

RONALDO'S TIP

If you have any fresh herbs hanging around, add a little bit to the dish to elevate the flavor.

EXCHANGES/CHOICES
2 starch, 1/2 fat

CALORIES 180 | **CALORIES FROM FAT** 25 | **TOTAL FAT** 3g | **SATURATED FAT** 0.5g | **TRANS FAT** 0g
CHOLESTEROL 0mg | **SODIUM** 370mg | **POTASSIUM** 970mg | **TOTAL CARBOHYDRATE** 34g
DIETARY FIBER 5g | **SUGARS** 8g | **PROTEIN** 6g | **PHOSPHORUS** 135mg

PAPAS CRIOLLAS DE TÍA MARÍA

¿Quién es María? Cuando yo era niño en Colombia, mi tía María vendía papitas amarillas fritas con sal. Eran mantecosas, suaves y deliciosas. Esta es mi versión de su plato, con un toque de sazón cubana.

TIEMPO DE PREPARACIÓN: 15 minutos
TIEMPO DE COCCIÓN: 55 minutos
RINDE: 4 porciones
TAMAÑO DE LA PORCIÓN: 4 onzas

1 libra de papitas amarillas, lavadas y partidas por la mitad

1/2 taza de cebolla amarilla, finamente picada

1/2 taza de cebolla roja, finamente picada

1/4 cdta. de orégano seco

Hojas de 4 ramitas de tomillo fresco, sin tallos

1 diente de ajo, pelado y finamente picado

1/4 cdta. de sal marina

1 cdta. de pimienta negra gruesa

1/4 cdta. de comino

2 cdtas. de aceite de aguacate

2 tazas de tomate enlatado, aplastado

1 taza de caldo de pollo sin sal

1. Calentar el horno a 400°F.

2. Colocar las papas en una lata y hornear 30 minutos.

3. Mientras las papas están en el horno, echar la cebolla, pimiento rojo, orégano, tomillo, ajo, sal, pimienta y comino a una vasija. Mezclar bien los ingredientes.

4. Calentar una sartén a fuego medio. Una vez que la sartén esté caliente, echar el aceite y espere 10 segundos hasta que se caliente. Agregar la mezcla de la vasija y saltear hasta que los vegetales estén traslúcidos o relucientes, aproximadamente 5 minutos.

5. Echar los tomates aplastados y el caldo a la sartén. Bajar el fuego y cocer a fuego lento 15 minutos.

6. Una vez que las papas estén cocidas, echarlas a la sartén y cocer a fuego lento unos 5 minutos. Servir.

CONSEJO DE RONALDO

Si tienen hierbas frescas por allí, échenle un poco al plato para darle más sabor.

SELECCIONES/INTERCAMBIOS
2 almidón, 1/2 grasa

CALORÍAS 180 | **CALORÍAS DE GRASA** 25 | **TOTAL DE GRASA** 3g | **GRASA SATURADA** 0.5g | **GRASA TRANS** 0g
COLESTEROL 0mg | **SODIO** 370mg | **POTASIO** 970mg | **TOTAL DE CARBOHYDRATOS** 34g
FIBRA ALIMENTARIA 5g | **AZÚCARES** 8g | **PROTEÍNA** 6g | **FÓSFORO** 135mg

Mashed Pumpkin Skillet with Baked Eggs

PREP TIME: 15 minutes
COOKING TIME: 25 minutes
SERVES: 2
SERVING SIZE: 1/2 of the skillet

1 cup peeled, cubed pumpkin
   (1/2-inch cubes)
Parchment paper
1/8 teaspoon pumpkin pie spice
1/8 teaspoon ground nutmeg
1 whole egg
3 tablespoons egg whites
1 teaspoon canola oil
1/4 cup peeled and cubed yellow onion
   (1/8-inch cubes)
1/4 teaspoon sea salt
1/4 teaspoon cracked black pepper
1/8 teaspoon ground thyme

1. Preheat oven to 400°F.

2. Place pumpkin cubes on baking sheet lined with parchment paper. Sprinkle pumpkin pie spice and nutmeg on pumpkin. Place in oven for 15 minutes, or until fork tender. Remove from oven and set aside.

3. Crack egg into a bowl, add egg whites, and whisk briskly for 30 seconds.

4. Preheat skillet or ovenproof pan over medium heat, add oil, and wait 10 seconds for oil to heat up. Add onions, salt, pepper, and thyme, and sauté until onions are translucent or shiny. Add pumpkin to the skillet and mash with fork. Add egg mixture to skillet and place it in oven for 8 minutes. Remove from oven and enjoy.

EXCHANGES/CHOICES
1/2 starch, 1 medium-fat protein

CALORIES 90 | **CALORIES FROM FAT** 45 | **TOTAL FAT** 5g | **SATURATED FAT** 1g | **TRANS FAT** 0g
CHOLESTEROL 95mg | **SODIUM** 310mg | **POTASSIUM** 310mg | **TOTAL CARBOHYDRATE** 7g
DIETARY FIBER 1g | **SUGARS** 3g | **PROTEIN** 7g | **PHOSPHORUS** 85mg

CAZUELA DE PURÉ DE CALABAZA CON HUEVOS AL HORNO

TIEMPO DE PREPARACIÓN: 15 minutos
TIEMPO DE COCCIÓN: 25 minutos
RINDE: 2 porciones
TAMAÑO DE LA PORCIÓN: 1/2 cazuela

1 taza de calabaza pelada y cortada en cubos de 1/2 pulgada

Papel mantequilla

1/8 cdta. de especias de tarta de calabaza (*pumpkin spice*)

1/8 cdta. de nuez moscada molida

1 huevo entero

3 cdas. de claras de huevo

1 cdta. de aceite de canola

1/4 taza de cebolla amarilla, pelada y cortada en cubos de 1/8 de pulgada

1/4 cdta. de sal marina

1/4 cdta. de pimienta negra gruesa

1/8 cdta. de tomillo en polvo

1. Calentar el horno a 400°F.

2. Colocar los cubitos de calabaza en una lata para hornear cubierta con papel mantequilla. Echar las especias y nuez moscada a la calabaza. Hornear 15 minutos o hasta que la calabaza esté blanda cuando se pinche con un tenedor. Sacar del horno y poner de lado.

3. Partir el huevo en una vasija, agregar las claras de huevo y batir enérgicamente 30 segundos.

4. Calentar la sartén o recipiente que se pueda meter al horno a fuego medio, agregar el aceite y esperar 10 segundos para que se caliente. Agregar la cebolla, sal, pimienta y tomillo, y saltear hasta que la cebolla esté traslúcida o reluciente. Echar la calabaza a la sartén y aplastar con un tenedor. Agregar la mezcla de huevo a la sartén y meter al horno 8 minutos. Retirar del horno y disfrutar.

SELECCIONES/INTERCAMBIOS
1/2 almidón, 1 proteína con grasa moderada

CALORÍAS 90 | **CALORÍAS DE GRASA** 45 | **TOTAL DE GRASA** 5g | **GRASA SATURADA** 1g | **GRASA TRANS** 0g
COLESTEROL 95mg | **SODIO** 310mg | **POTASIO** 310mg | **TOTAL DE CARBOHYDRATOS** 7g
FIBRA ALIMENTARIA 1g | **AZÚCARES** 3g | **PROTEÍNA** 7g | **FÓSFORO** 85mg

PAISAS' SCRAMBLED EGGS

Want to get the family out of bed in the morning with an amazing smell? This recipe has an aroma as effective as a freshly brewed pot of coffee. I love breakfast, and it's a must that I eat some sort of egg dish. This recipe is my favorite way to cook eggs.

PREP TIME: 10 minutes
COOKING TIME: 10–15 minutes
SERVES: 2
SERVING SIZE: 1/2 of the eggs

1/2 cup washed and cubed Roma tomatoes
1/4 medium Spanish onion, cut into small cubes (about 1/2 cup)
1/4 teaspoon kosher salt
Pinch cracked black pepper
1/4 teaspoon garlic powder
6 tablespoons egg whites
2 whole eggs, whisked
2 tablespoons fat-free cottage cheese

1. Preheat a nonstick pan over medium heat. Once pan is hot, add tomatoes and onion, and sauté until they are soft. Add salt, pepper, and garlic powder, and mix well so flavors distribute evenly.

2. Add egg whites to the bowl with whisked eggs; whisk briefly to incorporate. Add egg mixture to the pan and scramble eggs until they are cooked through, about 1–2 minutes. Top each serving with 1 tablespoon cottage cheese and enjoy!

EXCHANGES/CHOICES
1/2 starch, 1 medium-fat protein

CALORIES 110 | **CALORIES FROM FAT** 45 | **TOTAL FAT** 5g | **SATURATED FAT** 2g | **TRANS FAT** 0g
CHOLESTEROL 190mg | **SODIUM** 370mg | **POTASSIUM** 250mg | **TOTAL CARBOHYDRATE** 7g
DIETARY FIBER 1g | **SUGARS** 3g | **PROTEIN** 9g | **PHOSPHORUS** 135mg

HUEVOS REVUELTOS DE PAISAS

¿Quieren hacer que la familia se levante con un aroma fabuloso de mañana? Esta receta es tan eficaz como el café recién preparado. Me encanta el desayuno, y para mí es imprescindible comer algún platillo con huevo. Esta receta es mi manera favorita de preparar huevos.

TIEMPO DE PREPARACIÓN: 10 minutos
TIEMPO DE COCCIÓN: 10-15 minutos
RINDE: 2 porciones
TAMAÑO DE LA PORCIÓN: Mitad de los huevos

1/2 taza de tomates Roma, lavados y cortados en cubos pequeños

1/4 cebolla española mediana, cortada en cubos pequeños (aproximadamente 1/2 taza)

1/4 cdta. de sal *kosher*

1 pizca de pimienta negra gruesa

1/4 cdta. de ajo en polvo

6 cdas. de claras de huevo

2 huevos enteros, batidos

2 cdas. de requesón o queso cabaña descremado

1. Calentar una sartén antiadherente a fuego medio. Cuando esté caliente, echar el tomate y la cebolla, y saltear hasta que se pongan blandos. Agregar la sal, pimienta y ajo en polvo, y mezclar bien para que los sabores se distribuyan uniformemente.

2. Echar las claras de huevo a la vasija con los huevos batidos y batir brevemente para incorporar. Agregar la mezcla de huevo a la sartén y revolver los huevos hasta que estén cocidos, aproximadamente 1-2 minutos. Echar a cada porción 1 cda. de requesón ¡y disfrutar!

SELECCIONES/INTERCAMBIOS
1/2 almidón, 1 proteína con grasa moderada

CALORÍAS 110 | **CALORÍAS DE GRASA** 45 | **TOTAL DE GRASA** 5g | **GRASA SATURADA** 2g | **GRASA TRANS** 0g
COLESTEROL 190mg | **SODIO** 370mg | **POTASIO** 250mg | **TOTAL DE CARBOHYDRATOS** 7g
FIBRA ALIMENTARIA 1g | **AZÚCARES** 3g | **PROTEÍNA** 9g | **FÓSFORO** 135mg

Green Vegetable Egg Tortilla

Adding lots of greens to your morning meal charges your body with some incredible nutrition. This recipe is a great way to get you through the first part of the day. Breakfast doesn't have to mean hitting the drive-through window at a doughnut or coffee shop. The time we spend waiting to place our order at the drive-through could be spent making an awesome, healthy breakfast like this one. Have a great day!

PREP TIME: 10 minutes
COOKING TIME: 15 minutes
SERVES: 4
SERVING SIZE: 1/4 of the tortilla

2 stalks green onion, finely sliced
2 crowns broccoli, finely sliced
  (about 1 cup)
1/2 cup washed and cubed Roma
  tomatoes
1 cup spinach, washed and thinly sliced
1/2 teaspoon kosher salt
1 teaspoon garlic powder
1 teaspoon dried oregano
1/4 teaspoon cracked black pepper
1/2 teaspoon Spanish smoked paprika
4 eggs, whisked
1/2 cup fat-free milk

1. Preheat oven to 350°F.

2. To a bowl, add green onion, broccoli, tomato, spinach, salt, garlic powder, oregano, pepper, and smoked paprika. Toss ingredients well to make sure greens are covered with the spices.

3. Preheat an ovenproof nonstick pan over medium heat. Add vegetables from the bowl and sauté until ingredients are cooked through, about 2 minutes.

4. Add milk to the bowl with whisked eggs and whisk briefly to combine. Add egg mixture to pan and stir with a wooden or plastic spoon. Make sure all ingredients are evenly spread out.

5. Place pan in the middle rack of your oven and cook for 10 minutes. To check if the tortilla (egg and vegetable mixture) is done, insert a toothpick in the middle; if it comes out clean, the tortilla is cooked through.

6. Remove from oven and let it rest on the stovetop for 1–2 minutes so eggs settle and don't fall apart when serving. Enjoy!

EXCHANGES/CHOICES
1 vegetable, 1 medium-fat protein

CALORIES 100 | **CALORIES FROM FAT** 45 | **TOTAL FAT** 5g | **SATURATED FAT** 2g | **TRANS FAT** 0g
CHOLESTEROL 185mg | **SODIUM** 340mg | **POTASSIUM** 350mg | **TOTAL CARBOHYDRATE** 7g
DIETARY FIBER 1g | **SUGARS** 3g | **PROTEIN** 9g | **PHOSPHORUS** 165mg

OMELET DE VERDURAS

Agregar muchas verduras a su comida matutina los recarga de energía con excelentes nutrientes. Esta receta es una estupenda manera de empezar el día. No es necesario comprar el desayuno en la ventanilla de la pastelería o cafetería. El tiempo que nos toma ir al restaurante y esperar para pedir el desayuno en el drive-through lo podemos pasar preparando un desayuno saludable como este. ¡Que tengan un día maravilloso!

TIEMPO DE PREPARACIÓN: 10 minutos
TIEMPO DE COCCIÓN: 15 minutos
RINDE: 4 porciones
TAMAÑO DE LA PORCIÓN: 1/4 de tortilla

Tallos de 2 cebollines (*green onion*), cortados en rodajas finas

2 cabezas de brócoli, en rodajas finas (aproximadamente 1 taza)

1/2 taza de tomates Roma, lavados y cortados en cubos pequeños

1 taza de espinaca, lavada y cortada en tiras delgadas

1/2 cdta. de sal kosher

1 cdta. de ajo en polvo

1 cdta. de orégano seco

1/4 cdta. de pimienta negra gruesa

1/2 cdta. de pimentón español ahumado (*paprika*)

4 huevos, batidos

1/2 taza de leche descremada

1. Calentar el horno a 350°F.

2. En una vasija echar el cebollín, brócoli, tomate, espinaca, sal, ajo en polvo, orégano, pimienta y pimentón. Mezclar bien los ingredientes para asegurarse de que las especias cubran bien las verduras.

3. Calentar a fuego medio una sartén antiadherente que se pueda meter al horno. Agregar los vegetales de la vasija y sofreír hasta que los ingredientes estén cocidos por dentro, aproximadamente 2 minutos.

4. Echar la leche a la vasija con los huevos batidos y batir brevemente para incorporar. Agregar la mezcla de huevos a la sartén, y mezclar con un cucharón de madera o plástico. Asegurarse de que todos los ingredientes estén repartidos uniformemente.

5. Colocar la sartén en la rejilla del medio del horno y hornear 10 minutos. Para verificar que la tortilla esté lista, insertar un palito de dientes en el medio; si sale limpio, la tortilla está cocida por dentro.

6. Retirar del horno y enfriar en la estufa 1-2 minutos para que los huevos se cuajen más y no se desmoronen al servir. ¡A disfrutar!

SELECCIONES/INTERCAMBIOS
1 vegetal, 1 proteína con grasa moderada

CALORÍAS 100 | **CALORÍAS DE GRASA** 45 | **TOTAL DE GRASA** 5g | **GRASA SATURADA** 2g | **GRASA TRANS** 0g
COLESTEROL 185mg | **SODIO** 340mg | **POTASIO** 350mg | **TOTAL DE CARBOHYDRATOS** 7g
FIBRA ALIMENTARIA 1g | **AZÚCARES** 3g | **PROTEÍNA** 9g | **FÓSFORO** 165mg

MORNING COCONUT PANCAKES

PREP TIME: 35 minutes
COOKING TIME: 3–4 minutes per pancake
SERVES: 8
SERVING SIZE: 1 pancake

1/2 cup coconut flour
1 teaspoon baking soda
1/4 teaspoon salt
1/4 teaspoon ground nutmeg
1/4 teaspoon ground cinnamon
1 teaspoon vanilla extract
6 tablespoons egg whites (about 2 eggs
    minus the yolk)
1 whole egg
1 cup 2% milk
1 cup blueberries
2 teaspoons avocado oil, divided

1. To a bowl, add coconut flour, baking soda, salt, nutmeg, and cinnamon. Stir to combine ingredients.

2. Into a separate bowl add vanilla, egg whites, egg, milk, blueberries, and 1 teaspoon avocado oil. Whisk briskly until smooth. Add wet mixture to the dry ingredients and whisk once more until you have a smooth batter. Cover with plastic wrap and place in the refrigerator for 20 minutes.

3. Remove bowl from the refrigerator and fold mixture with a plastic spatula.

4. Preheat large nonstick pan over medium-high heat, add remaining 1 teaspoon oil, and wait for oil to heat up. Using a ladle, pour pancake mix into the pan to create a 4 × 4-inch pancake. Cook each side of the pancake for about 1 minute 30 seconds. Repeat until you have cooked all the batter. Serve.

RONALDO'S TIP

You may have to adjust the heat while cooking your pancakes. If the pan gets too hot, it increases the chance of your pancakes burning.

EXCHANGES/CHOICES
1/2 starch, 1/2 fat

CALORIES 70 | **CALORIES FROM FAT** 25 | **TOTAL FAT** 3g | **SATURATED FAT** 1.5g | **TRANS FAT** 0g
CHOLESTEROL 25mg | **SODIUM** 270mg | **POTASSIUM** 85mg | **TOTAL CARBOHYDRATE** 7g
DIETARY FIBER 2g | **SUGARS** 4g | **PROTEIN** 4g | **PHOSPHORUS** 45mg

PANQUEQUES DE COCO

TIEMPO DE PREPARACIÓN: 35 minutos
TIEMPO DE COCCIÓN: 3-4 minutos por
  panqueque
RINDE: 8 porciones
TAMAÑO DE LA PORCIÓN: 1 panqueque

1/2 taza de harina de coco
1 cdta. de bicarbonato de sodio
1/4 cdta. de sal
1/4 cdta. de nuez moscada molida
1/4 cdta. de canela molida
1 cdta. de extracto de vainilla
6 cdas. de claras de huevo
  (aproximadamente 2 huevos
  sin la yema)
1 huevo entero
1 taza de leche con 2% de grasa
1 taza de arándanos (*blueberries*)
2 cdtas. de aceite de aguacate,
  en partes

1. En una vasija, agregar la harina de coco, el bicarbonato, la sal, la nuez moscada y la canela. Mezclar todos los ingredientes.

2. En otra vasija, agregar la vainilla, claras de huevo, huevo, leche, arándanos y 1 cdta. de aceite de aguacate. Batir enérgicamente hasta que tenga consistencia uniforme. Agregar la mezcla de ingredientes húmedos a los secos y volver a batir hasta que la masa tenga consistencia uniforme. Tapar con plástico y meter en el refrigerador 20 minutos.

3. Retirar la vasija del refrigerador y mezclar con una espátula de plástico.

4. Calentar una sartén antiadherente grande a fuego medio-alto, agregar la cdta. restante de aceite y esperar que se caliente. Usando un cucharón, echar la mezcla en la sartén para crear un panqueque de 4 × 4 pulgadas. Cocer cada lado del panqueque 1 minuto y medio. Repetir hasta que la masa se acabe. Servir.

CONSEJO DE RONALDO

Quizá sea necesario usar una temperatura más alta o baja para los panqueques. Si la sartén se calienta demasiado, es más probable que los panqueques se quemen.

SELECCIONES/INTERCAMBIOS
1/2 almidón, 1/2 grasa

CALORÍAS 70 | **CALORÍAS DE GRASA** 25 | **TOTAL DE GRASA** 3g | **GRASA SATURADA** 1.5g | **GRASA TRANS** 0g | **COLESTEROL** 25mg | **SODIO** 270mg | **POTASIO** 85mg | **TOTAL DE CARBOHYDRATOS** 7g | **FIBRA ALIMENTARIA** 2g | **AZÚCARES** 4g | **PROTEÍNA** 4g | **FÓSFORO** 45mg

FARMERS' MARKET DISHES

PLATOS CON INGREDIENTES DEL
MERCADO DE AGRICULTORES

This chapter demonstrates how to use the ingredients you buy at the farmers' market. I've provided information on what to look for while shopping and how to choose the best vegetables, potatoes, and fruits in Why the Farmers' Market? (on page 8). In almost every town you'll find a market with local, inexpensive produce. What better way to introduce you to the joys of the farmers' market than with some delicious, farmers' market—inspired recipes!

Este capítulo demuestra cómo utilizar los ingredientes que se compran en el mercado de agricultores. Les aconsejo qué buscar y cómo escoger las mejores verduras, papas y frutas en ¿Por qué el mercado de agricultores? (en la pág. 9). En casi todas las ciudades se puede encontrar un mercado con productos locales de bajo costo. ¿Qué mejor manera de hacerles probar los tesoros del mercado de agricultores que unas cuantas recetas deliciosas que usan como fuente de inspiración el mercado de agricultores?

—Chef Ronaldo

Butternut Squash Soup

PREP TIME: 20 minutes
COOKING TIME: 40 minutes
SERVES: 8
SERVING SIZE: 1 cup soup and 1 tablespoon
 yogurt topping

1 tablespoon avocado oil

1 medium Spanish onion, peeled and
 finely chopped (about 1 cup)

1 poblano pepper, washed and finely
 chopped

1 (2-pound) butternut squash, peeled
 and cut into 1/2-inch cubes

1 teaspoon kosher salt

1 teaspoon cracked black pepper

1/4 teaspoon ground cumin

1/4 teaspoon ground cinnamon
 plus dash

1/4 teaspoon ground nutmeg plus dash

8 cups unsalted chicken stock, divided

1 tablespoon lime juice

1/2 cup fat-free plain Greek yogurt

1. To a large pot, add avocado oil, onions, and poblano pepper, and cook on medium heat until onions are translucent.

2. Add butternut squash, salt, pepper, cumin, cinnamon, and nutmeg. Stir ingredients together, add 2 cups stock, and simmer for 25 minutes or until squash is fork tender.

3. Turn off the heat and transfer ingredients to a blender. Working in a few batches to prevent splatter, purée the mixture. Once you have a smooth purée, pour mixture back into the pot along with the remaining stock and place over medium-low heat. Simmer for 10–15 minutes.

4. Meanwhile, add yogurt and a dash of nutmeg and cinnamon to a mixing bowl. Fold until all ingredients are incorporated.

5. Ladle soup into bowls. Top with 1 tablespoon yogurt topping, and serve. The end result should give you goose bumps.

EXCHANGES/CHOICES
1 starch, 1 vegetable, 1/2 fat

CALORIES 130 | CALORIES FROM FAT 25 | TOTAL FAT 3g | SATURATED FAT 1g | TRANS FAT 0g
CHOLESTEROL 0mg | SODIUM 330mg | POTASSIUM 700mg | TOTAL CARBOHYDRATE 20g
DIETARY FIBER 3g | SUGARS 5g | PROTEIN 7g | PHOSPHORUS 140mg

SOPA DE CALABAZA (TIPO *BUTTERNUT*)

TIEMPO DE PREPARACIÓN: 20 minutos
TIEMPO DE COCCIÓN: 40 minutos
RINDE: 8 porciones
TAMAÑO DE LA PORCIÓN: 1 taza de sopa
y 1 cda. de yogur para echar encima

1 cda. de aceite de aguacate

1 cebolla española, pelada y finamente picada (aproximadamente 1 taza)

1 chile poblano, lavado y finamente picado

1 calabaza (tipo *butternut*) de 2 libras, pelada y cortada en cubos de 1/2 pulgada

1 cdta. de sal *kosher*

1 cdta. de pimienta negra gruesa

1/4 cdta. de comino

1/4 cdta. de canela molida más una pizca

1/4 cdta. de nuez moscada, más una pizca

8 tazas de caldo de pollo sin sal, en partes

1 cda. de jugo de lima o limón verde

1/2 taza de yogur griego de sabor natural, descremado

1. En una olla grande, echar el aceite de aguacate, cebolla y chile poblano, y dorar a fuego medio hasta que la cebolla esté traslúcida.

2. Echar la calabaza, sal, pimienta, comino, canela y nuez moscada. Mezclar bien los ingredientes, añadir 2 tazas de caldo y cocer a fuego lento 25 minutos o hasta que la calabaza esté blanda cuando se pinche con un tenedor.

3. Apagar el fuego y pasar los ingredientes a la licuadora. Licuar la mezcla en tandas para evitar salpicar. Una vez que el puré tenga consistencia uniforme, echar la mezcla en la olla con el caldo restante, a fuego medio-bajo. Hervir a fuego lento 10–15 minutos.

4. Mientras tanto, poner en una vasija el yogur con una pizca de nuez moscada y canela. Mezclar los ingredientes con movimientos suaves para que se incorporen.

5. Llenar tazones de sopa con un cucharón. Echar encima 1 cda. del yogur y servir. El resultado final hará que se le ponga la piel de gallina.

SELECCIONES/INTERCAMBIOS
1 almidón, 1 vegetal, 1/2 grasa

CALORÍAS 130 | **CALORÍAS DE GRASA** 25 | **TOTAL DE GRASA** 3g | **GRASA SATURADA** 1g | **GRASA TRANS** 0g
COLESTEROL 0mg | **SODIO** 330mg | **POTASIO** 700mg | **TOTAL DE CARBOHIDRATOS** 20g
FIBRA ALIMENTARIA 3g | **AZÚCARES** 5g | **PROTEÍNA** 7g | **FÓSFORO** 140mg

PLANTAIN AND SWEET POTATO SOUP

PREP TIME: 25 minutes
COOKING TIME: 1 hour 30 minutes
SERVES: 10
SERVING SIZE: 3/4 cup

---

3 green plantains
1 large (1 1/2-pound) sweet potato, peeled and cut into 1/2-inch cubes
1 medium Spanish onion (about 1 cup), peeled and finely chopped
2 sticks celery, washed and finely diced
64 ounces unsalted chicken stock
1 teaspoon kosher salt
1 teaspoon fennel seed
1 teaspoon cracked black pepper
1 teaspoon ground cinnamon
2 tablespoons lime juice
3 tablespoons finely chopped cilantro

1. Cut both ends off plantains with a chef's knife. Insert tip of knife into the plantain and run from top to bottom with curved part of the plantain facing you. (Repeat 5 times per plantain to make peeling easier.) Once you have made the slits, place plantains in a pot filled with hot water for about 5 minutes, until the water loosens the shell from the plantains. Working on one plantain at a time, remove from water and peel shell with your thumb. Cut plantains into 1/2-inch cubes and return to the water.

2. To a large pot, add plantains, sweet potato, onion, celery, chicken stock, salt, fennel seed, pepper, and cinnamon. Stir ingredients well with a large ladle. Bring soup up to a gentle simmer. Simmer on low for about 1 hour 30 minutes.

3. Serve each portion garnished with lime juice and cilantro.

EXCHANGES/CHOICES
2 1/2 starch

CALORIES 180 | **CALORIES FROM FAT** 10 | **TOTAL FAT** 1g | **SATURATED FAT** 0g | **TRANS FAT** 0g
CHOLESTEROL 0mg | **SODIUM** 300mg | **POTASSIUM** 780mg | **TOTAL CARBOHYDRATE** 41g
DIETARY FIBER 4g | **SUGARS** 14g | **PROTEIN** 6g | **PHOSPHORUS** 115mg

SOPA DE PLÁTANO Y BATATA

TIEMPO DE PREPARACIÓN: 25 minutos
TIEMPO DE COCCIÓN: 1 hora y media
RINDE: 10 porciones
TAMAÑO DE LA PORCIÓN: 3/4 taza

3 plátanos verdes

1 batata o boniato grande
(1 1/2 libras), pelado y cortado en
cubos de 1/2 pulgada

1 cebolla española mediana
(aproximadamente 1 taza), pelada
y finamente picada

2 tallos de apio, lavados y finamente
picados

64 onzas de caldo de pollo sin sal

1 cdta. de sal *kosher*

1 cdta. de semillas de hinojo

1 cdta. de pimienta negra gruesa

1 cdta. de canela molida

2 cdas. de jugo de lima o limón verde

3 cdas. de cilantro finamente picado

1. Cortar ambos extremos de los plátanos con un cuchillo de chef. Meter la punta de un cuchillo en el plátano y cortar de arriba a abajo (con la parte curva hacia arriba). (Repetir 5 veces por plátano para poder pelarlos más fácilmente). Una vez que se hagan los cortes, colocar los plátanos en una olla llena de agua caliente unos 5 minutos, hasta que el agua afloje la cáscara de los plátanos. Sacar los plátanos del agua, uno por uno, y pelar la cáscara con el pulgar. Cortar los plátanos en cubos de 1/2 pulgada y volver a echar al agua.

2. En una olla grande, echar los plátanos, batata, cebolla, apio, caldo de pollo, sal, hinojo, pimienta y canela. Mezclar bien los ingredientes con un cucharón grande de sopa. Hervir la sopa a fuego lento aproximadamente 1 hora y media.

3. Servir cada porción con jugo de limón verde y cilantro.

SELECCIONES/INTERCAMBIOS
2 1/2 almidones

CALORÍAS 180 | **CALORÍAS DE GRASA** 10 | **TOTAL DE GRASA** 1g | **GRASA SATURADA** 0g | **GRASA TRANS** 0g
COLESTEROL 0mg | **SODIO** 300mg | **POTASIO** 780mg | **TOTAL DE CARBOHIDRATOS** 41g
FIBRA ALIMENTARIA 4g | **AZÚCARES** 14g | **PROTEÍNA** 6g | **FÓSFORO** 115mg

MI MADRE'S SLAW

My mom would make slaw as a topping for burgers when we were kids. That slaw was so good it could stand on its own; maybe it was all the mayonnaise she added. Here is my healthier, dressed-up version of her slaw.

1. Add the cabbage, onion, cilantro, apple, and avocado to a bowl, and toss gently. Set aside.

2. To make the dressing, add all dressing ingredients to a separate bowl. Whisk briskly for 30 seconds.

3. Pour dressing over cabbage mixture, making sure you get all the dressing from the bowl. Toss cabbage mixture with your hands to finish the slaw.

PREP TIME: 15 minutes
ASSEMBLY TIME: 5 minutes
SERVES: 4
SERVING SIZE: 1 cup

SLAW
2 1/2 cups finely shredded white cabbage

1 small red onion, peeled and thinly sliced (about 1 cup)

3 tablespoons finely chopped cilantro

1 Granny Smith apple, peeled and thinly sliced

1 (4-ounce) Hass avocado, flesh scooped out

DRESSING
2 tablespoons fresh lime juice

1 tablespoon finely chopped chives

2 tablespoons finely chopped cilantro

1 tablespoon low-fat mayonnaise

1/2 teaspoon kosher salt

1/2 teaspoon cracked black pepper

EXCHANGES/CHOICES
3 vegetable, 1 fat

CALORIES 110 | **CALORIES FROM FAT** 45 | **TOTAL FAT** 5g | **SATURATED FAT** 1g | **TRANS FAT** 0g
CHOLESTEROL 0mg | **SODIUM** 280mg | **POTASSIUM** 380mg | **TOTAL CARBOHYDRATE** 17g
DIETARY FIBER 5g | **SUGARS** 7g | **PROTEIN** 2g | **PHOSPHORUS** 55mg

ENSALADA DE COL DE MI MADRE

Cuando éramos niños, mi mamá hacía ensalada de col como salsa para la hamburguesa. Era tan rica que se podía comer sola, tal vez debido a toda la mayonesa que le echaba. Esta es mi versión más saludable de su ensalada de col, con unos cuantos toques propios.

TIEMPO DE PREPARACIÓN: 15 minutos
TIEMPO PARA ARMAR: 5 minutos
RINDE: 4 porciones
TAMAÑO DE LA PORCIÓN: 1 taza

ENSALADA DE COL

2 1/2 tazas de col o repollo blanco, finamente rallado

1 cebolla roja pequeña, pelada y en tajadas finas (aproximadamente 1 taza)

3 cdas. de cilantro finamente picado

1 manzana tipo Granny Smith, pelada y en tajadas delgadas

Pulpa de 1 aguacate Hass (de 4 onzas)

ALIÑO

2 cdas. de jugo de limón verde recién exprimido

1 cda. de cebolleta finamente picada

2 cdas. de cilantro finamente picado

1 cda. de mayonesa con poca grasa

1/2 cdta. de sal *kosher*

1/2 cdta. de pimienta negra gruesa

1. Echar la col, cebolla, cilantro, manzana y aguacate a una vasija y mezclar con movimientos suaves. Poner de lado.

2. Para hacer el aliño, echar todos los ingredientes en un recipiente separado. Batir a mano enérgicamente 30 segundos.

3. Echar el aliño a la ensalada de col, asegurándose de usar todo el aliño en la vasija. Mezclar la ensalada con las manos como toque final.

SELECCIONES/INTERCAMBIOS
3 vegetales, 1 grasa

CALORÍAS 110 | **CALORÍAS DE GRASA** 45 | **TOTAL DE GRASA** 5g | **GRASA SATURADA** 1g | **GRASA TRANS** 0g
COLESTEROL 0mg | **SODIO** 280mg | **POTASIO** 380mg | **TOTAL DE CARBOHIDRATOS** 17g
FIBRA ALIMENTARIA 5g | **AZÚCARES** 7g | **PROTEÍNA** 2g | **FÓSFORO** 55mg

Cucumber Tuna Boats

PREP TIME: 15 minutes
REFRIGERATION TIME: 10 minutes
SERVES: 8
SERVING SIZE: 2 tuna boats

7 ounces low-sodium canned tuna
(canned in water)

2 radishes, washed and finely chopped

1 plum tomato, washed and finely
chopped

2 tablespoons finely chopped cilantro

2 tablespoons lime juice

1 (4-ounce) Hass avocado, flesh
scooped out and mashed

1/2 teaspoon garlic powder

1/4 teaspoon ground ginger

1 teaspoon kosher salt

1/4 teaspoon cracked black pepper

2 large cucumbers
(about 1 1/2 pounds total)

1. In a mixing bowl, combine tuna, radishes, tomato, cilantro, lime juice, avocado, garlic powder, ginger, salt, and pepper. Incorporate ingredients well with wooden spoon. Place mixture in the refrigerator to rest while you prepare the boats.

2. Peel cucumbers and cut them in half lengthwise. Remove seeds from the center to make room for the tuna mixture.

3. Remove tuna mixture from refrigerator and add tuna to the center of all 4 cucumber halves. Cut each half into 4 equal pieces and serve.

EXCHANGES/CHOICES
1 vegetable, 1 fat

CALORIES 80 | **CALORIES FROM FAT** 25 | **TOTAL FAT** 3g | **SATURATED FAT** 0g | **TRANS FAT** 0g
CHOLESTEROL 5mg | **SODIUM** 330mg | **POTASSIUM** 380mg | **TOTAL CARBOHYDRATE** 6g
DIETARY FIBER 2g | **SUGARS** 3g | **PROTEIN** 8g | **PHOSPHORUS** 90mg

Canoas de pepinos rellenas con atún

TIEMPO DE PREPARACIÓN: 15 minutos
TIEMPO DE REFRIGERACIÓN: 10 minutos
RINDE: 8 porciones
TAMAÑO DE LA PORCIÓN: 2 canoas de atún

7 onzas de atún con poco sodio (enlatado en agua)

2 rábanos, lavados y finamente picados

1 tomate ciruela, lavado y finamente picado

2 cdas. de cilantro finamente picado

2 cdas. de jugo de lima o limón verde

Pulpa aplastada de 1 aguacate Hass (de 4 onzas)

1/2 cdta. de ajo en polvo

1/4 cdta. de jengibre en polvo

1 cdta. de sal *kosher*

1/4 cdta. de pimienta negra gruesa

2 pepinos grandes (aproximadamente 1 1/2 libras en total)

1. En una vasija, mezclar el atún, rábanos, tomate, cilantro, jugo de limón, aguacate, ajo en polvo, jengibre, sal y pimienta. Incorporar los ingredientes con un cucharón de madera. Colocar la mezcla en el refrigerador mientras prepara los pepinos.

2. Pelar los pepinos y cortarlos por la mitad, a lo largo. Extraer las semillas del centro a fin de hacer espacio para la mezcla de atún.

3. Sacar la mezcla de atún del refrigerador y echar el atún en el centro de cada una de las 4 mitades de pepino. Cortar cada mitad en 4 partes iguales y servir.

SELECCIONES/INTERCAMBIOS
1 vegetal, 1 grasa

CALORÍAS 80 | **CALORÍAS DE GRASA** 25 | **TOTAL DE GRASA** 3g | **GRASA SATURADA** 0g | **GRASA TRANS** 0g
COLESTEROL 5mg | **SODIO** 330mg | **POTASIO** 380mg | **TOTAL DE CARBOHIDRATOS** 6g
FIBRA ALIMENTARIA 2g | **AZÚCARES** 3g | **PROTEÍNA** 8g | **FÓSFORO** 90mg

PICKLED WATERMELON

PREP TIME: 15 minutes
REFRIGERATION TIME: 2 hours
SERVES: 4
SERVING SIZE: 1/2 cup

2 cups seeded, cubed watermelon
  (1/2-inch cubes)
1/2 teaspoon sea salt
1 teaspoon cracked black pepper
1 1/2 cups apple cider vinegar
1/2 teaspoon minced fresh ginger
1/2 teaspoon chili powder
1/2 cup water

1. Add all ingredients to a large bowl. Fold ingredients together with a plastic spatula or wooden spoon.

2. Cover tightly with plastic wrap, making sure there are no loose ends. Store in refrigerator for 2 hours (or overnight to get a deeper flavor profile). Serve chilled.

RONALDO'S TIP

This side dish is best served with fish. The tanginess and sweetness of the watermelon pair well with the flavors of fish.

EXCHANGES/CHOICES
1/2 other carbohydrate

CALORIES 45 | **CALORIES FROM FAT** 0 | **TOTAL FAT** 0g | **SATURATED FAT** 0g | **TRANS FAT** 0g
CHOLESTEROL 0mg | **SODIUM** 250mg | **POTASSIUM** 170mg | **TOTAL CARBOHYDRATE** 7g
DIETARY FIBER 1g | **SUGARS** 5g | **PROTEIN** 1g | **PHOSPHORUS** 20mg

SANDÍA ENCURTIDA

TIEMPO DE PREPARACIÓN: 15 minutos
TIEMPO DE REFRIGERACIÓN: 2 horas
RINDE: 4 porciones
TAMAÑO DE LA PORCIÓN: 1/2 taza

2 tazas de sandía sin semillas, en cubos de 1/2 pulgada

1/2 cdta. de sal marina

1 cdta. de pimienta negra gruesa

1 1/2 tazas de vinagre de sidra de manzana

1/2 cdta. de jengibre fresco, finamente picado

1/2 cdta. de chile en polvo

1/2 taza de agua

1. Echar todos los ingredientes en una vasija grande. Mezclar los ingredientes con una espátula de plástico o cucharón de madera.

2. Tapar bien con plástico, asegurándose de que el sello sea hermético. Meter en el refrigerador 2 horas (o toda la noche para que los sabores sean más intensos). Servir fría.

CONSEJO DE RONALDO

Lo mejor es servir este plato con pescado. La acidez y dulzura de la sandía van bien con el sabor del pescado.

SELECCIONES/INTERCAMBIOS
1/2 otro carbohidrato

CALORÍAS 45 | **CALORÍAS DE GRASA** 0 | **TOTAL DE GRASA** 0g | **GRASA SATURADA** 0g | **GRASA TRANS** 0g
COLESTEROL 0mg | **SODIO** 250mg | **POTASIO** 170mg | **TOTAL DE CARBOHIDRATOS** 7g
FIBRA ALIMENTARIA 1g | **AZÚCARES** 5g | **PROTEÍNA** 1g | **FÓSFORO** 20mg

Pickled Caramelized Red Onions

COOKING TIME: 10 minutes
REFRIGERATION TIME: 2-3 hours
SERVES: 16
SERVING SIZE: 1/4 cup

2 teaspoons avocado oil

4 small red onions, peeled, cut in half, and sliced into 1/4-inch slices (about 4 cups)

1 teaspoon kosher salt, divided

1/2 teaspoon cracked black pepper, divided

2 cups apple cider vinegar

2 teaspoons Old Bay seasoning

1/2 teaspoon ground coriander

1. Preheat a large pan over medium heat and add oil. Wait a few seconds for oil to heat up. Add onions, 1/2 teaspoon salt, and 1/4 teaspoon pepper to the pan. Cook onions down until they are translucent and shiny, about 5 minutes (make sure to move onions around with a spoon so they cook evenly). Reduce heat to low and sweat onions for about 5 minutes.

2. To a sealable container, add apple cider vinegar, Old Bay seasoning, coriander, 1/2 teaspoon salt, and 1/4 teaspoon black pepper. Add onions to the container and seal tight. Place in refrigerator for 2-3 hours (or overnight) to develop nice deep flavors. Serve.

RONALDO'S TIP

These onions are perfect for topping tacos.

EXCHANGES/CHOICES
1 vegetable

CALORIES 30 | **CALORIES FROM FAT** 10 | **TOTAL FAT** 1g | **SATURATED FAT** 0g | **TRANS FAT** 0g
CHOLESTEROL 0mg | **SODIUM** 120mg | **POTASSIUM** 80mg | **TOTAL CARBOHYDRATE** 4g
DIETARY FIBER 1g | **SUGARS** 2g | **PROTEIN** 0g | **PHOSPHORUS** 15mg

CEBOLLA ROJA CARAMELIZADA Y ENCURTIDA

TIEMPO DE COCCIÓN: 10 minutos
TIEMPO DE REFRIGERACIÓN: 2-3 horas
RINDE: 16 porciones
TAMAÑO DE LA PORCIÓN: 1/4 taza

2 cdtas. de aceite de aguacate

4 cebollas rojas pequeñas, peladas y en tajadas finas de 1/4 de pulgada (aproximadamente 4 tazas)

1 cdta. de sal *kosher*, en partes

1/2 cdta. de pimienta negra gruesa, en partes

2 tazas de vinagre de sidra de manzana

2 cdtas. de especias Old Bay

1/2 cdta. cilantro molido

1. Calentar una sartén a fuego medio y echar el aceite. Esperar unos segundos para que el aceite se caliente. Echar la cebolla, 1/2 cdta. de sal y 1/4 cdta. de pimienta a la sartén. Dorar la cebolla hasta que esté traslúcida y reluciente, aproximadamente 5 minutos (asegurarse de revolver la cebolla con un cucharón para que se cueza uniformemente). Poner a fuego lento y sudar la cebolla unos 5 minutos.

2. Echar en un recipiente con tapa hermética el vinagre de sidra, especias Old Bay, cilantro, 1/2 cdta. de sal y 1/4 cdta. de pimienta negra. Echar la cebolla al recipiente y tapar bien. Refrigerar 2–3 horas (o de un día para otro) para que el sabor sea intenso. Servir.

CONSEJO DE RONALDO

Esta salsa de cebolla es perfecta como relleno de tacos.

SELECCIONES/INTERCAMBIOS
1 vegetal

CALORÍAS 30 | **CALORÍAS DE GRASA** 10 | **TOTAL DE GRASA** 1g | **GRASA SATURADA** 0g | **GRASA TRANS** 0g
COLESTEROL 0mg | **SODIO** 120mg | **POTASIO** 80mg | **TOTAL DE CARBOHIDRATOS** 4g
FIBRA ALIMENTARIA 1g | **AZÚCARES** 2g | **PROTEÍNA** 0g | **FÓSFORO** 15mg

SALADS

ENSALADAS

This chapter covers delicious and nutritious leafy greens and other veggies. I take the traditional salad from a boring dish to one that is composed of different textures, flavors, and layers. Not every salad needs lettuce. I will show you how to make creative, tasty salads you'll love.

Este capítulo se dedica a las deliciosas y nutritivas verduras y otros vegetales. Hago que la ensalada convencional pase de ser un plato aburrido a uno compuesto por diferentes texturas, sabores y dimensiones. No es necesario que todas las ensaladas tengan lechuga. Les voy a enseñar a hacer ensaladas creativas y sabrosas que les encanten.

—Chef Ronaldo

CILANTRO-MINT WATERMELON SALAD

I love watermelon, especially when it's paired with cilantro and mint. The fat from the cheese and the slight kick from the chili powder in this recipe brighten the sweetness of the watermelon. This salad is perfect for when you are on the go. My little son, Liam, loves this salad too!

PREP TIME: 15 minutes
REFRIGERATION TIME: 5 minutes
SERVES: 2
SERVING SIZE: 1 cup

2 cups seedless watermelon cubes
1 teaspoon crumbled queso fresco
1 teaspoon finely chopped cilantro
1 teaspoon finely chopped mint
1 teaspoon fresh lime juice
1/8 teaspoon chili powder

1. Add all ingredients to a bowl and toss gently. Place in the refrigerator for 5 minutes to chill before serving. This allows the flavors of the watermelon to marry with the herbs, lime, and chili powder.

EXCHANGES/CHOICES
1 fruit

CALORIES 60 | CALORIES FROM FAT 10 | TOTAL FAT 1g | SATURATED FAT 0g | TRANS FAT 0g
CHOLESTEROL 0mg | SODIUM 20mg | POTASSIUM 210mg | TOTAL CARBOHYDRATE 13g
DIETARY FIBER 1g | SUGARS 10g | PROTEIN 2g | PHOSPHORUS 35mg

ENSALADA DE SANDÍA CON CILANTRO Y MENTA

Me encanta la sandía, especialmente cuando se condimenta con cilantro y menta. La grasa del queso y el toque picante del chile en polvo en esta receta realzan la dulzura de la sandía. Esta ensalada es perfecta para cuando estén ocupados. ¡A mi hijito Liam también le encanta esta ensalada!

TIEMPO DE PREPARACIÓN: 15 minutos
TIEMPO DE REFRIGERACIÓN: 5 minutos
RINDE: 2 porciones
TAMAÑO DE LA PORCIÓN: 1 taza

2 tazas de sandía en trozos sin semilla
1 cdta. de queso fresco desmenuzado
1 cdta. de cilantro finamente picado
1 cdta. de menta finamente picada
1 cdta. de jugo de limón verde recién exprimido
1/8 cdta. de chile en polvo

1. Echar todos los ingredientes en una vasija y mezclar un poco. Colocar en el refrigerador 5 minutos para que se enfríe antes de servir. Esto permite que la sandía se impregne del sabor de las hierbas, el limón verde y chile en polvo.

SELECCIONES/INTERCAMBIOS
1 fruta

CALORÍAS 60 | **CALORÍAS DE GRASA** 10 | **TOTAL DE GRASA** 1g | **GRASA SATURADA** 0g | **GRASA TRANS** 0g
COLESTEROL 0mg | **SODIO** 20mg | **POTASIO** 210mg | **TOTAL DE CARBOHIDRATOS** 13g
FIBRA ALIMENTARIA 1g | **AZÚCARES** 10g | **PROTEÍNA** 2g | **FÓSFORO** 35mg

Quinoa, Mango, and Jicama Salad

PREP TIME: 15 minutes
COOKING TIME: 20 minutes
SERVES: 6
SERVING SIZE: 1/2 cup

QUINOA
1 cup quinoa
1 1/2 cups water
1/4 teaspoon avocado oil
1/4 teaspoon kosher salt

SALAD
1 cup peeled and cubed jicama
  (1/4-inch cubes)
1/4 cup thinly sliced red onion
3 ounces mango, peeled and cubed
3 radishes, cut into thin rounds
1 tablespoon finely chopped cilantro
1/4 teaspoon cracked black pepper
1 tablespoon lime juice
1/4 teaspoon chili powder
1/4 teaspoon avocado oil

1. Rinse quinoa with cold water in a colander. Add quinoa, water, oil, and salt to a rice cooker, and cook for about 20 minutes. Once the quinoa is done, fluff it with a fork and spread it onto a baking sheet to cool. Set aside.

2. Once quinoa has cooled, transfer it to a large bowl. Add jicama, onion, mango, radishes, cilantro, and pepper. Toss gently to incorporate. Set aside.

3. In a small bowl, add lime juice, chili powder, and avocado oil, and whisk together for about 30 seconds to create a light, flavorful dressing. Add dressing to the bowl with all the ingredients and mix together gently so the dressing is fully incorporated with the salad ingredients.

EXCHANGES/CHOICES
1/2 starch, 1 fruit, 1/2 fat

CALORIES 130 | **CALORIES FROM FAT** 20 | **TOTAL FAT** 2g | **SATURATED FAT** 0g | **TRANS FAT** 0g
CHOLESTEROL 0mg | **SODIUM** 90mg | **POTASSIUM** 250mg | **TOTAL CARBOHYDRATE** 24g
DIETARY FIBER 4g | **SUGARS** 3g | **PROTEIN** 4g | **PHOSPHORUS** 140mg

ENSALADA DE QUINUA, MANGO Y JÍCAMA

TIEMPO DE PREPARACIÓN: 15 minutos
TIEMPO DE COCCIÓN: 20 minutos
RINDE: 6 porciones
TAMAÑO DE LA PORCIÓN: 1/2 taza

QUINUA

1 taza de quinua
1 1/2 tazas de agua
1/4 cdta. de aceite de aguacate
1/4 cdta. de sal *kosher*

ENSALADA

1 taza de jícama, pelada y cortada en cubos de 1/4 de pulgada
1/4 taza de cebolla roja en rodajas delgadas
3 onzas de mango pelado, en cubos
3 rábanos, cortados en rodajas finas
1 cda. de cilantro finamente picado
1/4 cdta. de pimienta negra gruesa
1 cda. de jugo de lima o limón verde
1/4 cdta. de chile en polvo
1/4 cdta. de aceite de aguacate

1. Enjuagar la quinua con agua fría en un colador. Poner la quinua, agua, aceite y sal en una arrocera y prenderla. Estará lista en unos 20 minutos. Una vez que la quinua esté lista, granearla con un tenedor y esparcirla en una lata de hornear para que se enfríe. Poner de lado.

2. Una vez que la quinua esté fría, pasarla a una vasija grande. Agregar la jícama, cebolla, mango, rábanos, cilantro y la pimienta. Mezclar delicadamente. Poner de lado.

3. En una vasija pequeña, echar el jugo de limón verde, chile en polvo y aceite de aguacate y mezclar aproximadamente 30 segundos para crear un sabroso aliño *light*. Agregar el aliño a la vasija con todos los ingredientes y mezclar con movimientos suaves para que el aliño se impregne en los ingredientes de la ensalada.

SELECCIONES/INTERCAMBIOS
1/2 almidón, 1 fruta, 1/2 grasa

CALORÍAS 130 | **CALORÍAS DE GRASA** 20 | **TOTAL DE GRASA** 2g | **GRASA SATURADA** 0g | **GRASA TRANS** 0g
COLESTEROL 0mg | **SODIO** 90mg | **POTASIO** 250mg | **TOTAL DE CARBOHIDRATOS** 24g
FIBRA ALIMENTARIA 4g | **AZÚCARES** 3g | **PROTEÍNA** 4g | **FÓSFORO** 140mg

Avocado Salad with Tomatillo *Chimichurri* Dressing

The first time I ever tried a version of this salad was about 10 years ago. My father made it for a customer who had specially requested it. From that day on, I've made this salad many times and in many different ways. This is the ultimate version of my recipe for this salad.

The citrus combined with the creamy avocado works wonders for your taste buds, and red onion gives the salad a slightly spicy kick, which completes the whole dish. The recipe is easy but packed with flavor, mi gente. Enjoy!

PREP TIME: 10 minutes
ASSEMBLY TIME: 15 minutes
SERVES: 2
SERVING SIZE: 2 ounces avocado

---

1 tomatillo, husk removed, washed, and cut into 1/4-inch cubes

2 tablespoons finely chopped cilantro

1/4 teaspoon kosher salt

1 teaspoon cracked black pepper

1/2 teaspoon rice vinegar

1/2 teaspoon lime juice

1 plum tomato, sliced into rounds

1/2 cup sliced red onion

1 (4-ounce) Hass avocado, pitted and cut into 1/2-inch cubes

1. In a bowl, combine the tomatillo, cilantro, salt, pepper, rice vinegar, and lime juice. Mix well to create the tomatillo *chimichurri* and set aside.

2. In a separate bowl, place the tomato, red onion, avocado, and 1 tablespoon tomatillo *chimichurri*, and mix well. Make sure that the ingredients get coated well, and serve. Enjoy! If you have any remaining *chimichurri*, you can refrigerate it for up to 3 days.

EXCHANGES/CHOICES
2 vegetable, 2 fat

CALORIES 130 | CALORIES FROM FAT 80 | TOTAL FAT 9g | SATURATED FAT 1.5g | TRANS FAT 0g
CHOLESTEROL 0mg | SODIUM 250mg | POTASSIUM 600mg | TOTAL CARBOHYDRATE 13g
DIETARY FIBER 6g | SUGARS 5g | PROTEIN 3g | PHOSPHORUS 70mg

ENSALADA DE AGUACATE CON ALIÑO DE CHIMICHURRI DE TOMATILLO

La primera vez de que probé una versión de esta ensalada fue hace unos 10 años. Mi padre la hizo para un cliente que la había solicitado. Desde ese día, he preparado esta ensalada muchas veces y de muchas maneras diferentes. Esta es la versión final de mi receta para esta ensalada. Los cítricos combinados con el cremoso aguacate producen maravillas en el paladar, y la cebolla morada le da a la ensalada un toque de sabor fuerte, que complementa el plato. La receta es fácil pero muy sabrosa, mi gente. ¡A disfrutar!

TIEMPO DE PREPARACIÓN: 10 minutos
TIEMPO PARA ARMAR: 15 minutos
RINDE: 2 porciones
TAMAÑO DE LA PORCIÓN: 2 onzas de aguacate

---

1 tomatillo pelado, lavado y cortado en cubos de 1/4 de pulgada

2 cdas. de cilantro finamente picado

1/4 cdta. de sal *kosher*

1 cdta. de pimienta negra gruesa

1/2 cdta. de vinagre de arroz

1/2 cdta. de jugo de lima o limón verde

1 tomate ciruela, cortado en rodajas

1/2 taza de cebolla roja cortada en rodajas

1 aguacate Hass (de 4 onzas), sin pepa y cortado en cubos de 1/2 pulgada

1. En una vasija, mezclar el tomatillo, cilantro, sal, pimienta, vinagre de arroz y jugo de limón verde. Mezclar bien para preparar el chimichurri de tomatillo y poner de lado.

2. En otra vasija, colocar el tomate, cebolla roja, aguacate y 1 cda. de chimichurri de tomatillo y mezclar bien. Asegurarse de que los ingredientes se recubran bien y servir. ¡A disfrutar! Si les queda un poco de chimichurri, lo pueden refrigerar hasta 3 días.

SELECCIONES/INTERCAMBIOS
2 vegetales, 2 grasas

CALORÍAS 130 | **CALORÍAS DE GRASA** 80 | **TOTAL DE GRASA** 9g | **GRASA SATURADA** 1.5g | **GRASA TRANS** 0g
COLESTEROL 0mg | **SODIO** 250mg | **POTASIO** 600mg | **TOTAL DE CARBOHIDRATOS** 13g
FIBRA ALIMENTARIA 6g | **AZÚCARES** 5g | **PROTEÍNA** 3g | **FÓSFORO** 70mg

CUCUMBER AVOCADO SALAD

I love cucumbers, guys! They are crisp, juicy, and so refreshing. This salad highlights the cucumber well. Like a referee between two fighters, the cucumber in this salad is able to subdue the other flavors to create the perfect taste for your palate.

PREP TIME: 10 minutes
ASSEMBLY TIME: 10 minutes
SERVES: 2
SERVING SIZE: 1/2 the salad

DRESSING
1 1/2 tablespoons lime juice
1/4 teaspoon lime zest
1 tablespoon minced fresh dill
1 tablespoon minced cilantro
1 tablespoon apple cider vinegar
1/4 teaspoon kosher salt
1 teaspoon cracked black pepper

SALAD
2 cups peeled, seeded cucumber cubes
  (1/2-inch cubes)
10 cherry tomatoes, halved
1 (4-ounce) Hass avocado, pitted and
  cubed

1. To a bowl, add lime juice, lime zest, dill, cilantro, apple cider vinegar, salt, and pepper, and whisk until liquid emulsifies.

2. To the dressing, add the cucumber, cherry tomatoes, and avocado, and gently mix with a wooden spoon. Make sure to taste for seasoning once more before you serve.

EXCHANGES/CHOICES
2 vegetable, 2 fat

CALORIES 130 | **CALORIES FROM FAT** 80 | **TOTAL FAT** 9g | **SATURATED FAT** 1.5g | **TRANS FAT** 0g
CHOLESTEROL 0mg | **SODIUM** 250mg | **POTASSIUM** 700mg | **TOTAL CARBOHYDRATE** 12g
DIETARY FIBER 6g | **SUGARS** 5g | **PROTEIN** 3g | **PHOSPHORUS** 85mg

ENSALADA DE PEPINO Y AGUACATE

Señores, ¡me encanta el pepino! Son crujientes, jugosos y tan refrescantes. Esta ensalada realza mucho el pepino. Como un árbitro entre dos luchadores, el pepino en esta ensalada logra predominar sobre los demás sabores y crear el sabor perfecto para el paladar.

TIEMPO DE PREPARACIÓN: 10 minutos
TIEMPO PARA ARMAR: 10 minutos
RINDE: 2 porciones
TAMAÑO DE LA PORCIÓN: 1/2 ensalada

ALIÑO
1 1/2 cdas. de jugo de lima o limón verde

1/4 cdta. de ralladura de limón verde

1 cda. de eneldo fresco, picado

1 cda. de cilantro picado

1 cda. de vinagre de sidra de manzana

1/4 cdta. de sal *kosher*

1 cdta. de pimienta negra gruesa

ENSALADA
2 tazas de pepino pelado, sin semillas, en cubos de 1/2 pulgada

10 tomates cerezos, cortados por la mitad

1 aguacate Hass (de 4 onzas), sin la pepa y cortado en cubos

1. En una vasija, echar el jugo de limón verde, ralladura de limón verde, eneldo, cilantro, vinagre de manzana, sal y pimienta, y batir hasta que el líquido se emulsione.

2. Agregar al aliño el pepino, tomates cerezos y aguacate, y mezclar suavemente con un cucharón de madera. Antes de servir, asegurarse de probar una vez más para ver si está bien condimentada.

SELECCIONES/INTERCAMBIOS
2 vegetales, 2 grasas

CALORÍAS 130 | **CALORÍAS DE GRASA** 80 | **TOTAL DE GRASA** 9g | **GRASA SATURADA** 1.5g | **GRASA TRANS** 0g | **COLESTEROL** 0mg | **SODIO** 250mg | **POTASIO** 700mg | **TOTAL DE CARBOHIDRATOS** 12g | **FIBRA ALIMENTARIA** 6g | **AZÚCARES** 5g | **PROTEÍNA** 3g | **FÓSFORO** 85mg

Island Beet Salad

PREP TIME: 15 minutes
COOKING TIME: 1 hour 30 minutes
SERVES: 6
SERVING SIZE: 1 cup

DRESSING
1 tablespoon lime juice
1/4 teaspoon lime zest
1 teaspoon avocado oil
1 tablespoon finely chopped cilantro
1 teaspoon Chinese ginger powder
1/4 teaspoon kosher salt
1 teaspoon cracked black pepper

SALAD
2 teaspoons avocado oil
6 beets (about 18 ounces total)
2 teaspoons chopped almonds
1 ounce feta cheese, crumbled
1/4 cup sliced red onion
2 Roma tomatoes, washed and sliced

1. Add all dressing ingredients to a bowl and whisk briskly for about 30 seconds to form an emulsion. Set aside.

2. Preheat oven to 400°F.

3. Rub 2 teaspoons avocado oil on the beets, place beets in baking dish, and cover with foil. Bake for 1 hour 30 minutes, or until beets can be easily pierced with fork. Once beets are done, place in a bowl with ice water to cool the beets and to loosen the skins. Once cooled, remove beets from ice bath and peel off skin with paper towel. Cut beets into cubes and set aside.

4. Preheat a small pan over medium heat, add chopped almonds, and toss for about 30 seconds to toast. Remove from pan and set aside.

5. To a bowl, add beets, feta cheese, toasted almonds, red onion, and tomato. Add to the dressing and toss lightly to coat ingredients well with dressing. Taste salad to check seasoning before serving.

RONALDO'S TIP

Remember, you can roast the beets ahead of time or the night before to cut down on cooking time. A lot of my recipes have ingredients that you can prepare ahead of time.

EXCHANGES/CHOICES
2 vegetable, 1 fat

CALORIES 80 | CALORIES FROM FAT 25 | TOTAL FAT 3g | SATURATED FAT 1g | TRANS FAT 0g
CHOLESTEROL 0mg | SODIUM 190mg | POTASSIUM 370mg | TOTAL CARBOHYDRATE 11g
DIETARY FIBER 3g | SUGARS 7g | PROTEIN 3g | PHOSPHORUS 65mg

Ensalada isleña de remolacha

TIEMPO DE PREPARACIÓN: 15 minutos
TIEMPO DE COCCIÓN: 1 hora y media
RINDE: 6 porciones
TAMAÑO DE LA PORCIÓN: 1 taza

ALIÑO

1 cda. de jugo de lima o limón verde
1/4 cdta. de ralladura de limón verde
1 cdta. de aceite de aguacate
1 cda. de cilantro finamente picado
1 cdta. de jengibre chino en polvo
1/4 cdta. de sal *kosher*
1 cdta. de pimienta negra gruesa

ENSALADA

2 cdtas. de aceite de aguacate
6 remolachas o betabeles (aproximadamente 18 onzas en total)
2 cdtas. de almendras picadas
1 onza de queso feta, desmenuzado
1/4 taza de cebolla roja, en rodajas
2 tomates Roma, lavados y en tajadas

1. Echar todos los ingredientes del aliño a una vasija y batir enérgicamente unos 30 segundos para emulsionarlos. Poner de lado.

2. Calentar el horno a 400°F.

3. Frotar 2 cdtas. de aceite de aguacate en la remolacha, colocar las remolachas en una lata de hornear y cubrir con papel de aluminio. Hornear 1 hora y media o hasta que se puedan pinchar fácilmente las remolachas con un tenedor. Una vez que las remolachas estén listas, colocarlas en una vasija con agua y hielo para enfriarlas y hacer que se les afloje la piel. Una vez frías, retirar las remolachas del baño de hielo y pelar la piel usando una toalla de papel. Cortar la remolacha en cubos y poner de lado.

4. Para tostar las almendras, calentar una sartén pequeña a fuego medio, agregar las almendras y tostar unos 30 segundos. Retirar de la sartén y poner de lado.

5. En una vasija echar la remolacha, queso feta, almendras tostadas, cebolla roja y tomate. Echarlos al aliño y mezclar ligeramente para cubrir los ingredientes bien. Antes de servir, probar la ensalada para ver si está bien condimentada.

CONSEJO DE RONALDO

Recuerden que pueden asar la remolacha con anticipación o la noche previa para disminuir el tiempo de preparación. Muchas de mis recetas incluyen ingredientes que se pueden preparar antes de tiempo.

SELECCIONES/INTERCAMBIOS
2 vegetales, 1 grasa

CALORÍAS 80 | **CALORÍAS DE GRASA** 25 | **TOTAL DE GRASA** 3g | **GRASA SATURADA** 1g | **GRASA TRANS** 0g
COLESTEROL 0mg | **SODIO** 190mg | **POTASIO** 370mg | **TOTAL DE CARBOHIDRATOS** 11g
FIBRA ALIMENTARIA 3g | **AZÚCARES** 7g | **PROTEÍNA** 3g | **FÓSFORO** 65mg

Roasted Beet, Apple, and Queso Fresco Salad

PREP TIME: 15 minutes
COOKING TIME: 1 hour 10 minutes
SERVES: 4
SERVING SIZE: 1 cup

1 teaspoon canola oil
3 beets (about 12 ounces total)
2 teaspoons avocado oil
1 tablespoon freshly squeezed lime juice
1/4 teaspoon kosher salt
1/4 teaspoon cracked black pepper
2 cups peeled and cubed Golden
  Delicious apples (1/2-inch cubes)
1 tablespoon finely chopped cilantro
1 tablespoon crumbled queso fresco
1/4 cup sliced yellow onion

1. Preheat oven to 400°F.

2. Rub canola oil on beets, making sure to cover the whole surface. Pierce a few holes in beets so heat can circulate and speed up the cooking process. Place beets in a small baking dish and cover tightly with foil. Roast beets for 1 hour 10 minutes, until you can easily pierce the flesh of the beet with a fork. Remove from oven and place beets directly into a bowl with ice water. This will cool down the beets rapidly, stop the cooking process, and make removing the skins that much easier. When beets are cooled, peel off skins with a paper towel. Cut beets into 1/2-inch cubes and set aside.

3. Add avocado oil, lime juice, salt, and black pepper to a bowl and whisk briskly for 30 seconds to create your dressing. Set aside.

4. In a separate bowl, add apples, 2 cups beet cubes, cilantro, queso fresco, and onions, and toss gently. Add dressing and toss once more. Now it's ready to serve. Enjoy!

EXCHANGES/CHOICES
3 vegetable, 1 fat

CALORIES 110 | **CALORIES FROM FAT** 35 | **TOTAL FAT** 4g | **SATURATED FAT** 1g | **TRANS FAT** 0g
CHOLESTEROL 0mg | **SODIUM** 200mg | **POTASSIUM** 350mg | **TOTAL CARBOHYDRATE** 18g
DIETARY FIBER 3g | **SUGARS** 13g | **PROTEIN** 3g | **PHOSPHORUS** 55mg

Ensalada de Remolacha Asada, Manzana y Queso Fresco

TIEMPO DE PREPARACIÓN: 15 minutos
TIEMPO DE COCCIÓN: 1 hora y 10 minutos
RINDE: 4 porciones
TAMAÑO DE LA PORCIÓN: 1 taza

1 cdta. de aceite de canola

3 remolachas o betabeles (aproximadamente 12 onzas en total)

2 cdtas. de aceite de aguacate

1 cda. de jugo de lima o limón verde, recién exprimido

1/4 cdta. de sal *kosher*

1/4 cdta. de pimienta negra gruesa

2 tazas de manzanas Golden Delicious, peladas y cortadas en cubos de 1/2 pulgada

1 cda. de cilantro finamente picado

1 cda. de queso fresco desmenuzado

1/4 taza de cebolla amarilla en rodajas

1. Calentar el horno a 400°F.

2. Frotar las remolachas con el aceite de canola asegurándose de cubrir toda la superficie. Hacer unos cuantos agujeros en las remolachas para que el calor pueda circular y acelerar el proceso de cocción. Colocar las remolachas en un recipiente pequeño que se pueda meter al horno y tapar bien con papel de aluminio. Asar las remolachas 1 hora y 10 minutos, hasta que se puedan pinchar fácilmente con un tenedor. Sacar del horno y colocar las remolachas en una vasija con agua helada. Esto las enfriará rápidamente, detendrá el proceso de cocción y hará que pelarlas sea más fácil. Cuando las remolachas se enfríen, pelarlas usando una toalla de papel. Cortar la remolacha en cubos de 1/2 pulgada y poner de lado.

3. Echar el aceite de aguacate, jugo de limón verde, sal y pimienta negra en una vasija y batir enérgicamente 30 segundos para preparar el aliño. Poner de lado.

4. En otra vasija, echar la manzana, 2 tazas de remolacha en cubitos, cilantro, queso fresco y cebolla, y revolver delicadamente. Echar el aliño y mezclar una vez más. Ahora está lista para servir. ¡A disfrutar!

SELECCIONES/INTERCAMBIOS
3 vegetales, 1 grasa

CALORÍAS 110 | **CALORÍAS DE GRASA** 35 | **TOTAL DE GRASA** 4g | **GRASA SATURADA** 1g | **GRASA TRANS** 0g
COLESTEROL 0mg | **SODIO** 200mg | **POTASIO** 350mg | **TOTAL DE CARBOHIDRATOS** 18g
FIBRA ALIMENTARIA 3g | **AZÚCARES** 13g | **PROTEÍNA** 3g | **FÓSFORO** 55mg

QUINOA CUBAN SALAD

I love quinoa in just about anything. In this dish we are marrying quinoa with some greens, chicken, great spices, and a lot of flavor. The great thing about this salad is that none of the ingredients get lost; they all taste fresh, bright, and crisp. This is a great meal to prep on Sunday for the week ahead (mix the dressing right before serving). It is sure to keep your taste buds dancing. Toma!

PREP TIME: 15 minutes
COOKING TIME: 25 minutes
SERVES: 1
SERVING SIZE: 1 salad

1/4 cup dried quinoa, rinsed
1/2 cup water
1/8 teaspoon kosher salt
1 teaspoon avocado oil
1 cup asparagus pieces, cut on the bias (1/4-inch pieces)
4 ounces chicken breast, thinly sliced
1/2 teaspoon garlic powder
1/4 teaspoon dried rosemary
1/4 teaspoon dried oregano
1/8 teaspoon cracked black pepper
1/8 teaspoon ground cumin
Nonstick cooking spray
1 tablespoon lime juice
1 teaspoon canola oil
1 tablespoon finely chopped green onion
1 tablespoon crumbled queso fresco
1 cup kale, cut into strips
1 tablespoon finely chopped cilantro

1. Add 1/4 cup rinsed quinoa, water, 1/8 teaspoon salt, and avocado oil to a rice cooker or small pot. If using the rice cooker, just hit the cook button and let the cooker work its magic. If using a small pot, bring the mixture to a simmer, cover, and reduce heat to low for about 20 minutes. Quinoa will puff up and be tender when done. Fluff with fork before removing from pot. Set 1/4 cup of cooked quinoa aside to cool for the salad. Save any remaining quinoa for another occasion.

2. While quinoa cooks, place a small pot of water on the stove and bring to a boil over high heat. Add asparagus, cook for 30 seconds, and remove from water. Set aside to cool.

3. Place chicken strips into a resealable plastic bag and add garlic powder, dried rosemary, dried oregano, black pepper, and cumin. Close the bag and massage spices into the chicken.

4. Preheat a nonstick pan over medium-high heat and spray with nonstick cooking spray. Add chicken to the pan and brown on both sides. This should take about 5 minutes. Keep an eye on the pan; if it gets too hot, turn the heat down slightly to avoid burning the chicken. Set chicken aside.

5. In a small bowl whisk together the lime juice and canola oil. Set dressing aside.

6. Combine quinoa, asparagus, green onion, queso fresco, kale, cilantro, chicken, and dressing. Toss well to incorporate all ingredients. Enjoy!

EXCHANGES/CHOICES
2 starch, 4 lean protein, 1 fat

CALORIES 380 | **CALORIES FROM FAT** 140 | **TOTAL FAT** 15g | **SATURATED FAT** 2.5g | **TRANS FAT** 0g
CHOLESTEROL 90mg | **SODIUM** 350mg | **POTASSIUM** 1250mg | **TOTAL CARBOHYDRATE** 29g
DIETARY FIBER 8g | **SUGARS** 6g | **PROTEIN** 36g | **PHOSPHORUS** 500mg

ENSALADA CUBANA DE QUINUA

Me encanta la quinua en prácticamente cualquier cosa. En este platillo combinamos la quinua con unas cuantas verduras, pollo, especias fabulosas y mucho sabor. Lo bueno de esta ensalada es que ninguno de los ingredientes se pierde; todos saben frescos, intensos y crujientes. Esta receta es perfecta para prepararla el domingo y comerla durante la semana siguiente (echar el aliño y mezclar justo antes de servir). Sentirán una fiesta en su boca. ¡Toma!

TIEMPO DE PREPARACIÓN: 15 minutos
TIEMPO DE COCCIÓN: 25 minutos
RINDE: 1 porción
TAMAÑO DE LA PORCIÓN: 1 ensalada

1/4 taza de quinua seca, enjuagada
1/2 taza de agua
1/8 cdta. de sal *kosher*
1 cdta. de aceite de aguacate
1 taza de espárragos, cortados en diagonal en trozos de 1/4 de pulgada
4 onzas de pechuga de pollo, en tajadas delgadas
1/2 cdta. de ajo en polvo
1/4 cdta. de romero seco
1/4 cdta. de orégano seco
1/8 cdta. de pimienta negra gruesa
1/8 cdta. de comino
Aceite en aerosol
1 cda. de jugo de lima o limón verde
1 cdta. de aceite de canola
1 cda. de cebollín, finamente picado
1 cda. de queso fresco desmenuzado
1 taza de col rizada, cortada en tiras
1 cda. de cilantro finamente picado

1. Echar 1/4 de taza de quinua enjuagada, agua, 1/8 cdta. de sal y aceite de aguacate en una arrocera u olla pequeña. Si usa la arrocera, basta con apretar el botón para prenderla y dejar que haga su magia. Si se usa una ollita, hervir unos minutos, tapar y poner a fuego lento. Estará lista en unos 20 minutos. La quinua se hinchará y pondrá blanda cuando esté lista. Granearla con un tenedor antes de sacar de la olla. Poner de lado 1/4 taza de quinua cocida para enfriar y luego usar en la ensalada. Si queda quinua, guardarla para otra ocasión.

2. Mientras la quinua se cuece, poner sobre la estufa una ollita con agua y hervir a fuego alto, añadir los espárragos, cocer 30 segundos y retirarlos del agua. Poner de lado para que se enfríen.

3. Colocar el pollo en tiras en una bolsa de plástico que se pueda cerrar y echar el ajo en polvo, romero seco, orégano seco, pimienta negra y comino. Cerrar la bolsa y masajear el pollo con las especias.

4. Calentar una sartén antiadherente a fuego medio-alto y echarle aceite en aerosol. Echar el pollo a la sartén y dorarlo por ambos lados. Esto debe tomar unos 5 minutos. Estar atento a la sartén; si está demasiado caliente, bajar el fuego un poco para evitar que el pollo se queme. Poner el pollo de lado.

5. En una vasija pequeña, batir el jugo de limón verde y el aceite de canola. Poner de lado.

6. Echar la quinua, espárragos, cebolla verde, queso fresco, col rizada, cilantro, pollo y aliño. Mezclar bien para que todos los ingredientes se incorporen. ¡A disfrutar!

SELECCIONES/INTERCAMBIOS
2 almidón, 4 proteína magra, 1 grasa

CALORÍAS 380 | **CALORÍAS DE GRASA** 140 | **TOTAL DE GRASA** 15g | **GRASA SATURADA** 2.5g | **GRASA TRANS** 0g
COLESTEROL 90mg | **SODIO** 350mg | **POTASIO** 1250mg | **TOTAL DE CARBOHIDRATOS** 29g
FIBRA ALIMENTARIA 8g | **AZÚCARES** 6g | **PROTEÍNA** 36g | **FÓSFORO** 500mg

Spinach, Apple, and Pear Salad

We all know the saying, "An apple a day keeps the doctor away." This salad has all the nutritional benefits of apples and more. Packed with flavor, fruits, and greens, this salad is sure to rock your taste buds and impress your guests. Pears are a great source of fiber, vitamin B2, and vitamin C. Apples add antioxidants, which are disease-fighting compounds. Enjoy!

PREP TIME: 10 minutes
ASSEMBLY TIME: 10 minutes
SERVES: 3
SERVING SIZE: 1 cup

DRESSING
1 tablespoon minced cilantro
1 tablespoon fresh lime juice
1/2 teaspoon kosher salt
1/8 teaspoon cracked black pepper
1/8 teaspoon ground ginger
2 teaspoons avocado oil

SALAD
1 cup spinach, chopped
1 Granny Smith apple, peeled and (medium) diced
1 pear, peeled and (medium) diced
1 tablespoon crumbled queso fresco
1 stalk green onion, washed and thinly sliced
1 dried fig, sliced

1. Add all dressing ingredients to a mixing bowl. Whisk briskly for 30 seconds to create an emulsion. Place dressing in the refrigerator.

2. To a separate bowl, add spinach, apple, pear, queso fresco, onion, and dried fig. Toss ingredients gently. Add dressing and toss lightly once more. Mix with a spoon, making sure dressing is distributed well throughout the salad. Serve and enjoy!

EXCHANGES/CHOICES
1 fruit, 1 vegetable, 1 fat

CALORIES 130 | **CALORIES FROM FAT** 35 | **TOTAL FAT** 4g | **SATURATED FAT** 1g | **TRANS FAT** 0g
CHOLESTEROL 0mg | **SODIUM** 340mg | **POTASSIUM** 270mg | **TOTAL CARBOHYDRATE** 22g
DIETARY FIBER 4g | **SUGARS** 13g | **PROTEIN** 2g | **PHOSPHORUS** 45mg

ENSALADA DE ESPINACA, MANZANA Y PERA

Todos conocemos el refrán, "Cada día una manzana, para una vida sana". Esta ensalada tiene todos los beneficios nutricionales de las manzanas y mucho más. Esta ensalada con frutas y verduras está repleta de sabor, y sin duda les sabrá a maravillas e impresionará a sus invitados. Las peras son una excelente fuente de fibra, vitamina B2 y vitamina C. Las manzanas aportan antioxidantes, que combaten las enfermedades. ¡A disfrutar!

TIEMPO DE PREPARACIÓN: 10 minutos
TIEMPO PARA ARMAR: 10 minutos
RINDE: 3 porciones
TAMAÑO DE LA PORCIÓN: 1 taza

ALIÑO

1 cda. de cilantro picado
1 cda. de jugo de limón verde recién exprimido
1/2 cdta. de sal *kosher*
1/8 cdta. de pimienta negra gruesa
1/8 cdta. de jengibre en polvo
2 cdtas. de aceite de aguacate

ENSALADA

1 taza de espinaca, picada
1 manzana Granny Smith, pelada y picada en cubitos medianos
1 pera pelada y picada en cubitos medianos
1 cda. de queso fresco desmenuzado
1 tallo de cebollín, lavado y finamente picado
1 higo seco, en rodajas

1. Echar todos los ingredientes del aliño a una vasija. Batir enérgicamente 30 segundos para que se emulsionen. Refrigerar el aliño.

2. En otra vasija, echar la espinaca, manzana, pera, queso fresco, cebolla e higo seco. Mezclar los ingredientes delicadamente. Echar el aliño y mezclar un poco una vez más. Mezclar con un cucharón, asegurándose de que el aliño se distribuya bien por toda la ensalada. ¡Servir y disfrutar!

SELECCIONES/INTERCAMBIOS
1 fruta, 1 vegetal, 1 grasa

CALORÍAS 130 | **CALORÍAS DE GRASA** 35 | **TOTAL DE GRASA** 4g | **GRASA SATURADA** 1g | **GRASA TRANS** 0g
COLESTEROL 0mg | **SODIO** 340mg | **POTASIO** 270mg | **TOTAL DE CARBOHIDRATOS** 22g
FIBRA ALIMENTARIA 4g | **AZÚCARES** 13g | **PROTEÍNA** 2g | **FÓSFORO** 45mg

WARM PURPLE POTATO SALAD WITH YOGURT-CILANTRO DRESSING

As a child my mother (mi madre) would make a version of this, but it had a little more hip-hugging fat. Lots of mayonnaise was the main ingredient besides the potato. Mom used a small white potato for this; we are using purple potatoes, because they are packed with antioxidants, and they taste so good.

They have a slightly nutty flavor, creamy texture, and stand up well to other ingredients. The yogurt-cilantro dressing pairs perfectly with the potatoes and brings the whole thing together. Enjoy!!!

PREP TIME: 10 minutes
COOKING TIME: 40 minutes
SERVES: 6
SERVING SIZE: 1 cup

POTATO SALAD
1 1/2 pounds baby purple potatoes, washed and halved
Parchment paper
1/4 teaspoon kosher salt
1/4 teaspoon cracked black pepper

CILANTRO DRESSING
1/2 cup fat-free plain Greek yogurt
3 tablespoons minced cilantro
2 1/2 teaspoons Spanish smoked paprika
1/4 teaspoon kosher salt

1. Preheat oven to 400°F.

2. Place potatoes on a parchment paper-lined baking sheet. Sprinkle salt and pepper evenly over the potatoes. Place in the oven for 40 minutes. Remove from oven and let cool until just warm.

3. Meanwhile, make the cilantro dressing. To a mixing bowl, add the yogurt, cilantro, smoked paprika, and salt, and whisk briskly together for 30 seconds. Cover with plastic wrap and place in the refrigerator until ready to use.

4. To put this dish together, remove dressing from refrigerator and add potatoes. Gently mix with a large spoon. As always, mix it well so the *sazón* spreads throughout the dish. Serve.

EXCHANGES/CHOICES
1 starch, 1/2 lean protein

CALORIES 90 | **CALORIES FROM FAT** 0 | **TOTAL FAT** 0g | **SATURATED FAT** 0g | **TRANS FAT** 0g
CHOLESTEROL 0mg | **SODIUM** 200mg | **POTASSIUM** 590mg | **TOTAL CARBOHYDRATE** 20g
DIETARY FIBER 2g | **SUGARS** 3g | **PROTEIN** 3g | **PHOSPHORUS** 105mg

ENSALADA CALIENTE DE PAPA MORADA CON ALIÑO DE YOGUR Y CILANTRO

Cuando era niño, mi madre preparaba una versión de esto, pero tenía un poco más de grasa, de esa que se va directamente a las caderas. El principal ingrediente, aparte de las papas, era un montón de mayonesa. Mamá usaba una papa blanca pequeña para esto, pero aquí estamos utilizando papas moradas porque tienen muchos antioxidantes y saben muy bien.

Tienen un ligero sabor a nuez, textura cremosa y van bien con otros ingredientes. El aliño de yogur con cilantro es perfecto para la papa y es el toque final perfecto. ¡A disfrutar!

TIEMPO DE PREPARACIÓN: 10 minutos
TIEMPO DE COCCIÓN: 40 minutos
RINDE: 6 porciones
TAMAÑO DE LA PORCIÓN: 1 taza

ENSALADA DE PAPA

1 1/2 libras de papas moradas p
equeñas, lavadas y cortadas
por la mitad
Papel mantequilla
1/4 cdta. de sal *kosher*
1/4 cdta. de pimienta negra gruesa

ALIÑO DE CILANTRO

1/2 taza de yogur griego de sabor
natural, descremado
3 cdas. de cilantro finamente picado
2 1/2 cdtas. de pimentón español
ahumado *(paprika)*
1/4 cdta. de sal *kosher*

1. Calentar el horno a 400°F.

2. Colocar las papas en una lata con papel mantequilla. Echar sal y pimienta uniformemente a las papas. Hornear 40 minutos. Sacar del horno y dejar enfriar hasta que estén tibias.

3. Mientras tanto, preparar el aliño de cilantro. En una vasija echar el yogur, cilantro, pimentón y sal, y batir enérgicamente 30 segundos. Tapar con plástico y refrigerar hasta que sea la hora de usarlo.

4. Para armar este plato, sacar el aliño del refrigerador y echárselo a las papas. Mezclar delicadamente con un cucharón grande. Como siempre, mezclar bien para que la sazón se impregne por todo el plato. Servir.

SELECCIONES/INTERCAMBIOS
1 almidón, 1/2 proteína magra

CALORÍAS 90 | CALORÍAS DE GRASA 0 | TOTAL DE GRASA 0g | GRASA SATURADA 0g | GRASA TRANS 0g
COLESTEROL 0mg | SODIO 200mg | POTASIO 590mg | TOTAL DE CARBOHIDRATOS 20g
FIBRA ALIMENTARIA 2g | AZÚCARES 3g | PROTEÍNA 3g | FÓSFORO 105mg

Caribbean Mango Salad

PREP TIME: 10 minutes
ASSEMBLY TIME: 5 minutes
SERVES: 4
SERVING SIZE: 1 cup

MANGO SALAD

6 ounces mango, peeled and cut into medium cubes

2 radishes, washed and thinly sliced

1 1/2 cups pineapple cubes

1/4 cup thinly sliced Spanish onion

1 tablespoon finely chopped cilantro

DRESSING

1 tablespoon fat-free plain Greek yogurt

1 teaspoon rice vinegar

1/2 teaspoon kosher salt

1 teaspoon cracked black pepper

2 teaspoons avocado oil

1. Add mango, radishes, pineapple, onion, and cilantro to a bowl and set aside.

2. To make the dressing, grab a mixing bowl and add all dressing ingredients. Whisk briskly for 20 seconds.

3. Add the dressing a little bit at a time to the mango and pineapple mixture. Toss gently until the dressing is incorporated with all the ingredients. Serve.

RONALDO'S TIP

You don't have to use all the dressing, guys. A little goes a long way in this salad. Trust me, the *sazón* will be present.

EXCHANGES/CHOICES
1 fruit, 1/2 fat

CALORIES 90 | **CALORIES FROM FAT** 25 | **TOTAL FAT** 3g | **SATURATED FAT** 0g | **TRANS FAT** 0g
CHOLESTEROL 0mg | **SODIUM** 250mg | **POTASSIUM** 180mg | **TOTAL CARBOHYDRATE** 15g
DIETARY FIBER 2g | **SUGARS** 13g | **PROTEIN** 1g | **PHOSPHORUS** 25mg

ENSALADA CARIBEÑA DE MANGO

TIEMPO DE PREPARACIÓN: 10 minutos
TIEMPO PARA ARMAR: 5 minutos
RINDE: 4 porciones
TAMAÑO DE LA PORCIÓN: 1 taza

ENSALADA DE MANGO

6 onzas de mango, pelado y cortado en cubos medianos

2 rábanos, lavados y en rodajas finas

1 1/2 tazas de piña o ananá en cubos

1/4 taza de cebolla española, en rodajas finas

1 cda. de cilantro finamente picado

ALIÑO

1 cda. de yogur griego de sabor natural, descremado

1 cdta. de vinagre de arroz

1/2 cdta. de sal *kosher*

1 cdta. de pimienta negra gruesa

2 cdtas. de aceite de aguacate

1. Echar el mango, rábanos, piña, cebolla y cilantro en una vasija, y poner de lado.

2. Para hacer el aliño, echar todos los ingredientes en otra vasija. Batir a mano enérgicamente 20 segundos.

3. Echar el aliño poco a poco a la mezcla de mango y piña. Mezclar delicadamente hasta que el aliño se incorpore a todos los ingredientes. Servir.

CONSEJO DE RONALDO

No es necesario usar todo el aliño, amigos. Un poco es más que suficiente para esta ensalada. Confíen en mí, está repleto de sazón.

SELECCIONES/INTERCAMBIOS
1 fruta, 1/2 grasa

CALORÍAS 90 | **CALORÍAS DE GRASA** 25 | **TOTAL DE GRASA** 3g | **GRASA SATURADA** 0g | **GRASA TRANS** 0g
COLESTEROL 0mg | **SODIO** 250mg | **POTASIO** 180mg | **TOTAL DE CARBOHIDRATOS** 15g
FIBRA ALIMENTARIA 2g | **AZÚCARES** 13g | **PROTEÍNA** 1g | **FÓSFORO** 25mg

Summary Peach and Corn Salad

Talk about a summer treat! This salad is so good. When you brown the peaches and corn, they tend to take on completely different flavor profiles. Be ready for an explosion of flavor.

PREP TIME: 20 minutes
COOKING TIME: 25 minutes
SERVES: 6
SERVING SIZE: 1 cup

SALAD
5 ripe peaches, washed and cut into quarters
1/4 teaspoon vanilla extract
1/4 teaspoon ground nutmeg
1/4 teaspoon ground cinnamon
2 teaspoons avocado oil, divided
5 ears corn, husks removed, washed
1 small red onion, peeled and thinly sliced (about 1 cup)

DRESSING
3 tablespoons fat-free plain Greek yogurt
1/2 teaspoon kosher salt
1 teaspoon cracked black pepper
1 teaspoon fennel seed
1/4 teaspoon ground cumin
1 teaspoon ground coriander
1 tablespoon avocado oil
2 tablespoons lime juice
1 tablespoon finely chopped cilantro

1. To a large bowl, add peaches, vanilla, nutmeg, cinnamon, and 1 teaspoon avocado oil, and toss gently.

2. Preheat a medium nonstick pan over medium heat. Add peaches to the pan and lightly brown them on both sides. Transfer to a small baking sheet and place in the refrigerator.

3. Place corn in a pot of cold water and bring to a boil until corn is cooked through, about 10–15 minutes. Remove from water and cut in half.

4. Preheat a medium nonstick pan over medium heat and add 1 teaspoon avocado oil. Wait 10 seconds and then add corn. Lightly brown all sides of the corn. Transfer corn to a small baking sheet and place in the refrigerator.

5. Once peaches and corn are cool, remove from the refrigerator. Cut the corn kernels off the ear; add to a bowl along with the peaches and add onions.

6. To a separate bowl, add all dressing ingredients. Whisk together until it reaches a smooth consistency. Add dressing to corn, peaches, onions, and toss gently. Serve.

EXCHANGES/CHOICES
1 starch, 1 fruit, 1 fat

CALORIES 180 | **CALORIES FROM FAT** 50 | **TOTAL FAT** 6g | **SATURATED FAT** 1g | **TRANS FAT** 0g
CHOLESTEROL 0mg | **SODIUM** 180mg | **POTASSIUM** 580mg | **TOTAL CARBOHYDRATE** 33g
DIETARY FIBER 5g | **SUGARS** 19g | **PROTEIN** 5g | **PHOSPHORUS** 125mg

ENSALADA VERANIEGA DE MAÍZ Y DURAZNO

¡Esta ensalada es un placer veraniego! Es buenísima. Cuando se doran los duraznos y el maíz, adquieren un sabor totalmente diferente. Prepárense para una explosión de sabor.

TIEMPO DE PREPARACIÓN: 20 minutos
TIEMPO DE COCCIÓN: 25 minutos
RINDE: 6 porciones
TAMAÑO DE LA PORCIÓN: 1 taza

ENSALADA

5 duraznos maduros, lavados y cortados en cuatro
1/4 cdta. de extracto de vainilla
1/4 cdta. de nuez moscada molida
1/4 cdta. de canela molida
2 cdtas. de aceite de aguacate, en partes
5 mazorcas de maíz o elote, peladas y lavadas
1 cebolla roja pequeña, pelada y en tajadas finas (aproximadamente 1 taza)

ALIÑO

3 cdas. de yogur griego de sabor natural, descremado
1/2 cdta. de sal *kosher*
1 cdta. de pimienta negra gruesa
1 cdta. de semillas de hinojo
1/4 cdta. de comino
1 cdta. de cilantro molido
1 cda. de aceite de aguacate
2 cdas. de jugo de lima o limón verde
1 cda. de cilantro finamente picado

1. En una vasija grande, echar los duraznos, vainilla, nuez moscada, canela y 1 cdta. de aceite de aguacate, y mezclar delicadamente.

2. Calentar una sartén antiadherente mediana a fuego medio. Echar los duraznos a la sartén y dorarlos ligeramente por ambos lados. Pasarlos a una lata de hornear pequeña y refrigerar.

3. Meter el maíz en una olla con agua fría y hervir hasta que el maíz esté cocido, unos 10-15 minutos. Retirar del agua y cortar por la mitad.

4. Calentar una olla antiadherente mediana a fuego medio y agregar 1 cdta. de aceite de aguacate. Esperar 10 segundos y echar el maíz. Dorar el maíz ligeramente por todas partes. Pasar el maíz a una lata de hornear pequeña y refrigerar.

5. Una vez que los duraznos y maíz se enfríen, sacar del refrigerador. Desgranar el maíz; echar en la vasija con los duraznos y agregar la cebolla.

6. En otra vasija, echar los ingredientes del aliño. Batir hasta lograr una crema uniforme. Echar el aliño al maíz, duraznos, cebolla y mezclar delicadamente. Servir.

SELECCIONES/INTERCAMBIOS
1 almidón, 1 fruta, 1 grasa

CALORÍAS 180 | **CALORÍAS DE GRASA** 50 | **TOTAL DE GRASA** 6g | **GRASA SATURADA** 1g | **GRASA TRANS** 0g
COLESTEROL 0mg | **SODIO** 180mg | **POTASIO** 580mg | **TOTAL DE CARBOHIDRATOS** 33g
FIBRA ALIMENTARIA 5g | **AZÚCARES** 19g | **PROTEÍNA** 5g | **FÓSFORO** 125mg

SURF & TURF

MAR Y TIERRA

This chapter covers some nuevo Latino beef, pork, poultry, and seafood dishes. All of these recipes are healthy, flavorful, and easy to make. In the pages ahead, we will also explore some cool cooking techniques from braising to roasting and sautéing.

Este capítulo incluye algunos platos de res, cerdo, aves y mariscos de la nueva cocina latina. Todas estas recetas son saludables, sabrosas y de preparación fácil. En las próximas páginas exploraremos unas fabulosas técnicas culinarias para guisar, asar y saltear los alimentos.

—Chef Ronaldo

HERB-RUBBED *BOLICHE* ROAST

The Cuban version of pot roast, Boliche Roast is a favorite dish among Cubans. My father taught me to make this roast by stuffing the center with chorizo. As the roast cooks, the chorizo flavor blends with the meat and bastes it from the inside out. The end result is a tender, juicy, incredible roast the family will love.

PREP TIME: 25 minutes
COOKING TIME: 3 hours 10 minutes
SERVES: 8
SERVING SIZE: 1 (4-ounce) slice

---

2 pounds eye-of-round beef roast
   (about 1 roast)
1 ounce chorizo, chopped
   (preferably Colombian chorizo)
2 cups sliced Spanish onion
1/2 teaspoon sea salt
1/2 teaspoon cracked black pepper
2 teaspoons dried thyme
1 teaspoon dried oregano
1 teaspoon garlic powder
1/4 teaspoon ground cumin
1 teaspoon avocado oil
1 teaspoon canola oil
2 cups unsalted chicken stock

1. Preheat oven to 350°F.

2. Insert a long, thin knife (boning knife) into each end of the roast, creating a pathway to stuff your chorizo. Stuff the chorizo inside the cavity. Set roast aside.

3. Place sliced onions in a casserole dish large enough for the roast; make sure onions form a bed for the roast to cook on.

4. To a small bowl, add salt, pepper, thyme, oregano, garlic powder, cumin, and avocado oil. Mix to create a paste. Rub paste all over the roast.

5. Preheat a large nonstick pan over medium-high heat, add canola oil, and brown roast on all sides. Once browned, place roast in casserole dish. Pour chicken stock over the meat and seal tightly with foil. Cook for 2 hours, then remove foil and cook for 1 additional hour.

6. Remove from oven and let meat rest for at least 20 minutes. Slice roast on the bias and serve.

RONALDO'S TIP

Do not discard the juices and onions left in the casserole dish. Skim off any fat and transfer the mixture to a blender. Purée to create a smooth sauce for your roast.

EXCHANGES/CHOICES
4 lean protein

CALORIES 190 | **CALORIES FROM FAT** 50 | **TOTAL FAT** 6g | **SATURATED FAT** 2g | **TRANS FAT** 0g
CHOLESTEROL 70mg | **SODIUM** 380mg | **POTASSIUM** 480mg | **TOTAL CARBOHYDRATE** 4g
DIETARY FIBER 1g | **SUGARS** 1g | **PROTEIN** 29g | **PHOSPHORUS** 285mg

BOLICHE CON HIERBAS

El boliche asado es la versión cubana de la carne a la olla, y uno de los platos preferidos de los cubanos. Mi padre me enseñó a preparar este asado relleno de chorizo. A medida que la carne se cocina, el sabor del chorizo la impregna y la baña de adentro hacia afuera. El resultado es un asado tierno, jugoso y delicioso que le encantará a la familia.

TIEMPO DE PREPARACIÓN: 25 minutos
TIEMPO DE COCCIÓN: 3 horas y 10 minutos
RINDE: 8 porciones
TAMAÑO DE LA PORCIÓN: 1 tajada (de 4 onzas)

2 libras de asado redondo o
    peceto de res *(eye of the round)*,
    (aproximadamente 1 boliche)
1 onza de chorizo, picado
    (preferiblemente chorizo colombiano)
2 tazas de cebolla española en rodajas
1/2 cdta. de sal marina
1/2 cdta. de pimienta negra gruesa
2 cdtas. de tomillo seco
1 cdta. de orégano seco
1 cdta. de ajo en polvo
1/4 cdta. de comino
1 cdta. de aceite de aguacate
1 cdta. de aceite de canola
2 tazas de caldo de pollo sin sal

1. Calentar el horno a 350°F.

2. Meter la punta de un cuchillo largo y delgado (para deshuesar) en cada extremo del boliche, abriendo camino para rellenarlo de chorizo. Meter el chorizo en la cavidad. Poner el boliche de lado.

3. Colocar la cebolla en rodajas en una cazuela lo suficientemente grande para el asado, asegurándose de que la cebolla forme una base sobre la cual cocer el asado.

4. En una vasija pequeña, echar la sal, pimienta, tomillo, orégano, ajo en polvo, comino y aceite de aguacate. Mezclar para crear una pasta. Frotar la pasta en todo el asado.

5. Calentar una olla grande antiadherente a fuego medio-alto, agregar el aceite de canola y dorar toda la superficie del asado. Una vez que esté dorado, colocar la carne en una asadera. Echar el caldo de pollo sobre la carne y sellar herméticamente con papel de aluminio. Cocer 2 horas al horno y luego retirar el papel y cocer 1 hora adicional.

6. Sacar la carne del horno y ponerla de lado por lo menos 20 minutos. Cortar el boliche en diagonal y servir.

CONSEJO DE RONALDO

No desechen los jugos y la cebolla en la cazuela. Descarten la capa superior de grasa y licúen la mezcla para crear una salsa de consistencia uniforme para el boliche.

SELECCIONES/INTERCAMBIOS
4 proteínas magras

CALORÍAS 190 | **CALORÍAS DE GRASA** 50 | **TOTAL DE GRASA** 6g | **GRASA SATURADA** 2g | **GRASA TRANS** 0g
COLESTEROL 70mg | **SODIO** 380mg | **POTASIO** 480mg | **TOTAL DE CARBOHIDRATOS** 4g
FIBRA ALIMENTARIA 1g | **AZÚCARES** 1g | **PROTEÍNA** 29g | **FÓSFORO** 285mg

Curry *Adobo*-Rubbed Flank Steak

Wanting to cause a little controversy at home with my cooking, I take a different approach to cooking traditional Ropa Vieja. A while back I took a trip to Jamaica, and it was an experience I'll never forget thanks to the people, the sound of the waves crashing against the cliffs, the reggae music, and some of the best food that my palate has ever come in contact with. One of the best memories from the trip was Jamaican "curry." It was savory and sweet. Nothing says Jamaica better than that curry. I created this dish as a way to keep that flavor (and the memories behind it) alive.

PREP TIME: 15 minutes
COOKING TIME: 1 hour
SERVES: 8
SERVING SIZE: 4 ounces meat and vegetables

1/2 teaspoon curry powder
1/2 teaspoon amchar masala
1 teaspoon kosher salt
1/2 teaspoon cracked black pepper
1/2 teaspoon Chinese ginger powder
1/2 teaspoon ground cumin
1 1/2 pounds flank steak
1 teaspoon avocado oil
1/2 cup sliced Spanish onion
1/2 cup sliced red pepper
1 tablespoon tomato paste
1 1/2 cups unsalted chicken stock
1 tablespoon minced cilantro

1. Preheat oven 400°F.

2. To create the *adobo*, mix curry powder, amchar masala, salt, pepper, Chinese ginger, and cumin together in a small bowl. Set aside.

3. Lay flank steak on a cutting board. (Round side is the top and flat side is the bottom.) With a meat mallet, gently pound the meat to tenderize it. Rub *adobo* on the round side of the flank steak; make sure to massage the rub into every inch of the meat.

4. Preheat a large sauté pan over high heat, add avocado oil, and wait 10 seconds so oil heats up. Place flank steak rub side down, press it to the pan, and sear for 3 minutes. Flip meat over and sear for 3 minutes. Set meat aside.

5. In same pan add onion, red peppers, and tomato paste, and sauté until vegetables are translucent. Add chicken stock to the pan and simmer for about 1 minute. Add vegetable mixture to a large casserole dish. Place flank steak on top of vegetables in casserole dish and cover with foil. Place in oven for 40 minutes. Once finished, remove dish from oven and place meat on a rack to rest for 10 minutes.

6. Meanwhile, add sauce from casserole into a blender and purée. Transfer sauce to a sauté pan and simmer for 3 minutes. Fold in cilantro.

7. Slice meat on the bias, place on plate, and pour sauce over it to serve.

EXCHANGES/CHOICES
3 lean protein

CALORIES 150 | **CALORIES FROM FAT** 50 | **TOTAL FAT** 6g | **SATURATED FAT** 2g | **TRANS FAT** 0g | **CHOLESTEROL** 55mg | **SODIUM** 320mg | **POTASSIUM** 390mg | **TOTAL CARBOHYDRATE** 3g | **DIETARY FIBER** 1g | **SUGARS** 1g | **PROTEIN** 20g | **PHOSPHORUS** 190mg

ROPA VIEJA CON ADOBO DE CURRY

Para generar un poco de polémica en casa con mi cocina, uso un método diferente para preparar la tradicional ropa vieja. Un tiempo atrás hice un viaje a Jamaica y fue una experiencia que nunca voy a olvidar gracias a la gente, el sonido de las olas que rompían contra los acantilados, la música reggae y una comida que está entre la mejor que jamás he probado. Uno de mis mejores recuerdos del viaje a Jamaica es el curry. Es salado y dulce a la vez. Nada es más representativo de Jamaica que ese curry. Creé este plato como una manera de conservar ese sabor (y los recuerdos que trae).

TIEMPO DE PREPARACIÓN: 15 minutos
TIEMPO DE COCCIÓN: 1 hora
RINDE: 8 porciones
TAMAÑO DE LA PORCIÓN: 4 onzas de carne
   y vegetales

1/2 cdta. de curry en polvo

1/2 cdta. de *amchar masala*
   (mezcla de especias indias)

1 cdta. de sal *kosher*

1/2 cdta. de pimienta negra gruesa

1/2 cdta. de jengibre chino en polvo

1/2 cdta. de comino

1 1/2 libras de falda de res
   (flank steak)

1 cdta. de aceite de aguacate

1/2 taza de cebolla española en rodajas

1/2 taza de pimiento rojo en rodajas

1 cda. de pasta de tomate

1 1/2 tazas de caldo de pollo sin sal

1 cda. de cilantro picado

1. Calentar el horno a 400°F.

2. Para crear el adobo, mezclar el curry en polvo, *amchar masala*, sal, pimienta, jengibre chino y comino en una vasija pequeña. Poner de lado.

3. Poner la falda de res en la tabla de cortar. (El lado redondo va hacia arriba y el plano abajo). Con un mazo de carne, golpear suavemente la carne para ablandarla. Frotar el adobo en la parte redonda de la carne, asegurándose de echarle las especias a toda la carne.

4. Calentar una sartén grande a fuego alto, echar el aceite de aguacate y esperar 10 segundos para que se caliente. Colocar la carne con las especias hacia abajo y dorarla en la sartén, presionándola, 3 minutos. Voltear la carne y dorar 3 minutos. Poner la carne de lado.

5. En la misma sartén echar la cebolla, pimientos rojos y pasta de tomate, y sofreír hasta que los vegetales estén traslúcidos. Echar el caldo de pollo y cocer a fuego lento aproximadamente 1 minuto. Echar la mezcla de vegetales a una cazuela grande. Colocar la carne sobre los vegetales en la cazuela y tapar con papel de aluminio. Hornear 40 minutos. Una vez listo, sacar la cazuela del horno y colocar la carne sobre una rejilla 10 minutos.

6. Mientras tanto, licuar la salsa de la cazuela. Echar la salsa a la sartén y cocer a fuego lento 3 minutos. Echar el cilantro y revolver.

7. Cortar la carne en diagonal, ponerla en una fuente y echarle la salsa antes de servirla.

SELECCIONES/INTERCAMBIOS
3 proteínas magras

CALORÍAS 150 | **CALORÍAS DE GRASA** 50 | **TOTAL DE GRASA** 6g | **GRASA SATURADA** 2g | **GRASA TRANS** 0g | **COLESTEROL** 55mg | **SODIO** 320mg | **POTASIO** 390mg | **TOTAL DE CARBOHIDRATOS** 3g | **FIBRA ALIMENTARIA** 1g | **AZÚCARES** 1g | **PROTEÍNA** 20g | **FÓSFORO** 190mg

Latin Herb-Crusted Beef Tenderloin with Avocado *Chimichurri*

PREP TIME: 25 minutes
COOKING TIME: 55 minutes
SERVES: 25
SERVING SIZE: 1 (3 1/2-ounce) slice beef and 2 teaspoons sauce

HERB CRUST
1 tablespoon dried thyme
1 teaspoon ground cumin
1 tablespoon dried oregano
1 tablespoon garlic powder
1 tablespoon dried rosemary
1 tablespoon kosher salt
1 tablespoon cracked black pepper
1 teaspoon avocado oil

AVOCADO *CHIMICHURRI*
1 1/2 limes, juiced (2 tablespoons juice)
1 (4-ounce) Hass avocado
1 teaspoon ground coriander
2 teaspoons rice vinegar
1 teaspoon kosher salt
1/2 teaspoon cracked black pepper
3 tablespoons avocado oil
2 cups packed cilantro, finely chopped
1/2 medium Spanish onion, cut into 1/8-inch cubes (1/2 cup)

TENDERLOIN
1 (5-pound) beef tenderloin (ask your butcher to clean it for you)
2 teaspoons avocado oil
3 cups sliced Spanish onion
4 cloves garlic, peeled and finely chopped

1. Preheat oven to 400°F.

2. Add all herb crust ingredients to a bowl and mix well with a spoon to create a lovely paste. Set aside.

3. Add all avocado *chimichurri* ingredients to a food processor. Pulsate until mixture comes together, resembling a slightly chunky salsa. Taste again to check the seasoning; if it is not correct, adjust as necessary. Transfer mixture to a bowl, cover with plastic wrap, and place in the refrigerator.

4. Cut off 4 inches from the skinny end of the beef tenderloin and reserve for another recipe. Rub the herb crust mixture onto the top of the tenderloin, making sure to rub it into the meat and cover every inch. (This is important because you want the herb crust to fuse with the tenderloin.) Set aside for 5 minutes at room temperature so herb crust can settle into the meat.

5. Preheat a large flat skillet or any pan big enough to hold tenderloin over medium-high heat. Add avocado oil to pan, wait a few seconds so oil heats up. Place meat herb crust down and sear for 3 minutes. Repeat on the other side. Remove meat from pan and set aside.

6. To the same pan, add onions and garlic, and cook onions down over low heat. Transfer mixture to a baking sheet, creating a bed for the meat. Place tenderloin on baking sheet with herb crust facing up. Cook in the oven for 45 minutes.

7. Once done, remove baking sheet from the oven and place tenderloin on a cutting board to rest for 10 minutes before cutting. This allows the juices to settle. Store onions in a bowl, cover with plastic wrap, and set aside.

8. To serve, cut a 3 1/2-ounce slice of meat and top with 2 tablespoons onions and 2 teaspoons avocado *chimichurri*.

EXCHANGES/CHOICES
3 lean protein, 1 fat

CALORIES 170 | **CALORIES FROM FAT** 70 | **TOTAL FAT** 8g | **SATURATED FAT** 2g | **TRANS FAT** 0g
CHOLESTEROL 55mg | **SODIUM** 350mg | **POTASSIUM** 350mg | **TOTAL CARBOHYDRATE** 4g
DIETARY FIBER 1g | **SUGARS** 1g | **PROTEIN** 21g | **PHOSPHORUS** 215mg

LOMO DE CARNE CON COSTRA DE HIERBAS LATINAS Y CHIMICHURRI DE AGUACATE

TIEMPO DE PREPARACIÓN: 25 minutos
TIEMPO DE COCCIÓN: 55 minutos
RINDE: 25 porciones
TAMAÑO DE LA PORCIÓN: 1 tajada de carne de res (3 1/2 onzas) y 2 cdtas. de salsa

COSTRA DE HIERBAS
1 cda. de tomillo seco
1 cdta. de comino
1 cda. de orégano seco
1 cda. de ajo en polvo
1 cda. de romero seco
1 cda. de sal *kosher*
1 cda. de pimienta negra gruesa
1 cdta. de aceite de aguacate

CHIMICHURRI DE AGUACATE
Jugo de 1 1/2 limas o limones verdes
  (2 cdas. de jugo)
1 aguacate Hass (de 4 onzas)
1 cdta. cilantro molido
2 cdtas. de vinagre de arroz
1 cdta. de sal *kosher*
1/2 cdta. de pimienta negra gruesa
3 cdas. de aceite de aguacate
2 tazas bien colmadas de cilantro,
  finamente picado
1/2 cebolla española mediana, cortada
  en cubos de 1/8 de pulgada (1/2 taza)

LOMO
1 lomo de res (de 5 libras) (Pedirle al
  carnicero que lo desgrase)
2 cdtas. de aceite de aguacate
3 tazas de cebolla española en rodajas
4 dientes de ajo, pelados y finamente
  picados

1. Calentar el horno a 400°F.

2. Echar todos los ingredientes de la costra de hierbas a una vasija y mezclar bien con un cucharón para crear una pasta preciosa. Poner de lado.

3. Poner todos los ingredientes del chimichurri de aguacate en el procesador de alimentos. Prender y apagar hasta que se mezcle bien y forme una salsa con trozos pequeños. Volver a probar que esté bien condimentada; si no, hacer los cambios correspondientes. Poner la mezcla en una vasija, tapar con plástico y refrigerar.

4. Cortar 4 pulgadas del extremo delgado del lomo y guardar para otra receta. Frotar la mezcla de la costra de hierbas en la parte superior del lomo, asegurándose de que la carne la absorba y que cubra cada pulgada. (Esto es importante porque lo ideal es que la costra de hierbas se funda con el lomo). Poner de lado 5 minutos a temperatura ambiente para que la costra de hierbas se adhiera bien a la carne.

5. Calentar una sartén plana o una sartén regular a fuego medio-alto. La sartén debe ser lo suficientemente grande para el lomo. Echar el aceite de aguacate a la sartén y esperar unos segundos para que se caliente. Con la costra de hierbas hacia abajo, dorar la carne 3 minutos. Repetir por el otro lado. Retirar la carne de la sartén y poner de lado.

6. En la misma sartén, echar la cebolla y el ajo, y cocer a fuego lento. Pasar la mezcla a una lata de hornear, creando una cama para la carne. Colocar el lomo en la lata, con la costra de hierbas hacia arriba. Hornear 45 minutos.

7. Una vez que el lomo esté listo, sacarlo del horno y ponerlo de lado sobre una tabla y esperar 10 minutos antes de cortar. Esto permite que los jugos se asienten. Poner la cebolla en una vasija, tapar con plástico y poner de lado.

8. Para servir, cortar una tajada de carne de 3 1/2 onzas y echar encima 2 cdas. de cebolla y 2 cdtas. de chimichurri de aguacate.

SELECCIONES/INTERCAMBIOS
3 proteínas magras, 1 grasa

CALORÍAS 170 | **CALORÍAS DE GRASA** 70 | **TOTAL DE GRASA** 8g | **GRASA SATURADA** 2g | **GRASA TRANS** 0g | **COLESTEROL** 55mg | **SODIO** 350mg | **POTASIO** 350mg | **TOTAL DE CARBOHIDRATOS** 4g | **FIBRA ALIMENTARIA** 1g | **AZÚCARES** 1g | **PROTEÍNA** 21g | **FÓSFORO** 215mg

Roasted Chicken in *Mojo* Citrus Sauce

PREP TIME: 40 minutes
COOKING TIME: About 2 hours, plus resting time
SERVES: 10
SERVING SIZE: 4 ounces chicken and 2 tablespoons citrus sauce

4 cloves garlic, thinly sliced
1 lemon, cut into 1/4-inch rounds
2 ripe oranges, cut into 1/4-inch rounds
2 limes, cut into 1/4-inch rounds
1 teaspoon kosher salt
1 teaspoon cracked black pepper
1 teaspoon ground thyme
1 teaspoon dried sage
1 boneless, skinless whole chicken
  (about 2 1/2 pounds)
30 inches butcher's twine
1 teaspoon avocado oil
1 cup finely chopped Spanish onion
1/2 cup finely chopped red pepper
1/2 cup finely chopped green pepper
1 cup unsalted chicken stock
2 tablespoons finely chopped cilantro

1. Preheat oven to 350°F.

2. Add garlic, lemon, oranges, limes, salt, pepper, thyme, and sage to a bowl and mix well with a spoon. Set aside.

3. Truss your chicken using butcher's twine (if you're not sure how to truss a chicken, you can find instructional videos online) and rub the skinless surface of the chicken with the herb-citrus mixture. (Trust me, this chicken will be delicious even without the skin.) Place all of the citrus rounds on the surface of the chicken in a uniform fashion. Set aside.

4. Preheat a nonstick pan over medium-high heat, add avocado oil, and wait 10 seconds for oil to heat up. Add onion, red pepper, and green pepper to the pan, and cook until vegetables are cooked through, about 5 minutes.

5. Place vegetable mixture in a roasting pan to create a bed for the chicken. Place chicken on top, breast side up. Place roasting pan in the oven for 1 hour 30 minutes to 2 hours, or until the internal temperature reaches 160°F. (Always check temperature at the thickest part of the breast and inner thigh.)

6. Remove chicken from oven, place on a dripping tray, and let it rest about 10 minutes so the juices redistribute. Transfer drippings and citrus to a clear jar. Skim off and discard any fat that rises to the top.

7. To make the citrus sauce, preheat a large nonstick pan over medium heat and add reserved chicken drippings to the pan along with chicken stock. Let it simmer for 10 minutes, then transfer mixture to a blender and purée. (Work in 3 batches to avoid any splatter.) Fold in cilantro to finish the sauce. Serve sauce with chicken.

EXCHANGES/CHOICES
1/2 other carbohydrate, 3 1/2 lean protein

CALORIES 180 | **CALORIES FROM FAT** 35 | **TOTAL FAT** 4g | **SATURATED FAT** 1g | **TRANS FAT** 0g
CHOLESTEROL 85mg | **SODIUM** 250mg | **POTASSIUM** 540mg | **TOTAL CARBOHYDRATE** 9g
DIETARY FIBER 2g | **SUGARS** 4g | **PROTEIN** 27g | **PHOSPHORUS** 270mg

POLLO ASADO EN MOJO DE CÍTRICOS

TIEMPO DE PREPARACIÓN: 40 minutos
TIEMPO DE COCCIÓN: Aproximadamente 2
  horas y media
RINDE: 10 porciones
TAMAÑO DE LA PORCIÓN: 4 onzas de pollo y
  2 cdas. de salsa de cítricos

4 dientes de ajo, en rodajas delgadas

1 limón, cortado en rodajas de
  1/4 de pulgada

2 naranjas maduras, cortadas en rodajas
  de 1/4 de pulgada

2 limas o limones verdes, cortados en
  rodajas de 1/4 de pulgada

1 cdta. de sal *kosher*

1 cdta. de pimienta negra gruesa

1 cdta. de tomillo en polvo

1 cdta. de salvia seca

1 pollo entero deshuesado, sin piel
  (aproximadamente 2 1/2 libras)

30 pulgadas de pita de cocina

1 cdta. de aceite de aguacate

1 taza de cebolla española, finamente
  picada

1/2 taza de pimiento rojo, finamente
  picado

1/2 taza de pimiento verde, finamente
  picado

1 taza de caldo de pollo sin sal

2 cdas. de cilantro finamente picado

1. Calentar el horno a 350°F.

2. Echar el ajo, limón, naranjas, limones verdes, sal, pimienta, tomillo y salvia a una vasija, y mezclar bien con un cucharón. Poner de lado.

3. Atar el pollo usando pita de cocina (si no están seguros de cómo atar el pollo, pueden encontrar videos en Internet que enseñan a hacerlo). Frotar la superficie del pollo sin piel con la mezcla de hierbas y cítricos. (Confíen en mí, este pollo es delicioso incluso sin la piel). Colocar todos los cítricos en rodajas sobre la superficie del pollo de manera uniforme. Poner de lado.

4. Calentar una sartén antiadherente a fuego medio-alto, agregar el aceite de aguacate y esperar unos segundos para que se caliente. Echar la cebolla, pimiento rojo y pimiento verde a la sartén. y cocer hasta que estén completamente cocidos, unos 5 minutos.

5. Colocar la mezcla de vegetales en una asadera para crear una cama para el pollo. Colocar encima el pollo, con la pechuga hacia arriba. Meter la asadera al horno de 1 hora y media a 2 horas, o hasta que la temperatura interna sea 160° F. (Siempre tomar la temperatura en la parte más gruesa de la pechuga y muslos).

6. Sacar el pollo del horno, escurrirlo sobre una rejilla, y poner de lado unos 10 minutos para que el jugo se redistribuya. Pasar el jugo y los cítricos a un frasco traslúcido. Eliminar la grasa que suba a la parte superior.

7. Para preparar la salsa de cítricos, calentar una sartén antiadherente grande a fuego medio y echar el jugo de pollo que se desgrasó y el caldo de pollo. Hervir a fuego lento 10 minutos y luego licuar la mezcla. (Hacerlo en 3 tandas para evitar salpicar). Echar el cilantro y mezclar para terminar de preparar la salsa. Servir la salsa con el pollo.

SELECCIONES/INTERCAMBIOS
1/2 otro carbohidrato, 3 1/2 proteínas magras

CALORÍAS 180 | **CALORÍAS DE GRASA** 35 | **TOTAL DE GRASA** 4g | **GRASA SATURADA** 1g | **GRASA TRANS** 0g
COLESTEROL 85mg | **SODIO** 250mg | **POTASIO** 540mg | **TOTAL DE CARBOHIDRATOS** 9g
FIBRA ALIMENTARIA 2g | **AZÚCARES** 4g | **PROTEÍNA** 27g | **FÓSFORO** 270mg

Braised Whole Chicken with Yucca

PREP TIME: 20 minutes
COOKING TIME: 2 hours 30 minutes
SERVES: 8
SERVING SIZE: 1 1/4 cups

Nonstick cooking spray

1/2 cup cubed Spanish onion
(1/8-inch cubes)

32 ounces unsalted chicken stock

2 teaspoons garlic powder

2 teaspoons dried sage

1 teaspoon curry powder

1 teaspoon dried oregano

1 teaspoon Spanish smoked paprika

1/4 teaspoon ground nutmeg

1 teaspoon kosher salt

1/2 teaspoon cracked black pepper

3 dried bay leaves

1 (2-pound) whole chicken, skin
removed

1 pound yucca, outer brown and inner
pink skins peeled, cut into 1/2-inch
cubes

1. Preheat Dutch oven or large pot over high heat and spray with nonstick cooking spray. Add onions and sauté until they are translucent. Add chicken stock, garlic powder, sage, curry powder, oregano, smoked paprika, nutmeg, kosher salt, cracked black pepper, and bay leaves. Stir well.

2. Place chicken and yucca inside Dutch oven or pot. Cover with lid slightly ajar and cook for 2 hours 30 minutes over low heat to slowly cook the dish. This allows all the flavors to develop properly. Once finished, remove from oven and serve.

RONALDO'S TIP

You can ask your butcher to butcher the whole chicken before you cook it. Ask the butcher to cut it into: two drumsticks, two thighs, two breasts, and two wings. Make sure the skin is removed!

When this dish is finished, the meat should be pulling apart, tender, juicy, and full of beautiful flavors. I like to remove the chicken from the Dutch oven after it is cooked and turn up the heat to thicken the sauce a bit. Before serving, you can add a squeeze of lime to the dish for acidity. Enjoy!

EXCHANGES/CHOICES
1 1/2 starch, 2 1/2 lean protein

CALORIES 240 | **CALORIES FROM FAT** 70 | **TOTAL FAT** 8g | **SATURATED FAT** 2g | **TRANS FAT** 0g
CHOLESTEROL 55mg | **SODIUM** 320mg | **POTASSIUM** 400mg | **TOTAL CARBOHYDRATE** 26g
DIETARY FIBER 2g | **SUGARS** 2g | **PROTEIN** 17g | **PHOSPHORUS** 150mg

GUISO DE POLLO ENTERO CON YUCA

TIEMPO DE PREPARACIÓN: 20 minutos
TIEMPO DE COCCIÓN: 2 horas y media
RINDE: 8 porciones
TAMAÑO DE LA PORCIÓN: 1 1/4 tazas

Aceite en aerosol

1/2 taza de cebolla española
(en cubos de 1/8 de pulgada)

32 onzas de caldo de pollo sin sal

2 cdtas. de ajo en polvo

2 cdtas. de salvia seca

1 cdta. de curry en polvo

1 cdta. de orégano seco

1 cdta. de pimentón español ahumado
(paprika)

1/4 cdta. de nuez moscada molida

1 cdta. de sal kosher

1/2 cdta. de pimienta negra gruesa

3 hojas de laurel

1 pollo entero (de 2 libras), sin piel

1 libra de yuca, sin la cáscara marrón ni
la piel rosa interior, cortada en cubos
de 1/2 pulgada

1. Calentar una olla pesada o grande a fuego alto y echarle aceite en aerosol. Echar la cebolla y saltear hasta que esté traslúcida. Echar el caldo de pollo, ajo en polvo, salvia, curry en polvo, orégano, pimentón, nuez moscada, pimienta, sal kosher y hojas de laurel. Mezclar bien.

2. Poner el pollo y la yuca en la olla. Tapar pero dejando la olla un poco entreabierta y cocer 2 horas y media a fuego bajo. Cocerlo lentamente permite que todos los sabores se intensifiquen debidamente. Una vez que esté listo, retirar de la olla y servir.

CONSEJO DE RONALDO

Antes de cocinar, le pueden pedir al carnicero que corte el pollo entero en presas. Pídanle que lo corte en: dos piernas, dos muslos, dos pechugas y dos alas. ¡Asegúrense de que le quite la piel!

Cuando este plato está listo, la carne debe desprenderse del hueso fácilmente y estar tierna, jugosa y muy sabrosa. Una vez que el pollo está cocido, me gusta sacarlo de la olla y subir la temperatura para espesar la salsa un poco. Antes de servir, pueden echarle un chorrito de limón verde al plato para darle un toque de acidez. ¡A disfrutar!

SELECCIONES/INTERCAMBIOS
1 1/2 almidones, 2 1/2 proteínas magras

CALORÍAS 240 | CALORÍAS DE GRASA 70 | TOTAL DE GRASA 8g | GRASA SATURADA 2g | GRASA TRANS 0g
COLESTEROL 55mg | SODIO 320mg | POTASIO 400mg | TOTAL DE CARBOHIDRATOS 26g
FIBRA ALIMENTARIA 2g | AZÚCARES 2g | PROTEÍNA 17g | FÓSFORO 150mg

Cuban Chicken Stir-Fry

This is one of my favorite dishes to make when I'm on the go. The recipe is easy to handle and, let me tell you, the dish comes out delicious. This recipe is also a great way to get rid of vegetables that have been left in the refrigerator a day too long. Feel free to substitute ingredients, but make sure you follow the steps for a successful, healthy dish.

PREP TIME: 15 minutes
COOKING TIME: 15 minutes
SERVES: 2
SERVING SIZE: 1 1/2 cups

2 teaspoons avocado oil
8 ounces chicken breasts, sliced into 1/8-inch slices
1 cup chopped broccoli, washed
1/4 cup red pepper strips
1/4 cup green pepper strips
2 cloves garlic, peeled and finely chopped
1/2 cup sliced Spanish onion (about 1/2 medium onion)
4 white button mushrooms, washed and sliced
1/2 cup fresh corn kernels
1 teaspoon cracked black pepper
1/2 teaspoon Chinese ginger powder
1/2 teaspoon white rice vinegar
2 teaspoons low-sodium soy sauce

1. Preheat large sauté pan over medium heat, add avocado oil, and wait 10 seconds for oil to heat up. Add sliced chicken to the pan and cook all the way through, about 3–5 minutes, tossing continuously so the chicken doesn't burn.

2. Add broccoli, red pepper, green pepper, garlic, onion, mushrooms, and corn to a bowl. Mix ingredients well with a spoon. Add pepper, Chinese ginger, white rice vinegar, and low-sodium soy sauce. Add mixture to sauté pan and cook for 5–7 minutes, tossing every 2 minutes to make sure the mixture cooks evenly.

3. This dish is best served in a bowl to keep it warm. Eat it with a pair of chopsticks if you are up for it.

EXCHANGES/CHOICES
1 starch, 4 lean protein

CALORIES 270 | **CALORIES FROM FAT** 70 | **TOTAL FAT** 8g | **SATURATED FAT** 1.5g | **TRANS FAT** 0g
CHOLESTEROL 85mg | **SODIUM** 240mg | **POTASSIUM** 990mg | **TOTAL CARBOHYDRATE** 20g
DIETARY FIBER 4g | **SUGARS** 6g | **PROTEIN** 31g | **PHOSPHORUS** 390mg

SALTADO DE POLLO A LA CUBANA

Este es uno de mis platos preferidos para hacer al paso. La receta es fácil y, permítanme decirles, el plato sale delicioso. Esta receta también es una excelente manera de aprovechar los vegetales que quedan en el refrigerador y ya no están tan frescos. Siéntanse en libertad de sustituir ingredientes, pero asegúrense de seguir los pasos necesarios para que su platillo sea saludable y un éxito.

TIEMPO DE PREPARACIÓN: 15 minutos
TIEMPO DE COCCIÓN: 15 minutos
RINDE: 2 porciones
TAMAÑO DE LA PORCIÓN: 1 1/2 tazas

2 cdtas. de aceite de aguacate

8 onzas de pechugas de pollo, en tajadas de 1/8 de pulgada

1 taza de brócoli, lavado y picado

1/4 taza de pimiento rojo, en tiras

1/4 taza de pimiento verde, en tiras

2 dientes de ajo, pelados y finamente picados

1/2 taza de cebolla española, en tajadas (aproximadamente 1/2 cebolla mediana)

4 champiñones blancos, lavados y picados

1/2 taza de maíz o elote fresco, desgranado

1 cdta. de pimienta negra gruesa

1/2 cdta. de jengibre chino en polvo

1/2 cdta. de vinagre de arroz blanco

2 cdtas. de salsa de soya con poco sodio

1. Calentar una sartén grande a fuego medio, agregar el aceite de aguacate y esperar 10 segundos para que se caliente. Echar el pollo en tajadas a la sartén y cocer bien, de 3-5 minutos, revolviendo constantemente para que no se queme el pollo.

2. Echar el brócoli, pimiento rojo, pimiento verde, ajo, cebolla, champiñones y maíz en una vasija. Mezcle bien los ingredientes con un cucharón. Agregar la pimienta, jengibre chino, vinagre de arroz blanco y salsa de soya. Echar la mezcla a la sartén y cocer 5-7 minutos, revolviendo cada 2 minutos para asegurarse de que la mezcla se cueza uniformemente.

3. Lo mejor es servir este plato en un tazón para que se mantenga caliente. Tal vez deseen comerlo con palitos chinos.

SELECCIONES/INTERCAMBIOS
1 almidón, 4 proteínas magras

CALORÍAS 270 | **CALORÍAS DE GRASA** 70 | **TOTAL DE GRASA** 8g | **GRASA SATURADA** 1.5g | **GRASA TRANS** 0g
COLESTEROL 85mg | **SODIO** 240mg | **POTASIO** 990mg | **TOTAL DE CARBOHIDRATOS** 20g
FIBRA ALIMENTARIA 4g | **AZÚCARES** 6g | **PROTEÍNA** 31g | **FÓSFORO** 390mg

SEARED SCALLOPS WITH ROASTED GRAPE TOMATOES

PREP TIME: 10 minutes
COOKING TIME: 20 minutes
SERVES: 2
SERVING SIZE: 2 scallops and 1/2 of the sauce

---

7 ounces dry sea scallops (approximately 4 scallops; they can be found in most seafood sections)

2 teaspoons avocado oil, divided

1/2 cup cubed Spanish onion (1/4-inch cubes)

2 cloves garlic, peeled and finely chopped

1/2 teaspoon kosher salt

1/2 teaspoon cracked black pepper, divided

10 ounces grape tomatoes, washed and cut in half

1/2 cup unsalted chicken stock

1 teaspoon lime juice

2 teaspoons finely chopped cilantro

1. Preheat oven to 400°F.

2. Remove the small side muscle from the scallops, rinse scallops with cold water, and pat dry. Place in the refrigerator.

3. Preheat an ovenproof nonstick sauté pan over medium heat, add 1 teaspoon avocado oil, and wait 10 seconds for oil to heat up. Add onions and cook until translucent, about 2 minutes. Stir constantly so onions cook evenly. Add garlic, salt, and 1/4 teaspoon pepper, and stir for about 1 minute. Add tomatoes and chicken stock, and place pan in the oven for 10 minutes.

4. With about 4 minutes remaining on the sauce, remove scallops from the refrigerator. Preheat another nonstick pan over medium-high heat. Add remaining 1 teaspoon avocado oil and wait a few seconds for oil to heat up. Sprinkle 1/4 teaspoon pepper over both sides of scallops. Place scallops flat side down in the pan, press gently so they kiss the pan, and cook for 45 seconds. Repeat on the other side. Once cooked, set scallops aside.

5. Remove sauce from the oven and stir in lime juice and cilantro. Serve by placing half the sauce on bottom of each plate and 2 scallops on top.

EXCHANGES/CHOICES
2 vegetable, 2 lean protein

CALORIES 160 | **CALORIES FROM FAT** 50 | **TOTAL FAT** 6g | **SATURATED FAT** 1g | **TRANS FAT** 0g
CHOLESTEROL 25mg | **SODIUM** 420mg | **POTASSIUM** 550mg | **TOTAL CARBOHYDRATE** 13g
DIETARY FIBER 2g | **SUGARS** 4g | **PROTEIN** 15g | **PHOSPHORUS** 390mg

CONCHAS DORADAS CON TOMATES CEREZOS ASADOS

TIEMPO DE PREPARACIÓN: 10 minutos
TIEMPO DE COCCIÓN: 20 minutos
RINDE: 2 porciones
TAMAÑO DE LA PORCIÓN: 2 conchas y la mitad de la salsa

---

7 onzas de conchas *(scallops)* secas (aproximadamente 4 conchas; se encuentran en la sección de mariscos de la mayoría de los supermercados)

2 cdtas. de aceite de aguacate, en partes

1/2 taza de cebolla española (en cubos de 1/4 de pulgada)

2 dientes de ajo, pelados y finamente picados

1/2 cdta. de sal *kosher*

1/2 cdta. de pimienta negra gruesa, en partes

10 onzas de tomates cerezos lavados y cortados por la mitad

1/2 taza de caldo de pollo sin sal

1 cdta. de jugo de lima o limón verde

2 cdtas. de cilantro finamente picado

1. Calentar el horno a 400°F.

2. Retirar el musculito lateral de las conchas, enjuagarlas con agua fría y secarlas con una toalla de papel. Refrigerar.

3. Calentar una sartén antiadherente para sofreír que se pueda meter al horno, a fuego medio, agregar 1 cdta. de aceite de aguacate y esperar 10 segundos hasta que se caliente. Agregar la cebolla y cocer hasta que esté traslúcida aproximadamente 2 minutos. Revolver constantemente para que la cebolla se cueza de manera uniforme. Agregar el ajo, sal y 1/4 cdta. de pimienta, y revolver aproximadamente 1 minuto. Agregar los tomates y el caldo de pollo, y meter la sartén al horno 10 minutos.

4. Cuando queden aproximadamente 4 minutos para que la salsa esté lista, sacar las conchas del refrigerador. Calentar otra sartén antiadherente a fuego medio-alto. Añadir la cdta. restante de aceite de aguacate y esperar unos segundos hasta que se caliente. Echar 1/4 cdta. de pimienta a ambos lados de las conchas. Colocar las conchas con el lado plano hacia abajo en la sartén presionándolas ligeramente y cocer 45 segundos. Repetir por el otro lado. Cuando estén cocidas, ponerlas de lado.

5. Retirar la salsa del horno, agregar el jugo de limón verde y cilantro, y revolver. Servir colocando la salsa en el plato y luego dos conchas encima.

SELECCIONES/INTERCAMBIOS
2 vegetales, 2 proteínas magras

CALORÍAS 160 | **CALORÍAS DE GRASA** 50 | **TOTAL DE GRASA** 6g | **GRASA SATURADA** 1g | **GRASA TRANS** 0g
COLESTEROL 25mg | **SODIO** 420mg | **POTASIO** 550mg | **TOTAL DE CARBOHIDRATOS** 13g
FIBRA ALIMENTARIA 2g | **AZÚCARES** 4g | **PROTEÍNA** 15g | **FÓSFORO** 390mg

Red Leaf Lettuce Tilapia Tacos

PREP TIME: 20 minutes
COOKING TIME: 10 minutes
SERVES: 6
SERVING SIZE: 1 taco

---

3 ounces plum tomatoes, washed and cut into 1/4-inch cubes

2 tablespoons finely chopped cilantro

1 tablespoon lime juice

3 ounces Hass avocado, cut into 1/4-inch cubes

1/2 teaspoon garlic powder

1/4 teaspoon kosher salt, divided

12 ounces tilapia fillets

1/2 teaspoon cracked black pepper

6 leaves red leaf lettuce, washed and dried

2 ounces radishes, washed and cut into thin slices

1 lime, cut into 6 wedges

1. In a small mixing bowl combine tomatoes, cilantro, lime juice, avocado, garlic powder, and 1/8 teaspoon salt. Mix gently but well with a spoon. Place taco topping in the refrigerator to allow flavors to develop.

2. Season both sides of the tilapia with remaining 1/8 teaspoon salt and the pepper and cut into 2-ounce strips (6 strips total). Preheat a nonstick pan over medium heat. Cook fish strips for 1 minute per side. Once you have seared both sides, cover fish and turn off the heat. The residual heat will finish cooking the fish through (which will result in a juicy piece of fish).

3. Remove red leaf lettuce and taco topping from refrigerator. To build a taco, place 1 lettuce leaf on a plate, add 1 piece fish, 1 tablespoon topping mixture, 2 pieces radish, and 1 lime wedge. Repeat with remaining ingredients. Enjoy!

EXCHANGES/CHOICES
1 vegetable, 1 1/2 lean protein

CALORIES 90 | **CALORIES FROM FAT** 80 | **TOTAL FAT** 9g | **SATURATED FAT** 0.5g | **TRANS FAT** 0g
CHOLESTEROL 30mg | **SODIUM** 200mg | **POTASSIUM** 350mg | **TOTAL CARBOHYDRATE** 4g
DIETARY FIBER 2g | **SUGARS** 1g | **PROTEIN** 12g | **PHOSPHORUS** 120mg

TACOS DE TILAPIA CON LECHUGA ROJA

TIEMPO DE PREPARACIÓN: 20 minutos
TIEMPO DE COCCIÓN: 10 minutos
RINDE: 6 porciones
TAMAÑO DE LA PORCIÓN: 1 taco

3 onzas de tomates ciruelos, lavados y cortados en cubos de 1/4 de pulgada

2 cdas. de cilantro finamente picado

1 cda. de jugo de lima o limón verde

3 onzas de aguacate Hass, cortado en cubos de 1/4 de pulgada

1/2 cdta. de ajo en polvo

1/4 cdta. de sal *kosher*, en partes

12 onzas de filetes de tilapia

1/2 cdta. de pimienta negra gruesa

6 hojas de lechuga roja, lavada y secada

2 onzas de rábanos, lavados y cortados en rodajas finas

1 lima o limón verde, cortado en 6 trozos

1. En una vasija pequeña mezclar el tomate, cilantro, jugo de limón, aguacate, ajo en polvo y 1/8 cdta. de sal. Mezclar bien pero delicadamente con un cucharón. Refrigerar la salsa de los tacos para permitir que los sabores se intensifiquen.

2. Sazonar ambos lados de la tilapia con los 1/8 cdta. de sal y pimienta que queda, y cortar en tiras de 2 onzas (6 tiras en total). Calentar una sartén antiadherente a fuego medio. Cocer las tiras de pescado 1 minuto por lado. Una vez que se dore cada lado, tapar el pescado y apagar el fuego. El calor residual terminará de cocer el pescado por dentro (lo que producirá un jugoso trozo de pescado).

3. Sacar la lechuga roja y salsa de taco del refrigerador. Para armar un taco, colocar 1 hoja de lechuga en un plato, agregar 1 trozo de pescado, 1 cda. de la salsa, 2 trozos de rábano y 1 trozo de limón verde. Repetir con el resto de los ingredientes. ¡A disfrutar!

SELECCIONES/INTERCAMBIOS
1 vegetal, 1 1/2 proteínas magras

CALORÍAS 90 | **CALORÍAS DE GRASA** 80 | **TOTAL DE GRASA** 9g | **GRASA SATURADA** 0.5g | **GRASA TRANS** 0g
COLESTEROL 30mg | **SODIO** 200mg | **POTASIO** 350mg | **TOTAL DE CARBOHIDRATOS** 4g
FIBRA ALIMENTARIA 2g | **AZÚCARES** 1g | **PROTEÍNA** 12g | **FÓSFORO** 120mg

"CALLE OCHO" RED SNAPPER CEVICHE

Oh, let me tell you about this dish. Is it delicious? Yes! Is it easy to make? Yes! Will you impress your friends (and yourself) with this dish? Yes! I love to make ceviche, but it's a dish that many people find unapproachable or intimidating. Don't worry! I have fixed that with this easy approach.

PREP TIME: 15 minutes
REFRIGERATION TIME: 20–30 minutes
SERVES: 3
SERVING SIZE: 3 ounces red snapper

---

9 ounces red snapper fillet, cleaned and
   sliced on the bias
3 ounces light coconut milk
3 limes, juiced
1 tablespoon lime zest
1 tablespoon finely chopped red pepper
1 cup finely chopped cilantro
1 tablespoon finely chopped Spanish
   onion
1/4 teaspoon sea salt
1/8 teaspoon cracked black pepper

1. Add red snapper, coconut milk, lime juice, lime zest, red pepper, cilantro, Spanish onion, sea salt, and cracked black pepper to a mixing bowl. Mix well, tightly seal the bowl, and refrigerate 20–30 minutes. Mix once more before serving.

RONALDO'S TIP

Trust me, the acid from the lime cooks the fish beautifully. A good rule of thumb is the longer the fish sits in the lime juice, the more it will cook. In my opinion, 20 minutes is the perfect resting time to get just the right texture.

EXCHANGES/CHOICES
1 vegetable, 2 lean protein

CALORIES 110 | CALORIES FROM FAT 20 | TOTAL FAT 2g | SATURATED FAT 1.5g | TRANS FAT 0g
CHOLESTEROL 30mg | SODIUM 210mg | POTASSIUM 480mg | TOTAL CARBOHYDRATE 7g
DIETARY FIBER 2g | SUGARS 2g | PROTEIN 16g | PHOSPHORUS 190mg

CEVICHE DE PARGO ROJO DE LA CALLE OCHO

Ah, déjenme contarles sobre este plato. ¿Es delicioso? ¡Sí! ¿Es fácil de preparar? ¡Sí! ¿Impresionarán a sus amigos (y a sí mismos) con este plato? ¡Sí! Me encanta hacer ceviche, pero es un plato que muchas personas encuentran fuera de su alcance o intimidante. ¡No se preocupen! Lo he solucionado con este método fácil.

TIEMPO DE PREPARACIÓN: 15 minutos
TIEMPO DE REFRIGERACIÓN: 20-30 minutos
RINDE: 3 porciones
TAMAÑO DE LA PORCIÓN: 3 onzas de pargo rojo

9 onzas de pargo rojo o huachinango, limpio y cortado en diagonal

3 onzas de leche de coco light

3 limas o limones verdes, exprimidos

1 cda. de ralladura de limón verde

1 cda. de pimiento rojo, finamente picado

1 taza de cilantro finamente picado

1 cda. de cebolla española finamente picada

1/4 cdta. de sal marina

1/8 cdta. de pimienta negra gruesa

1. Echar el pargo rojo, leche de coco, jugo de limón verde, ralladura de limón verde, pimiento rojo, cilantro, cebolla española, sal marina y pimienta negra en una vasija. Mezclar bien, cerrar la vasija herméticamente y refrigerar 20-30 minutos. Mezclar una vez más antes de servir.

CONSEJO DE RONALDO

Confíen en mí: el ácido del limón verde cuece muy bien el pescado. Una buena regla es que cuanto más tiempo el pescado pase en el jugo de limón, más se cocerá. En mi opinión, 20 minutos es el tiempo perfecto para que alcance la textura correcta.

SELECCIONES/INTERCAMBIOS
1 vegetal, 2 proteínas magras

CALORÍAS 110 | **CALORÍAS DE GRASA** 20 | **TOTAL DE GRASA** 2g | **GRASA SATURADA** 1.5g | **GRASA TRANS** 0g
COLESTEROL 30mg | **SODIO** 210mg | **POTASIO** 480mg | **TOTAL DE CARBOHIDRATOS** 7g
FIBRA ALIMENTARIA 2g | **AZÚCARES** 2g | **PROTEÍNA** 16g | **FÓSFORO** 190mg

Pork Tenderloin with Yucca Filling

PREP TIME: 25 minutes
COOKING TIME: About 1 hour
SERVES: 7
SERVING SIZE: 3 ounces pork

2 1/2 teaspoons avocado oil, divided
1 poblano pepper
7 ounces yucca (about 1 medium yucca)
1/2 teaspoon kosher salt, divided
1/4 medium Spanish onion, peeled and
   finely chopped (about 1/4 cup)
4 cloves garlic, peeled and finely
   chopped, divided
4 slices low-sodium turkey bacon,
   cooked and finely chopped
2 teaspoons cracked black pepper
1 teaspoon ground cumin
1 teaspoon dried rosemary
1 pork tenderloin (about 20 ounces;
   ask butcher to clean it)
2 feet butcher's twine
1/2 cup cubed Spanish onion
   (1/4-inch cubes)
2 teaspoons tomato paste
4 ounces white wine
4 ounces unsalted chicken stock
2 teaspoons fresh thyme leaves

1. Preheat oven to 350°F.

2. Rub 1/2 teaspoon avocado oil on surface of poblano pepper. Place pepper over an open flame and rotate until skin is charred on all sides. Remove from flame and place in a resealable plastic bag for a few minutes to allow steam to loosen the skin. Remove pepper from bag, run under cold water, and peel the blistered skin away with a cloth. Finely chop pepper and set aside.

3. Cut yucca into thirds. Peel away the outer brown layer and the inner pink layer with a knife to reveal a white interior. Place peeled yucca in a pot with water, add 1/4 teaspoon salt, and simmer until yucca is tender, about 20 minutes. When yucca is done, turn the heat off and remove yucca to tray lined with parchment paper.

4. With potato masher or fork, mash yucca and mix in chopped onion, 2 cloves chopped garlic, turkey bacon, fire-roasted poblano, remaining 1/4 teaspoon salt, pepper, cumin, and rosemary. Fold mixture until well blended. Set yucca mixture aside.

5. Fillet open pork tenderloin. (It should resemble a square.) Place loin between 2 pieces of plastic wrap on a cutting board. Pound lightly to even out the thickness of the pork. Spread yucca mixture evenly across the entire surface of the pork and roll tightly. Tie loin with butcher's twine (look for videos online about how to truss a pork tenderloin).

6. Preheat a large ovenproof nonstick pan over medium heat, add remaining 2 teaspoons avocado oil, and wait 10 seconds for oil to heat up. Sear all sides of pork tenderloin. Set aside. To the same pan, add cubed onion, remaining garlic, and tomato paste, and cook for 2 minutes. Pour in white wine and simmer for 1 minute. Add chicken stock to the pan along with pork tenderloin.

7. Transfer pan to the oven and cook for 25 minutes, or until internal temperature of tenderloin reaches 150°F. Remove from oven, transfer pork tenderloin to a cooling rack, reserving the drippings. Residual cooking will bring internal temperature of pork up to 155°F for a nice medium cook.

8. Transfer drippings to a blender and purée until smooth. Add the sauce from the blender to a pan and simmer for about 2 minutes over low heat. Fold in the thyme. Remove the butcher's twine from the pork and serve with sauce.

EXCHANGES/CHOICES
1 starch, 3 lean protein

CALORIES 200 | **CALORIES FROM FAT** 45 | **TOTAL FAT** 5g | **SATURATED FAT** 1.5g | **TRANS FAT** 0g
CHOLESTEROL 60mg | **SODIUM** 350mg | **POTASSIUM** 530mg | **TOTAL CARBOHYDRATE** 15g
DIETARY FIBER 1g | **SUGARS** 2g | **PROTEIN** 20g | **PHOSPHORUS** 250mg

LOMO DE CERDO CON RELLENO DE YUCA

TIEMPO DE PREPARACIÓN: 25 minutos
TIEMPO DE COCCIÓN: Aproximadamente
  1 hora
RINDE: 7 porciones
TAMAÑO DE LA PORCIÓN: 3 onzas

2 1/2 cdtas. de aceite de aguacate, en partes

1 chile poblano

7 onzas de yuca (aproximadamente 1 yuca mediana)

1/2 cdta. de sal *kosher*, en partes

1/4 cebolla española, pelada y finamente picada (aproximadamente 1/4 taza)

4 dientes de ajo, pelados y finamente picados, en partes

4 lonjas de tocino de pavo, con poco sodio, cocido y finamente picado

2 cdtas. de pimienta negra gruesa

1 cdta. de comino

1 cdta. de romero seco

1 lomo de cerdo (aproximadamente 20 onzas; pedir al carnicero que lo desgrase)

2 pies de pita de cocina

1/2 taza de cebolla española (en cubos de 1/4 de pulgada)

2 cdtas. de pasta de tomate

4 onzas de vino blanco

4 onzas de caldo de pollo sin sal

2 cdtas. de hojas de tomillo fresco, sin tallos

1. Calentar el horno a 350°F.

2. Frotar 1/2 cdta. de aceite de aguacate en la superficie del chile poblano. Colocarlo sobre una llama y girar hasta que todo el chile se chamusque en contacto con el fuego. Cuando esté completamente chamuscado, sacarlo del fuego y ponerlo en una vasija con tapa unos 3 minutos, sin dejar que se escape el vapor para que la cáscara del chile se afloje. Sacar el chile de la vasija, enjuagarlo con agua fría y usar una toalla de papel para eliminar con cuidado la cáscara chamuscada. Picar el chile finamente y poner de lado.

3. Cortar la yuca en tres partes. Pelar la capa café externa y la capa interna de color rosa con un cuchillo para terminar con el interior blanco. Echar la yuca pelada a una olla con agua, agregar 1/4 cdta. de sal y hervir a fuego lento hasta que se ponga blanda, unos 20 minutos. Cuando la yuca esté lista, apagar el fuego y poner la yuca en una lata con papel mantequilla.

4. Con el prensapapas o un tenedor, aplastar la yuca y mezclar con la cebolla picada, 2 dientes de ajo picados, tocino de pavo, chile poblano, 1/4 cdta. de sal, pimienta, comino y romero. Mezclar todo bien. Poner de lado la mezcla de yuca.

5. Calentar el horno a 350°F. Filetear el lomo de cerdo para abrirlo. (Debe tener apariencia cuadrada). Colocar el lomo entre 2 pedazos de plástico, sobre una tabla de cortar. Golpear suavemente con un mazo hasta que la carne tenga un espesor uniforme. Echar la mezcla de yuca uniformemente en toda la superficie del cerdo y enrollar firmemente. Atar el lomo con pita de cocina (busquen videos en Internet sobre cómo amarrar un lomo de cerdo).

6. Calentar a fuego medio una sartén antiadherente grande que se pueda meter al horno, agregar las 2 cdtas. restantes de aceite de aguacate y esperar 10 segundos hasta que se caliente. Dorar toda la superficie del lomo. Poner de lado. En la misma sartén, echar la cebolla en cubos, los 2 dientes restantes de ajo y pasta de tomate, y cocer 2 minutos. Añadir el vino blanco y cocer a fuego lento 1 minuto. Agregar el caldo de pollo a la sartén, además del lomo de cerdo.

7. Meter la sartén al horno 25 minutos o hasta que la temperatura interna del lomo sea de 150°F. Sacar el lomo del horno y pasarlo a una rejilla para que enfríe. Guardar los jugos. El calor residual hará que la temperatura interna del lomo llegue a 155°F para que tenga un buen término medio.

8. Licuar los jugos hasta que tengan consistencia uniforme. Echar la salsa licuada a la sartén y hervir a fuego lento 2 minutos. Agregar el tomillo y mezclar. Quitar la pita de cocina del lomo y servir con la salsa.

SELECCIONES/INTERCAMBIOS
1 almidón, 3 proteínas magras

CALORÍAS 200 | **CALORÍAS DE GRASA** 45 | **TOTAL DE GRASA** 5g | **GRASA SATURADA** 1.5g | **GRASA TRANS** 0g
COLESTEROL 60mg | **SODIO** 350mg | **POTASIO** 530mg | **TOTAL DE CARBOHIDRATOS** 15g
FIBRA ALIMENTARIA 1g | **AZÚCARES** 2g | **PROTEÍNA** 20g | **FÓSFORO** 250mg

PORK TENDERLOIN WITH ZUCCHINI *SOFRITO* PASTA

PREP TIME: 20 minutes
COOKING TIME: 30 minutes
SERVES: 4
SERVING SIZE: 1 cup pasta and 4 ounces pork

1 (16-ounce) pork tenderloin
(ask your butcher to clean it)

1 navel orange, juiced

1 clove garlic, finely chopped

1 teaspoon ground thyme

1 teaspoon dried oregano

3/4 teaspoon kosher salt, divided

1 teaspoon cracked black pepper, divided

2 teaspoons avocado oil, divided

1 zucchini, washed

2 cloves garlic, peeled and washed

1 stalk green onion, washed and thinly sliced

3 plum tomatoes, washed and cut into 1/4-inch cubes

2 tablespoons finely chopped cilantro

1. Place pork tenderloin in a large resealable plastic bag. Add orange juice, chopped garlic, thyme, oregano, 1/2 teaspoon salt, and 1/2 teaspoon black pepper to the bag, and rub mixture into the pork. Place in the refrigerator for 20 minutes. Remove pork tenderloin from bag.

2. Preheat oven to 400°F.

3. Preheat large ovenproof sauté pan over medium heat, add 1 teaspoon avocado oil, and wait 10 seconds for oil to heat up. Place pork tenderloin in pan and sear for 2 minutes. Repeat on the other side. Remove tenderloin from pan and place on a rack on a baking sheet. Cook in the oven for 20 minutes.

4. When pork is done, remove from oven and rest for 5 minutes so juices redistribute in the meat.

5. While meat rests, make zucchini *sofrito* pasta. Peel zucchini with a peeler to create long flat "noodles." Set aside.

6. Preheat large sauté pan, add 1 teaspoon avocado oil, and wait 10 seconds for oil to heat up. Add garlic, green onion, and tomatoes, and sauté for 2 minutes. Reduce heat to medium-low, add zucchini, remaining salt, and remaining pepper, and toss gently for 2 minutes. Fold in cilantro and serve with pork.

EXCHANGES/CHOICES
2 vegetable, 3 lean protein

CALORIES 180 | **CALORIES FROM FAT** 45 | **TOTAL FAT** 5g | **SATURATED FAT** 1g | **TRANS FAT** 0g
CHOLESTEROL 75mg | **SODIUM** 430mg | **POTASSIUM** 740mg | **TOTAL CARBOHYDRATE** 9g
DIETARY FIBER 2g | **SUGARS** 5g | **PROTEIN** 25g | **PHOSPHORUS** 320mg

LOMO DE CERDO CON FIDEOS SOFRITOS DE CALABACÍN

TIEMPO DE PREPARACIÓN: 20 minutos
TIEMPO DE COCCIÓN: 30 minutos
RINDE: 4 porciones
TAMAÑO DE LA PORCIÓN: 1 taza de fideos y 4 onzas de carne de cerdo

---

1 lomo de cerdo (de 16 onzas)
(Pedirle al carnicero que lo desgrase)

1 naranja exprimida

1 diente de ajo, finamente picado

1 cdta. de tomillo en polvo

1 cdta. de orégano seco

3/4 cdta. de sal *kosher*, en partes

1 cdta. de pimienta negra gruesa, en partes

2 cdtas. de aceite de aguacate, en partes

1 calabacín o zapallito italiano, lavado

2 dientes de ajo, pelados y lavados

1 tallo de cebollín, lavado y finamente picado

3 tomates ciruelos, lavados y cortados en cubos de 1/4 de pulgada

2 cdas. de cilantro finamente picado

1. Colocar el lomo de cerdo en una bolsa grande de plástico con cierre. Agregar el jugo de naranja, ajo picado, tomillo, orégano, 1/2 cdta. de sal y 1/2 cdta. de pimienta negra a la bolsa y frotar la mezcla en el lomo. Refrigerar 20 minutos. Sacar el lomo de la bolsa.

2. Calentar el horno a 400°F.

3. Calentar a fuego medio una sartén antiadherente para sofreír que se pueda meter al horno, agregar 1 cdta. de aceite de aguacate y esperar 10 segundos hasta que se caliente. Poner el lomo en la sartén y dorar 2 minutos. Repetir por el otro lado. Retirar el lomo de la sartén y colocar en una rejilla sobre una lata de hornear. Hornear 20 minutos.

4. Cuando el lomo esté listo, retirarlo del horno y ponerlo de lado 5 minutos, para que los jugos se redistribuyan por toda la carne.

5. Mientras tanto, hacer los fideos sofritos de calabacín. Pelar el calabacín con un pelador, formando "fideos" largos. Poner de lado.

6. Calentar una sartén grande para sofreír, agregar 1 cdta. de aceite de aguacate y esperar 10 segundos hasta que se caliente. Agregar el ajo, cebolla verde y tomate, y saltear 2 minutos. Poner el fuego en medio-bajo, echar el calabacín, el resto de la sal y pimienta, y mezclar delicadamente 2 minutos. Echar el cilantro, revolver y servir con el lomo de cerdo.

SELECCIONES/INTERCAMBIOS
2 vegetales, 3 proteínas magras

CALORÍAS 180 | **CALORÍAS DE GRASA** 45 | **TOTAL DE GRASA** 5g | **GRASA SATURADA** 1g | **GRASA TRANS** 0g
COLESTEROL 75mg | **SODIO** 430mg | **POTASIO** 740mg | **TOTAL DE CARBOHIDRATOS** 9g
FIBRA ALIMENTARIA 2g | **AZÚCARES** 5g | **PROTEÍNA** 25g | **FÓSFORO** 320mg

RONALDO'S CUBAN SANDWICH

Sometimes we don't have a lot of time to prepare a whole meal and need something quick. I always have high-quality deli meat on hand for times like these. But not all deli meat is created equal; look for healthy, low-sodium deli meats when shopping. There is no substitute for a true Cuban sandwich, but this recipe is a light, delicious take on the classic.

PREP TIME: 10 minutes
COOKING TIME: 18 minutes
SERVES: 2
SERVING SIZE: 1/2 sandwich and 1/2 salad

SANDWICH
1 multigrain sandwich thin, split in half
Parchment paper
1 1/2 ounces low-fat sliced Swiss cheese
2 ounces sliced Hass avocado
1 1/2 ounces low-sodium sliced deli turkey
1 1/2 ounces low-sodium sliced deli ham

SALAD
1/2 cup baby arugula, washed
1/2 Roma tomato, sliced
1/8 cup sliced red onion
1/8 cup sliced cucumber
2 teaspoons chopped cilantro
2 teaspoons lime juice
1/8 teaspoon cracked black pepper

1. Preheat oven to 350°F.

2. Place both halves of multigrain roll on a baking sheet lined with parchment paper. Make sure the inside of the bun is facing up. To build the sandwich, layer Swiss cheese evenly on naked bun. Do the same with avocado, turkey, and ham. Place sandwich in the oven for 12 minutes. Remove sandwich from oven and close the roll.

3. Preheat a nonstick pan over medium heat. Place the sandwich in the middle of the pan and press down using a spatula or the bottom of a clean saucepan for 2–3 minutes. Flip the sandwich and repeat on the other side. This will give you the pressed look of a traditional Cuban sandwich. Cut in half.

4. Add arugula, tomato, red onion, cucumber, cilantro, lime juice, and black pepper to a bowl, and toss ingredients together. Serve with the sandwich. Now take a big bite of that delicious sandwich.

EXCHANGES/CHOICES
1 starch, 2 1/2 lean protein

CALORIES 190 | **CALORIES FROM FAT** 50 | **TOTAL FAT** 6g | **SATURATED FAT** 2g | **TRANS FAT** 0g
CHOLESTEROL 30mg | **SODIUM** 510mg | **POTASSIUM** 420mg | **TOTAL CARBOHYDRATE** 16g
DIETARY FIBER 3g | **SUGARS** 5g | **PROTEIN** 20g | **PHOSPHORUS** 290mg

SÁNDWICH CUBANO DE RONALDO

A veces no tenemos tiempo para preparar toda una comida y debemos hacer algo rápido. Siempre tengo embutidos de alta calidad a la mano para momentos como estos. Pero no todos los embutidos son iguales; cuando salgan de compras, busquen los saludables, con poco sodio. No existe sustituto para el verdadero sándwich cubano, pero esta receta es una versión light y deliciosa del sándwich clásico.

TIEMPO DE PREPARACIÓN: 10 minutos
TIEMPO DE COCCIÓN: 18 minutos
RINDE: 2 porciones
TAMAÑO DE PORCIONES: 1/2 sándwich y 1/2 ensalada

SÁNDWICH

1 panecillo delgado de sándwich de multicereales, partido por la mitad

Papel mantequilla

1 1/2 onzas de queso suizo con poca grasa

2 onzas de aguacate Hass en tajadas

1 1/2 onzas de embutido de pavo con poco sodio, en tajadas

1 1/2 onzas de embutido de jamón con poco sodio, en tajadas

ENSALADA

1/2 taza de retoños de rúcula o arúgula, lavada

1/2 tomate Roma, en tajadas

1/8 taza de cebolla roja, en rodajas

1/8 taza de pepino en rodajas

2 cdtas. de cilantro picado

2 cdtas. de jugo de lima o limón verde

1/8 cdta. de pimienta negra gruesa

1. Calentar el horno a 350°F.

2. Colocar ambas mitades del pan multicereales en una lata para hornear con papel mantequilla. Asegurarse de que el interior del pan quede hacia arriba. Para armar el sándwich, poner una tajada de queso suizo en el pan. Hacer lo mismo con el aguacate, pavo y jamón. Hornear el sándwich 12 minutos. Sacar el sándwich del horno y cerrar el pan.

3. Calentar una sartén antiadherente a fuego medio. Colocar el sándwich al centro de la sartén y presionarlo con una espátula o la base de una olla limpia por 2-3 minutos. Voltee el sándwich y vuelva a aplastar el otro lado. Así se verá como un sándwich cubano tradicional. Parta por la mitad

4. Echar la rúcula, tomate, cebolla roja, pepino, cilantro, jugo de limón y pimienta negra en una vasija y revolver los ingredientes. Servir con el sándwich. Es hora de meterle un gran bocado a este delicioso sándwich.

SELECCIONES/INTERCAMBIOS
1 almidón, 2 1/2 proteínas magras

CALORÍAS 190 | **CALORÍAS DE GRASA** 50 | **TOTAL DE GRASA** 6g | **GRASA SATURADA** 2g | **GRASA TRANS** 0g
COLESTEROL 30mg | **SODIO** 510mg | **POTASIO** 420mg | **TOTAL DE CARBOHIDRATOS** 16g
FIBRA ALIMENTARIA 3g | **AZÚCARES** 5g | **PROTEÍNA** 20g | **FÓSFORO** 290mg

INDEX

ÍNDICE DE MATERIAS